Children and Social Exclusion

Understanding Children's Worlds

Series Editor: Judy Dunn

The study of children's development can have a profound influence on how children are brought up, cared for, and educated. Many psychologists argue that, even if our knowledge is incomplete, we have a responsibility to attempt to help those concerned with the care, education, and study of children by making what we know available to them. The central aim of this series is to encourage developmental psychologists to set out the findings and the implications of their research for others – teachers, doctors, social workers, students, and fellow researchers – whose work involves the care, education, and study of young children and their families. The information and the ideas that have grown from recent research form an important resource which should be available to them. This series provides an opportunity for psychologists to present their work in a way that is interesting, intelligible, and substantial, and to discuss what its consequences may be for those who care for, and teach, children: not to offer simple prescriptive advice to other professionals, but to make important and innovative research accessible to them.

Children and Social Exclusion

Morality, Prejudice, and Group Identity

Melanie Killen and Adam Rutland

A John Wiley & Sons, Ltd., Publication

This edition first published 2011
© 2011 Melanie Killen and Adam Rutland

Blackwell Publishing was acquired by John Wiley & Sons in February 2007. Blackwell's publishing program has been merged with Wiley's global Scientific, Technical, and Medical business to form Wiley-Blackwell.

Registered Office
John Wiley & Sons Ltd, The Atrium, Southern Gate, Chichester, West Sussex, PO19 8SQ, United Kingdom

Editorial Offices
350 Main Street, Malden, MA 02148-5020, USA
9600 Garsington Road, Oxford, OX4 2DQ, UK
The Atrium, Southern Gate, Chichester, West Sussex, PO19 8SQ, UK

For details of our global editorial offices, for customer services, and for information about how to apply for permission to reuse the copyright material in this book please see our website at www.wiley.com/wiley-blackwell.

Library of Congress Cataloging-in-Publication Data
Killen, Melanie.
Children and social exclusion: morality, prejudice, and group identity / Melanie Killen, Adam Rutland.
p. cm. – (Understanding children's worlds; 18)
Includes bibliographical references and index.
ISBN 978-1-4051-7651-4 (hardback)
1. Social integration. 2. Children. 3. Group identity. 4. Identity (Psychology).
5. Prejudices. I. Rutland, Adam. II. Title.
HM683.K55 2011
302.4–dc22

2010047217

A catalogue record for this book is available from the British Library.

This book is published in the following electronic formats: ePDF 9781444396294; Wiley Online Library 9781444396317; ePub 9781444396300

Set in 10/12.5pt, Sabon-Roman by Thomson Digital, Noida, India
Printed in Malaysia by Ho Printing (M) Sdn Bhd
[1: 2011]

To Rob, Sasha, and Jacob for their love and affection,
and to Marcia, David, and Sean,
for their love and support (M.K.)

To Rachel, Kate, and Jonathan for their love and
endless inspiration, and to my late father, Peter, who
sadly died during the writing of this book, and Marion,
my mother, and Neil, my brother, for their continuous
love and support (A.R.)

Contents

Series Editor's Preface

This series, *Understanding Children's Worlds*, is concerned with children's social worlds, and their developing understanding of those worlds. The topics of exclusion and prejudice are clearly central to their social experiences, especially to their relationships with other children. What makes some children able to recognize and challenge stereotypic or prejudiced views of others? What experiences, in contrast, reinforce prejudice and bias? How well do we understand the development of individual differences in these early aspects of morality, and what are the trajectories in bias and prejudice from early childhood to adolescence and adulthood?

What is striking about this book is that Melanie Killen and Adam Rutland have brought together a notably wide range of ideas and research findings on these questions, a range that spans developmental psychology and social psychology – it is a bold vision that integrates very different ideas and theoretical approaches. Three themes stand out. First, Killen and Rutland summarize the early emergence of morality: how children view social exclusion as right or wrong, and the growth of their understanding of both explicit prejudicial views and implicit biases. Second, they consider children's ideas on group identity and exclusion, and carefully distinguish prejudice and exclusion. They examine, for instance, how children think about excluding individuals from within their own groups, and how they evaluate exclusion of individuals from a different group (intragroup versus intergroup exclusion). Third, importantly they move on to consider what we know about exclusion in diverse cultures – rather than solely in laboratory studies.

Particularly valuable, they then consider interventions that attempt to promote positive inclusion and a sense of shared identity among children from different groups. They assess how successful programs that vary intergroup contact, media exposure, and, importantly, cross-group friendship can be. Their integration of the ideas and findings of social and developmental psychology does indeed shed light on the developmental programs which, they argue, are fundamental for progress towards a fairer society.

Judy Dunn

Preface

Exclusion and inclusion are pervasive in children's lives and continue throughout adulthood. Understanding why exclusion happens, how children think about it, and what it means for social development involves an analysis of individuals, groups, and relationships. Writing this book from our various perspectives, which included social cognition, moral development, social identity, and intergroup attitudes, we took a new view on exclusion and inclusion in children's lives, one that enabled us to reflect on its fundamental role in social development. We have described how it is that through experiencing exclusion and inclusion, children develop morality (when to include, when not to exclude, and why) and form social identity (what groups do I belong to, what group norms do I care about?).

As a result of these developmental processes, children become capable of challenging or reinforcing prejudicial attitudes and stereotypic beliefs (sometimes explicitly and often implicitly). This is because children who develop social identity without invoking moral judgments appear to justify exclusion in contexts that reflect prejudice, discrimination, and bias. Yet children who develop an understanding of group dynamics and balance these concerns with fairness and equality are well positioned to reject or challenge stereotypic expectations and prejudicial beliefs. The factors and sources of experience that contribute to these diverse trajectories and perspectives reflect the core of this book. The tension between morality and social identity is complex, which makes it an intriguing and compelling topic to write about.

We emerged from this project with a strong sense that much is at stake in understanding children's perspectives about exclusion and inclusion because of the different consequences to social exclusion and inclusion. Issues as important as social justice and fairness are invoked.

Stereotyping, prejudice, and discrimination are unfortunate outcomes of exclusion decisions that are made without a balance of all of the factors that are implicated. Thus, exclusion takes many forms throughout social life and its meaning is vast and varied.

We began this book as an integrative collaboration, crossing the boundaries of developmental and social psychology to understand exclusion in the child. Over the past 10 years, researchers in the fields of developmental, social, neuroscience, and cognitive psychology have investigated ingroup bias and outgroup threat in their research designs and empirical projects; at the same time, researchers from many different subfields of social science have delved into morality and moral judgment in the child. The convergence of interest on these topics from such diverse areas is astounding and engaging. We found that the areas of intergroup attitudes and morality were often dichotomized, however, and not well integrated. Even closer to our own areas of study, we have found that developmental research has not traditionally examined morality in the context of intergroup relations, and social psychology research on social identity has not typically studied moral reasoning. Thus, one aim of this book was to take an integrative approach for describing how intergroup attitudes, morality, and social identity emerge in the child and create the conditions for exclusion and inclusion.

We would like to thank our respective colleagues and graduate students for discussions and collaborations on the topics in this book. Melanie Killen thanks her colleagues Dominic Abrams, William Arsenio, Natasha Cabrera, Robert Coplan, David Crystal, Ileana Enesco, Nathan Fox, Silvia Guerrero, Dan Hart, Charles Helwig, Stacey Horn, Peter Kahn, Sheri Levy, Tina Malti, Clark McKown, Drew Nesdale, Larry Nucci, Ken Rubin, Martin Ruck, Judi Smetana, Charles Stangor, Elliot Turiel, Cecilia Wainryb, Allan Wigfield, and Amanda Woodward for many collaborations and conversations about social cognition, social development, morality, and exclusion, as well as for many research collaborations that served as the basis for most of her research. In addition, she is grateful to William Damon and Elliot Turiel for inspiring her to study the development of morality, and for providing an intellectually engaging community in graduate school, one that has endured for several decades post-graduate, to Jonas Langer for his encouragement, to Judi Smetana for her mentorship, and to Larry Nucci for his guidance. Melanie Killen also thanks her former doctoral students for their many contributions to the research program on social and moral development, for pushing the research agenda into new and original research directions, and for becoming collaborators on many of the research projects described in this book, Alicia Ardila-Rey, Alaina Brenick, Christina Edmonds, Stacey Horn, Jennie Lee-Kim, Nancy Geyelin Margie, Heidi McGlothlin, Yoonjung Park, Christine Theimer Schuette, and Stefanie Sinno, and her current doctoral students Shelby Cooley, Alexandra Henning, Aline Hitti, Megan Clark Kelly, Kelly Lynn Mulvey, and Cameron Richardson, as well as Alexander O'Connor (at UC Berkeley), for their current participation in ongoing research avenues as well as for their lively discussions, feedback, and contributions on all phases of the research program. Thanks are extended to Joan Karr Tycko, who created the illustrations for the social exclusion studies described in chapter 6, and who provided helpful assistance on the development of the stimulus materials.

Adam Rutland thanks his colleagues Dominic Abrams, Rupert Brown, Lindsey Cameron, Marco Cinnirella, Jennifer Ferrell, Rosa Hossain, Sheri Levy, Peter McGeorge, Alan Milne, Drew Nesdale, Dennis Nigbur, Peter Noack, Joe Pelletier, and Charles Watters for numerous collaborations and lively discussions about social development, prejudice, social identity, group processes, intergroup attitudes, and social exclusion in childhood. Adam Rutland also thanks his former graduate students for all their help in creating an intellectually stimulating environment and furthering his knowledge of intergroup attitudes, social identity, biculturalism, cross-ethnic friendships among children and adolescents, Alison Benbow, Allard Feddes, Sarah FitzRoy, Philipp Jugert, and Caroline Kamu, and his current graduate students Samantha Lee and Claire Powell (also working with Dominic Abrams) for their contribution to our ongoing research program. In addition, we received helpful comments and substantive feedback on the manuscript from Dominic Abrams, Aline Hitti, Stacey Horn, Kelly Lynn Mulvey, Drew Nesdale, Larry Nucci, Yoonjung Park, Stefanie Sinno, Judith Smetana, and Elliot Turiel.

The research described in this book was supported by many external sources, including the National Science Foundation (Developmental and Learning Sciences) and the National Institutes of Health (NICHD) in the United States, to Melanie Killen, and the Economic and Social Research Council (ESRC), British Academy, Nuffield Foundation, and British Broadcasting Corporation (BBC) in the United Kingdom, to Adam Rutland. We are very grateful for the support from these funding agencies. The research described in this book was also supported by internal grants from our respective universities for which we are appreciative, the University of Maryland, College Park, US, and the University of Kent at Canterbury, UK. We extend our gratitude to Kelly Lynn

Mulvey for assisting us with organizational and technical details. We thank Andrew McLeer, Christine Cardone, Constance Adler, and Matt Bennett at Wiley-Blackwell publishers for their editorial and technical advice. Finally, we extend our deep appreciation to Judy Dunn for her support and encouragement throughout the project and for her wisdom and inspiration about the importance of children's lives.

Chapter 1

Introduction: Exclusion and Inclusion in Children's Lives

Acquiring morality, identifying with groups, and developing autonomy provide the foundation for social development in childhood and continue throughout adulthood. Understanding these foundational aspects of development helps to explain why children exclude and include peers, and how it is related to a larger part of becoming a member of a society and culture. When is exclusion legitimate and when it is wrong? What is involved when children exclude other peers and how is this related to exclusion as it happens in the adult world?

While children begin to understand the importance of including peers in their social exchanges, excluding other children from friendships and social groups is complicated. What is complicated is that inclusion is not always desirable, even from an adult perspective, and exclusion is not always wrong. Sports teams, music clubs, and social events often require abilities and talents that are necessary to join, and social events are often arranged in such a way that some type of decision rule about exclusion is used to make it work well. In fact, there are times when it would be viewed as negative to include someone in a group when the individual does not meet the expectations for the group goals (a slow runner will be excluded from a track team). In addition to meeting the criteria for inclusion there are other factors that are considered, which include what makes the group work well. For example, an overly aggressive individual or someone who has unhealthy intentions towards others might be excluded. This type of exclusion is more complicated because it refers to psychological traits which may be inferred by behavior that belies the actual talents of the individual. Moreover, psychological

Children and Social Exclusion: Morality, Prejudice, and Group Identity. Melanie Killen and Adam Rutland. © 2011 Melanie Killen and Adam Rutland. Published 2011 by Blackwell Publishing Ltd.

traits are often attributed to individuals based on their group membership (e.g., girls are not competitive) and not their behavior, which then makes an exclusion decision wrong or unfair. Nonetheless, there are clearly times when it is legitimate to exclude others from social groups when the criteria for exclusion are viewed as reasonable to make groups work well.

Children have to figure out the conditions and criteria for inclusion and exclusion, and this is not easy. In fact, it is a life-long challenge, changing as the scope, nature, and definition of the social group evolves. Figuring this out involves determining a set of fair criteria for inclusion, which involves understanding and anticipating the consequences of exclusion for both the excluder and the excluded.

What makes it more complicated in childhood is that children get many mixed messages from peers and adults about exclusion and inclusion. In early childhood adults typically communicate messages to children to convey the idea that everyone should be included in all activities regardless of merit, shared interests, or group goals for achievement. For example, in early childhood adults often express the view that "we're all friends." With age, however, adults recognize that children's friendships are a matter of personal choice and a result of psychological compatibility as opposed to a general expectation for pervasive inclusion. In fact, as children develop skills, interests, and talents, adults modify their expectations by condoning exclusion criteria for groups, such as competitive ones, as well as for achievement groups, such as tracking in schools based on academic skill, and even for friendship expectations.

To reinforce this pattern, most social groups in early childhood are mandated and created by adults. As children get older and form their own groups, however, they begin to establish their own boundaries, regulations, and norms, and adults often relinquish their role as "group norm creators." Children begin to set group norms that are often associated with their group identity. Given that there will be disagreements about norms, these aspects of groups become foci for exclusion. Thus, expectations for inclusion and exclusion evolve rapidly for children, often without clear or explicit guidelines from adults. And yet, children evolve ways of conceptualizing their groups, along with establishing the criteria for inclusion and exclusion, and the norms associated with group identity.

Together, these factors make it clear that exclusion and inclusion are complex decisions, with significant consequences for child development, as well as for becoming an adult and a member of society. Some forms of exclusion are viewed as relatively minor, such as not inviting someone to join a lunch table, but other forms of exclusion are fairly major, such as excluding someone from a group based on race or ethnicity. A central distinction between different forms of exclusion has to do with the reasons and motivations, such as excluding someone when there is no more room for someone to join or excluding someone because of their race, ethnicity, or religion. A fair amount of evidence suggests that the forms of exclusion that are negative in childhood are related to the types of bias, prejudice, and discrimination in adulthood that is reflected in exclusion decisions. When exclusion becomes extreme and turns into prejudice or victimization then the outcomes are negative for both the excluded and the excluder. By studying childhood exclusion we can learn about the roots of exclusion in the adult world.

Several major theories of development have been used to examine and explain exclusion and inclusion in childhood. These theories have focused on peer rejection in the context of children's friendships, groups, social interactions, and social relationships. In general, these theories describe how children learn to get along with others, when and why they reject each other, with implications for charting the developmental pathway for how children become members of societies and cultures.

Theories of Social Cognition, Social Relationships, and Exclusion

Social Domain theory (Turiel, 2006), which stems from Piagetian approaches to moral development, has shown that children's judgments about fairness emerges early in development, by 3.5 years of age, and that children distinguish rules about fairness from rules that make groups work well, referred to as societal understanding, or knowledge about the regulations that make groups function smoothly. This approach is important for understanding the basis for children's inclusion orientations in which they believe that it is important to treat others fairly and equally. Holding such views enables children to challenge exclusionary judgments from peers, as well as prejudicial attitudes. This model has also demonstrated the types of group norms, rules, and regulations that children develop and apply to social interactions which reflect their knowledge about society and group functioning.

The Social Domain approach provides a way for determining when children evaluate an act as wrong for moral reasons, such as concerns about fairness and equality, and when they view an act as wrong for societal reasons, such as consensus about group norms, traditions, customs, and regulations. Children also evaluate acts and rules as a matter of personal choice, in some contexts, which reflects a different domain of judgments and evaluations. Thus, this approach provides a way for understanding children's reasons for exclusion and inclusion decisions, and when children view exclusion as wrong and unfair, as legitimate and necessary for groups to work well, or as a personal choice.

A second theory that provides a guide to understanding exclusion is Social Identity Theory (Tajfel, 1970; Tajfel & Turner, 1979), which focuses on relationships between ingroups and outgroups, or intergroup attitudes and relationships. Intergroup attitudes refers to attitudes about social groups that focus on either the ingroup (the group that a person belongs to and identifies with) or the outgroup (a group that is different from one's own group and often varies in status from one's own group). In intergroup contexts individuals often do what they can to preserve their ingroup identity, which often means derogating or disliking the outgroup (Dovidio, Gaertner, & Validizic, 1998). Children and adults often exclude individuals from the outgroup to maintain a strong ingroup identity. This approach has demonstrated that intergroup attitudes often reflect stereotypic and prejudicial attitudes that underlie exclusionary decisions.

Children identity with different groups, some that are chosen, such as sports teams, and others that are not chosen, such as gender and race/ethnicity. When group identity becomes very salient and important to the child then there is a greater expectation that exclusion will happen and that children will condone it or justify it. Children have expectations about group norms that members of groups need to adhere to, and they will often exclude someone who does not conform to the group norms. Unfortunately, some norms have to do with how others should be treated and reflect prejudicial attitudes. Children often struggle with decisions about exclusion of peers from their own group who do not meet the expectations of their group as well as exclusion of others from different groups. This makes social interactions and relationships very complex.

A third theory that is relevant for understanding exclusion and inclusion is from the field of peer relationships and friendships. Hinde's multilevel theory of social interactions, groups, and relationships has been used to understand individual differences in patterns of peer rejection (Hinde, Titmus, Easton, & Tamplin, 1985; Rubin, Bukowski, & Parker, 2006). Children who reject others often display aggressive behaviors, whereas children who are rejected are often extremely shy, fearful, and wary. It is also often the case that children who reject others have also been rejected by their peers. Personality differences also contribute to the patterns of peer rejection, and individual differences in personality bear on the types of individual–group interactions that occur when a child is rejected by others.

For example, when children are asked to nominate who they like and who they dislike in a classroom context, some children are perceived as having a lot of friends and some are perceived as having no friends. This categorization system has shown that children who have no friends and are rejected by their peers are often the same children who bully others and are therefore rejected by their peers. Yet, sometimes children are rejected for reasons based on group membership (such as gender, race, and ethnicity) and which may have little to do with personality traits. Instead, it may have to do with group functioning, and who is perceived to "fit the group." This means that exclusion has to be understood by considering a number of factors, including personality traits as well as group membership and group dynamics.

Finally, theories about how children process information and interpret social cues in children's expressions, affect, and behavior have been useful for understanding exclusion and inclusion. Social Information Processing models (Crick & Dodge, 1994) focus on how children think about each step of a social encounter, particularly encounters that create conflict, such as exclusion and rejection. The first step involves interpretations of the intentions and social cues in the interaction, followed by decisions on how to act and what to accomplish. This work has been important for understanding exclusion because many situations in which children are excluded are the result of different interpretations (and misinterpretations) of the intentions of other children. For example, one child may be excluded from a game because the other children may think that he will be aggressive, that is, they expect the child to act like a bully, when, in fact, the expectations are based on stereotypes and not actual prior behavior. In this case, children's interpretations of the intentions of another child lead to the exclusion and create social conflict.

Different interpretations of others' actions are particularly related to exclusion when the intentions of the peer situation are ambiguous. One child may exclude another child from joining a lunch table because they think that the child does not want to join them due to being part of another group when, in fact, the child is shy and wants to join but does not know how to express it. This type of situation occurs often and contributes to exclusion. Thus, children's "reading of the social expectations" of others has important relevance for understanding exclusion. When children have different expectations of what others might do then this often leads to exclusion of others, creating negative consequences for children who are excluded.

What these different theories tell us is that exclusion is not the same as bullying. While some types of exclusion turn into bullying there are many instances of exclusion in which the exclusion is legitimate because it is done to make groups work well, or in which the exclusion has negative outcomes but is the result of different interpretations of the same situation. In general terms, exclusion, unlike bullying or victimization, is not always negative because sometimes excluding others has to do with group inclusion criteria that are viewed as fair and legitimate.

Types of Exclusion

As we have indicated, figuring out and understanding decision-making about exclusion is a social-cognitive challenge that emerges in childhood and continues through adulthood. Exclusion occurs among friends, in social groups, and by institutions. Exclusion decisions are sometimes explicit, based on the motivation to make a group function well ("Everyone in this group has to be good at drawing so if you're not good then you can't join"), or the personal desire to choose a friend or partner ("I don't want to play with her because we don't like the same things"). Being the recipient of exclusion often involves recognition of the importance of group functioning and social desires, but sometimes this also means an awareness that the decision was unfair or wrong ("They didn't let her in the club but that's not right because they think she's mean but she's not;" "That group doesn't let girls in and that's unfair because they have all of the toys").

How children develop morality and moral judgments, form group identities, and an understanding of groups, contribute to exclusionary decisions that have negative outcomes for social relationships as well as social development. In fact, our central thesis is that the basic conflict between moral orientations and prejudicial attitudes and biases that emerge in childhood are realized in situations involving inclusion and exclusion. Thus, studying why children include or exclude friends provides a window into their application of moral or prejudicial attitudes in *actual* social decision-making and exchanges. A child's first experiences of exclusion from social groups occurs in early peer interactions in the home or school context and then extends to larger groups, particularly for groups in which group identity and group membership becomes salient. Exclusion occurs at many levels, from the dyadic to groups, from interpersonal to intergroup, and reflecting different levels of intentions and goals (Abrams, Hogg, & Marques, 2005).

Goals of the Book

A central goal of this book, then, is to discuss the emergence and origins of morality as well as bias and prejudice in order to understand why individuals exclude others, and how this emerges in childhood. How do children and adolescents approach situations that involve exclusion? When do children view exclusion as a matter of right or wrong? When does implicit and explicit prejudice factor into exclusion decisions and how do group norms bear on this process? Prejudice typically refers to negative evaluations of individuals because of the social groups they belong to (see Brewer, 1999; Brown, 1995), and is often contrasted with bias in favor of one's own group (i.e., ingroup) over others' groups (i.e., outgroups), commonly known as ingroup bias, which does not necessarily involve the expression of negative attitudes towards other groups.

The consequences for children's peer relationships and interactions are that the experience of social exclusion creates negative consequences whether the exclusion was motivated by direct prejudice or by ingroup favoritism. For example, if an African-American boy has no one to play with during recess because all the European-American children in his class prefer to play with children from their own racial group then the child's experience is social exclusion even if no prejudiced attitudes were explicitly expressed. Further, the potential negative outcomes for social development exist for this child whether the exclusion was direct or indirect. What makes this issue so timely is that these types of exchanges are occurring around the world, with the increased mobility of ethnic groups and regional transitions of migration. Latino children in the United States, Muslim children in the Netherlands, Salvadoran children in Spain, and Serbian children in Switzerland are often in the situation of feeling left out of a group at school, and bringing the conditions that create this form of exclusion in childhood to light is an important first step towards creating more inclusive environments for all individuals.

Summary

Exclusion and inclusion from social groups is pervasive in social life. There are many reasons that exclusion occurs, and understanding explicit motivations as well as implicit biases that contribute to exclusion sheds light on the development of exclusion in children's lives. This book is divided into eight chapters. We begin in Chapter 2, with an examination of the emergence of morality in childhood to demonstrate when and how children's inclusive orientation manifests. We then turn to the emergence of categorization and prejudice in Chapter 3, in which we explain how biases and stereotyping gets expressed in childhood and adolescence. Next, in Chapter 4, we examine how group identity and prejudice develops, and demonstrate ways in which prejudice may be a function of group goals rather than "selfish" desires or psychopathology. Then, in Chapter 5 we describe exclusion in the context of peer relations. In Chapter 6, we discuss an integrative approach to examining peer exclusion from social domain and social identity theoretical perspectives, describing a set of studies on how children evaluate intragroup exclusion (when a group excludes a member of its own group) and intergroup exclusion (when a group excludes someone from a different group). Understanding the relationships between intragroup and intergroup exclusion reveals children's ideas about group dynamics, which contributes to decision-making about group identity, peer exclusion, and morality.

In Chapter 7, we review recent research on exclusion based on culture, nationality, and immigrant status given that most research reviewed focuses on gender, race, and ethnicity. In Chapter 8, we describe interventions designed to promote positive social inclusion amongst children in the form of intergroup contact, media exposure, and programs designed to facilitate cross-group friendships as well as a sense of shared identity among children from different social groups. In Chapter 9, we provide our integrative perspective on exclusion, prejudice, and morality, and contend that new theories are needed to help us understand how these constructs are interconnected and interrelated. We conclude with our overall reflection of the topic of this book as well as new directions for research on exclusion and inclusion in children's lives.

Chapter 2

The Emergence of Morality in Childhood

How do children acquire morality, how is morality measured, and what are the obstacles that children confront when applying morality to their daily social interactions and encounters? In this chapter, we will review research on morality in childhood, and how moral concepts such as justice and fairness are applied to situations involving social inclusion and exclusion. Understanding children's social exclusion requires knowing both the positive and negative side of child development. The positive side manifests in the early emergence of morality and a sense of fairness that children demonstrate spontaneously as early as 2 and 3 years of age. The negative side is reflected in children's distrust of others who are different, selfishness, and ingroup favoritism. Moral norms are the converse of prejudicial norms; to be prejudiced violates norms about equality and fairness. Thus, to understand when children exclude others in ways that are unfair, it is necessary to understand the contexts in which children value fairness.

In what types of contexts do children demonstrate morality and how does it become inhibited or suppressed in situations in which bias is revealed? We offer group identity as part of the key to the puzzle; group identity pulls children in directions away from fairness in some contexts and determining how this comes about is important. Thus, the dynamic between developing morality and group identity reflects the crux of prejudice as it emerges in childhood, and group membership becomes an important source of influence on children's ability and motivation to enact their emerging beliefs about fairness, inclusion, and equality.

Children and Social Exclusion: Morality, Prejudice, and Group Identity. Melanie Killen and Adam Rutland. © 2011 Melanie Killen and Adam Rutland. Published 2011 by Blackwell Publishing Ltd.

Morality in Childhood

We will first review how morality has been studied in childhood, and then describe research revealing morality in the context of intergroup attitudes and relationships. Morality, in general, has been defined as prescriptive norms regarding how people should treat one another, concerning concepts such as justice, fairness, and rights. Important experiences that contribute to forming and acting on these concepts include empathy, perspective-taking, reciprocity, and mutual respect. In contrast to what many child developmentalists theorized in the middle of the last century, children are capable of understanding these concepts, albeit in a more primitive form than that displayed by adults. Most lay definitions of morality are fairly general (to a fault, often, as in the "kitchen sink" metaphor), and research has demonstrated how morality is actually a very well-defined construct, at least when measuring it from a developmental perspective.

What Morality is Not

Many common conceptions about what morality entails center on "rule-following" behavior. This definition of morality stems from early psychological research in the mid-1900s, which was later re-examined by child developmental psychologists, who showed that rule-following behavior involves many aspects of social interactions that are not explicitly about morality. For example, rules about etiquette (where to place a knife and fork), conventions (what to wear to a wedding), and pragmatic regulations (do not touch a hot stove) are not prescriptive norms about interindividual treatment but are agreed-upon rules to regulate social interactions and ensure group functioning. Most centrally, violating a rule about etiquette does not involve a "victim;" disorder may result, and the violation may disrupt group functioning but this is not the same as creating harm or unfairness to another person or victim. In addition, many rules are contrary to moral principles. Thus, following the rules "Hit disobedient children," "Blacks and Whites cannot sit together," "All children must say a prayer" (in a public school in the United States) were deemed wrong from a moral viewpoint in courts of law in the United States, indicating that "rule-following" behavior is not specific enough as a definition of morality. Not all rules are moral rules. As it turns out, these distinctions are understood in childhood, as will be described below.

In the early part of the last century, morality was examined in a delimited way in childhood, focusing on cheating and lying, but often defined from the adult's perspective. As an illustration, two psychologists, Hartshorne and May (1928–1930), in the 1920s, studied children's cheating behavior. They compared children's responses to interview questions about cheating with their actual cheating on a paper-and-pencil exam. The actual cheating exam was deceptive because children were asked to trace a circle with their eyes closed, which signaled to the experimenter that all children who did the task correctly cheated given that it was impossible to perform the task without cheating (Hartshorne & May, 1928–1930). The findings indicated that the vast majority of the children cheated by peeking through their fingers to draw the circle correctly.

As it turned out, though, children's responses for their behavior were a more complete reflection of their moral judgment than their actual "rule-following" behavior. Children who lied about their cheating and insisted that they drew the circle with their eyes closed were more likely to cheat multiple times, whereas children who explained that they peeked because they wanted to do well on the test and they hoped to please the teacher by drawing a nice circle were less likely to cheat overall. These findings indicated that children's interpretation of their behavior is an important dimension of their morality, and that how morality is measured needs to go beyond mere behavioral observations. In fact, children's understanding about truthfulness, lying, and what makes cheating wrong is more reflective of morality than their specific rule-following behavior. To understand morality we need to know what individuals' intentions are regarding their actions, and to differentiate rules about conventions, regulations, and customs, from rules about fairness, equality, and justice (Smetana, 2006; Turiel, 1998). This was the goal of Piaget's (1932) research on moral judgment in childhood in the 1930s, to be described below.

Criteria, Definitions, and Measurements of Morality

Research on morality in the child over the past 50 years has provided a more complex characterization, demonstrating social-cognitive differentiations that children make regarding the large number of rules that they are confronted with in their daily lives, the origins of morality, how moral concepts are related to concepts about authority and punishment, the relation of moral judgments to moral emotions, the role of peer interactions and groups on morality, how family interactions and relationships contribute to moral understanding, and the social predispositions that contribute to the emergence of morality, to name a few (see *Handbook of Moral Development*, Killen & Smetana, 2006).

More specifically, over the past three decades studies have demonstrated that children evaluate social rules using different criteria, and that social events are conceptualized by children as moral, social-conventional, or psychological, reflecting different domains of knowledge (Turiel, 1983, 1998, 2006). The moral domain includes issues about fairness, equality, justice, rights, and other's welfare (physical and psychological harm); the societal domain includes concerns about group functioning, group regulations, social institutions, cultural norms, traditions, and cultural rituals; and the psychological domain includes personal goals, autonomy, identity, Theory of Mind, and individual prerogatives. In addition to measuring the criteria that children use to differentiate rules, research has examined the reasons that children give for their evaluation of transgressions. Before describing this research program in detail, however, studies that have documented the origins of moral judgment will be described. Then the methodology for analyzing children's underlying criteria for what makes an event or a rule moral or social-conventional, or a matter of individual choice and prerogatives, will be discussed.

Morality Encompasses Judgment, Emotions, Individuals, and Groups

In many views of morality, the central debate is whether morality is about judgments "or" emotions, whether the focus should be on the individual "or" the group. In fact, both judgments and emotions are central, and the focus for understanding morality in the child has to be on both the individual and the group. Children are developing new concepts, skills, beliefs, and perspectives about their individual identity, autonomy, and personhood at the same time that they are becoming attached to others, forming groups, and understanding group identity and group dynamics. Moral judgment emerges out of social interactions, and these interactions involve information about the emotional, mental, and motivational states of others. Children use this information, to varying degrees, as they begin to interact with others, and form concepts about fair and equal treatment of persons. Emotional reactions from recipients of unfair treatment, as well as emotional displays by transgressors, provides children with foundational information about the nature of social interactions and what makes an act right or wrong, good or bad, kind or mean (Arsenio & Gold, 2006; Dunn, 1988; Malti, Gasser, & Buchmann, 2009).

In order to understand how children acquire morality in the context of social interactions and groups, it is necessary to discuss the basic developmental constructs that guide what we know about the acquisition of morality and moral concepts in childhood, and to provide a historical context about how morality in childhood has been characterized. This also involves defining morality, how it emerges in early development, and what it means for children to apply moral principles to their interactions with others in multiple contexts. What are the "social precursors" of morality? What does morality in childhood look like and what are the major findings?

Social Precursors of Moral Judgment

Social relationships, preferences, predispositions, and mindreading

Research over the past two decades has changed the focus of the *emergence* of moral judgment from adolescence to childhood (Dunn, 2006; Nucci, 2001; Smetana, 1993; Turiel, 1998). In addition, research on what might be the precursors of morality has expanded to include the infant's first set of social interactions with parents and caregivers (Thompson, Laible, & Ontai, 2003), social interactions with extended family members, including siblings (Dunn, 2006), social-cognitive distinctions that reflect an understanding of intentionality of social goals of others (Woodward, 2009), and social distinctions reflecting early forms of cooperation (Tomasello, Carpenter, Call, Behne, & Moll, 2005). These different areas of research do not include all of the ways that precursors to morality have been documented in infancy and early childhood, but reflect important evidence that the "inclusive" part of human development emerges early. We will briefly illustrate what these lines of research have demonstrated about early moral development.

Social interactions and relationships

Precursors of morality include a wide range of responses to others in the family, regarding social-emotional and social-cognitive understanding. These findings reveal how infants come into the world with a social predisposition. Beginning with early social-cognition research on an infant's ability to differentiate people from other animate and inanimate objects on a number of dimensions (for a review, see Thompson, 2006), findings have shown that babies prefer to look at human faces than nonhuman faces, prefer human speech, and engage in focused social interaction very early. Thus, infants are predisposed to orient towards other social beings and, with age, these preferences become more differentiated, with babies preferring familiar "others" (such as family members) and same-age peers to strangers.

Importantly, babies begin to engage in social exchanges and reciprocity with parents as well, and these exchanges become part of the basic building blocks of being social, which contributes to the development of attachment and affiliation with others. An extensive history of attachment research has provided evidence for the adaptive nature of infant's social orientations towards others (Cassidy, 2008), and how social interactions and relationships from the first days of an infant's life set in motion a behavioral system that ensures close proximity and security between the infant and the caregiver. Secure attachment enables the child to be independent, explore, and engage in social relationships with peers that contributes to an orientation to be inclusive and prosocial.

The basis for attachment and affiliation that is necessary for constructing moral understanding develops during the preschool period. This is because understanding others is part of the motivation for acting morally, and developing principles about respect for others. Out of early social interactions emerges knowledge about people, emotions, conventions, self-awareness, and morality. As Thompson (2006) and Dunn (2006) have asserted, early morality stems from both knowledge about rules as well as from the emotional bonds and affective relationships that are reflected in early childhood.

Social-cognitive preferences and intentionality

A body of research has further documented how infants differentiate social goals and motivations, including intentionality (Woodward, 2008, 2009). For example, during the first year of life infants begin to understand the relation between a person who looks and the object of his or her gaze; whereas 10-month-old babies do not understand the relation, 12-month-old babies do. This is a very subtle relationship, one taken for granted by adults, but reflecting a social and cognitive achievement by the end of the first year of life. Woodward and her colleagues have shown how infants make inferences about the relationship between acts and intentions.

Along with cognition about intentions regarding acts and objects, researchers have examined how infants make connections regarding acts and intentions with social objects, that is, with peers and adults. In one study, infants watched a cartoon in which a square helped a triangle up a hill followed by a triangle that hindered the other triangle's "efforts" to go up the hill. Following the cartoon, infants reached out for the object that was depicted as a helper more often than the object that was depicted as a hinderer (Hamlin, Wynn, & Bloom, 2007). This tells us that infants have a bias towards objects that appear to be helping others than those that might be serving as an obstacle to obtain a goal. Further, Warneken and Tomasello (2007) demonstrated that infants at 14 months altruistically help others towards individual goals, and cooperate towards a shared goal. Coordinating their skills with other social partners, however, was more difficult for the 14-month-olds than for18- and 24-month-old children. Further, Vaish, Carpenter, and Tomasello (2009) demonstrated that children do not need to observe others' emotions to make judgments that inflicting harm on others is wrong. One implication of this finding is that while emotions often provide information about the connection between acts and consequences for young children, emotions are not the core feature of what makes an act moral. Instead, children appear to make inferences about acts of harm whether a negative emotion is associated with the act or not.

Early social interactions vary greatly by cultural contexts, and particularly in terms of the extent to which this exposure is with family, friends, siblings, or nonfamilial peers and adults (daycare settings). Research on early social interaction has been conducted in the Americas (North, Central, and South), Europe and the UK, as well as Asia (Japan, Korea, and China), and the findings provide a strong basis for the universality of early social interactions that contribute to the development of the person (Greenfield & Cocking, 1994; Thompson, 2006). The findings on early social interaction in preschool children indicate that exchanges with siblings and peers involve object disputes and turn-taking, which are negotiated by children. As will be discussed below, Ross and colleagues have demonstrated how social interactions in the family in early development form the basis for an understanding of justice (Ross, Ross, Stein, & Trabasso, 2006).

Through resolving conflicts with peers and siblings, children experience reciprocity and understand why inflicting harm on others is wrong. Over countless hours, children work through social conflicts, initiating attempts to bargain and negotiate as well as threaten and insist on their own way. Children gain feedback from siblings and peers about what works and what contributes to conflict resolution or conflict escalation. As it turns out, children who engage in constructive conflict resolution and negotiation are more socially competent in an array of social contexts, and have better success in school and with making friends (Rubin, Bukowski, & Parker, 2006). Along with Ross' work (Ross et al., 2006) on early negotiations in peer interactions, Hay (2006) has examined children's concepts of ownership, for example, and has demonstrated that conversational competence and discussions about ownership facilitate positive peer interactions in early childhood.

Dunn (2006) as well has demonstrated how precursors to morality along emotional, affective, linguistic, and cognitive dimensions emerge in family relationships and exchanges. Discussions between parents and children about the nature of acts and consequences of acts provide children with social-cognitive information about the negative outcome of an act, and how to give priority to considerations of others instead of the self. At the same time, the emotional components of family relationships are central. Rather than focusing solely on the mother–child relationship as a transmission process from adult to child, Dunn (2006) has demonstrated that the family context enables children to learn about the consequences of acts on others, and to make inferences based on witnessed exchanges, which involve emotional reactions, discourse, and conversations. How family discussions, arguments, debates, and teasing contribute to children's understanding about empathy, fairness, and Theory of Mind has received a fair amount of attention in the past decade.

The connection between a child's emerging Theory of Mind and moral development has been of great interest to scholars and researchers in both fields. An overwhelming amount of evidence has demonstrated that social interaction and social experiences during the first 4 years of life enable children to acquire a Theory of Mind, which enables children to understand that others have desires, intentions, and beliefs that are different from one's own (Astington & Olson, 1995; Baird & Astington, 2004; Carpendale & Lewis, 2006; Dunn, 2006; Wellman, 1990). The central way that this ability is related to moral judgment is that intentionality is an underlying construct of morality as well as part of what the child becomes capable of doing in the first few years of life. Morality involves understanding that an action is wrong based on one's intentions, not solely the "objective" consequences. This is initially applied to one's own actions, but to make more judgments about others it is essential to know that others have intentions that may be different from one's own (recent research on a child's theory of social mind, that is, when children understand that others may have different intentions with respect to group dynamics than the self, will be further elaborated on in the next chapter).

Dunn's careful social interaction research provides extensive evidence for how this aspect of moral judgment emerges through shared discourse in the family environment (Dunn, 2006). For example, children begin to understand the idea of responsibility, which means how children are accountable to others for their rule violations such as those involving hitting others. Dunn has shown how young children during the third year of life begin to blame others (especially siblings), reflecting a sense of blameworthiness for one's actions. Further, children become capable of differentiating others' feelings and emotions from their own, which is necessary for understanding others' perspectives and has implications for early morality.

Judgments and emotions

This characterization of the emergence of moral development differs from previous characterizations which have typically dichotomized morality as either stemming from cognition (Kantian "rationality") or emotions (Humean "sentiments"). Children acquire morality from their social experiences, and the emotional consequences of the actions of others provide information for them to determine how to act. Moreover, and importantly, the process of caring for others enables one to respond to others from a moral viewpoint. That is, feelings of attachment and affiliation provide the basis for the ability to make moral judgments.

At the same time, attachment to the group is related to group identity, which can provide the basis for prejudice and stereotyping. This is because being strongly attached to one's group and forming a group identity has been shown to contribute to ingroup preference and out-group dislike. Thus, how attachment and affiliation are interpreted by the child remains a very important component for determining when attachment contributes to morality and when it contributes to prejudice and bias. Traditional attachment research has focused on attachment to the caregiver (not the group), and how this emerges at the beginning of life, enabling children to develop healthy social relationships as well as to become independent and capable of exploration (Cassidy, 2008). Considering the implications of attachment to the group is quite different from the body of research on caregiver–child attachment.

The issue of attachment is complex, however, when predictions are made regarding attachment relationships and social development, particularly moral development. In fact, as will be discussed in Chapter 5, children's likelihood to commit moral transgressions, such as bullying or victimization, stems from, in part, the quality of their social relationships, and their cognition about the feeling states of others. Moral understanding derived from family interactions typically refers to interactions among others who are familiar to the self. As children engage and interact with others outside the home context, the formation of groups and group interactions enters into the social experiential base of moral judgments.

Recently, there has been more attention to moral judgments about moral emotions and the intersection of these abilities (Malti, Gummerum, Keller, & Buchmann, 2009). Malti and her colleagues have conducted a research program on how children and adolescents attribute emotions to others, and the relation of evaluations of transgressions along with the emotions that individuals attribute to victimizers and victims. Young children who have trouble coordinating different types of emotions often attribute positive emotions to transgressors due to the material gain or benefit derived from certain forms of bullying (such as pushing someone off a swing to get a turn). This has been referred to as the "happy victimizer" effect which appears to dissipate around 8–9 years of age. At this point, children begin to attribute both positive and negative emotions to transgressors. This research is integrative in that moral judgment is not pitted against moral emotion. Instead, the core of the approach is social cognition, and the analyses pertain to how individuals make judgments of the feelings that they expect others will have during social exchanges.

Early peer group interactions

For the most part, children's experiences in social peer groups begin early in development, as young as 3 and 4 years of age. The knowledge derived from these social encounters include an understanding of how to engage in social exchanges, establish social groups, acquire negotiation skills, learn how to resolve conflicts, understand the intentions of others (Theory of Mind) as well as how to apply moral concepts, such as fairness, equality, and empathy to social interactions with others. What makes new social interactions challenging, in contrast to family interactions, is the lack of prior knowledge about new playmates and peers. Children enter social groups with a lack of knowledge about what others are like, what they think, and whether there is a mutual compatibility or trust. Children's Theory of Mind becomes more explicit during this period as well. Interacting with new individuals involves a new set of challenges.

At the same time, these new challenges enable children to apply the knowledge acquired in familiar, family interactions to individuals with different traits, appearances, interests, and group identities. Through social negotiation, there is also the potential for group antagonism and favoring one's own ingroup, which can easily (but not necessarily) result in negative attitudes about those who are not in the child's "group," however that is defined.

Research in the area of peer interactions and relationships has identified different levels of peer groups that are much more differentiated than depicted in past research (Gelman & Wellman, 1991). These are sociometric categories of popular and rejected peers, social crowds, groups of friends, and groups of peers who "hang out" together in social cliques. How morality emerges in these types of groups has not been studied extensively and remains an area ripe for investigation.

Thus, the precursors for moral judgment are multidimensional, including establishing a Theory of Mind, forming attachments, engaging in social interaction, and interacting with family members regarding morally relevant exchanges. Moral judgment, which emerges during early childhood has reflected a long tradition of research in developmental psychology, with a focus on how morality is defined, measured, and analyzed. In the next section, we will discuss moral judgment research findings.

Moral Judgment and Interaction in Childhood

Piaget (1932), studying children's moral judgments in his classic book *The moral judgment of the child*, demonstrated how children change from focusing on authority mandates to determine what is right and wrong, to focusing on independent principles of justice by late childhood. With age, children do not define morality in terms of authority mandates but in terms of principles of fairness. Piaget drew on moral philosophical theories to assert that morality should not be defined by cultural norms and rules, but instead by principles stemming from reasoning about the treatment of others. Piaget (1932) showed that the origins of moral rationality, as theorized by Immanuel Kant (1785/1981), could be observed in childhood, and that the transformation from authority-based judgments to justice-based judgments takes place by 10 years of age, which reflects a developmental and universal social-cognitive transformation. What was important about this viewpoint was that Piaget designed studies to determine whether moral judgment was universal in childhood, and whether children could critically evaluate cultural norms and authority rules.

Moreover, Piaget theorized about moral emotions as reflected in respect for others but not as the fundamental basis of morality, which could only be judgment and rationality. This was quite different from the earlier accounts of children's moral reasoning because he: (1) investigated morality as a form of judgment, not strictly conformity to rules; (2) rejected a definition of morality as cultural norms or rules and relied on a definition that referred to principles of justice and fairness; (3) predicted that children constructed moral principles as they construct space, time, and causality, and that the knowledge related to morality was not solely learned from adults; and (4) proposed universally general moral developmental processes emerging in childhood.

Piaget's studies involved asking children about their rules for the game of marbles as well as their consciousness of the rules. He conducted detailed interviews with children regarding their judgments about their games as well as their evaluations of hypothetical dilemmas. He asked them what made the rules of the game fair or unfair, where the rules came from, and whether the rules could be changed. Using this methodology, he found that by 8 years of age, children view the basis of rules as something children negotiate by peers rather than as taught by adults, and that children reason about the wrongness of acts in terms of justice rather than what adults deem is right. He also found that children differentiate different forms of justice, such as distributive and retributive. Importantly, Piaget developed a methodology for soliciting children's perspectives on what makes an act right or wrong, and he established a way to analyze spontaneous reasoning from children regarding fundamental concepts, such as morality, authority, and social rules (Helwig, 2008; Turiel, 1998).

Further, Piaget's theory provided a rich basis for theorizing about children's morality in terms of judgment–action relations, morality and emotion, morality and authority, and the role of peer interaction in facilitating moral development. In particular, Piaget focused on how children's interactions with peers provide an essential experiential basis for constructing concepts of equality and fairness. Through a reciprocal process of identity and perspective-taking, children develop an understanding of why it is important to be fair and treat others equally. As one identifies with another then this becomes the source for understanding why it is wrong to inflict harm or deny others' resources ("I don't like it when someone takes my toy; he is like me so he must not like it when I take his toy").

Several studies by Damon (1977) examined children's discussions about fairness in peer exchanges, documenting age-related changes in concepts of distributive justice. In one study, children were videotaped in groups of three (without adults present) and were asked to divide up candy among their group after making bracelets. The findings showed that by 6 years of age, children spontaneously focused on principles of equality, and by 9–10 years of age, children referred to principles of merit and reciprocity. Interviews with children confirmed the generalizability of these concepts, which children applied to a wide range of peer settings (Damon & Killen, 1982).

To provide a detailed analysis of children's discourse during conflict interactions regarding the distribution of resources, Killen and Turiel (1991) videotaped children in groups of three playing with toys to determine how they approached conflicts that arose in the course of interaction (Figure 1.1). An example of an exchange in which three 3.5-year-olds are playing at a table with small toys while a video camera is on and no adults are present in the room, is the following:

[Three children are at a table asked to play with toys while no adults are present in the room]

RUTH: [holding up two Fisher-Price people] Hey, I want the green person. How about if we trade? Here, you can have this one [gives a blue person to Michael]. And I can have the green one. Okay? [reaches for the green person that Michael is holding in his hand]

Figure 2.1 Children negotiating toys at a table. (© 2010 Melanie Killen.)

MICHAEL: No! We already did trade. I want this one [holds on to the green one]. I want it now and you had it already.

LILY: Hey, you can both have my spoons, if you want? [shows her spoons to Michael and Ruth]

RUTH: No, I want the green person.

MICHAEL: I'm not trading any of mine. [hovers over his toys]

LILY: [sings] I'm not trading any of mine.

RUTH: [sings] I'm not trading any of mine.

LILY: Well, that's not fair because *I* don't have any people. [pouts]

MICHAEL: [to Ruth] Give her one of them.

RUTH: But you have three and she has none and I have one. So that's not fair.

LILY: Yeah, because I have none.

RUTH: [to Michael] You know what? If you give me the green and then I'll give her the red one and then we'll all have one.

MICHAEL: Well, if you don't give me the red one then I won't invite you to my birthday party.

LILY: But I don't have any people.

RUTH: Okay, I'll give you this one [to Lily] and I'll take this one from Michael and then we'll all have one, okay?

MICHAEL: [gives orange person to Ruth] Okay, but can we trade again tomorrow?

RUTH: [sings] Birthday party! [takes the orange person from Michael and gives the red person to Lily]

LILY: [sings] Birthday party!

MICHAEL: [sings] Birthday party!

This example, consistent with a Piagetian approach, reveals how children construct social and moral rules during their interactions. This differs from a view that examines whether children comply with rules as a means for determining the origins of morality. As reported by Killen and Turiel (1991), children's conflict resolution strategies were more varied and collaborative with age. Subsequently, the videotapes of these sessions (55 sessions conducted over 6 months, 2,000 discourse utterances) were analyzed from a child psycholinguistic framework (Killen & Naigles, 1995) and the findings indicated that children used "collaborative suggestions" most often, followed by "negotiations," "bargains," as well as "threats" (e.g., "I won't invite you to my birthday party"). Few references to the group were recorded in triadic settings with young children, aged 3.5 years. At 4.5 and 5.5 years, however, children begin to refer to their group, and to their collective identity.

At this point in development, collective identity typically has referred to the emergence of a group, that is, references to "us" rather than "you" and "me." For example, children at the youngest age were most likely to share between dyads, excluding the third child in the play session, and often in terms of access to the toys. While children often demonstrated spontaneous sharing between themselves and one other playmate, coordinating the interactions was difficult and children often excluded a third party from the discussions of how to share the toys. By 5.5 years of age, children in these peer group settings referred to one another in their discussions about sharing and came up with "third party reconciliation" resolution strategies. What requires more research is how this collective identity emerges, and how attitudes about ingroup and outgroup based on categories such as gender, race, and ethnicity bear on this process. This issue is the topic of the next two chapters (see Chapters 3 and 4) in which we describe the research on early categorization, prejudice, and group identity. During the preschool and elementary school periods, research has been conducted on the role of gender in same-gender and opposite-gender group encounters, with mixed findings (as discussed in the next chapter). Suffice it to say, Piaget's foundational research did not delve into these issues.

Thus, while Piaget's research set the stage to analyze children's construction of morality in social interactions, there were many limitations of his research, aside from the categories of social identity that contribute to ingroup/outgroup attitudes. One limitation of Piaget's analyses was that his observations of children's peer interactions were focused primarily on a narrow context, that is, children's discussion about the game of marbles (and all boys). Over the past few decades, developmental research has expanded the context of relevant interactions to the family, the home, school, and importantly to consider a range of issues for discussion and evaluation, including many varied social concepts (Smetana, 2006). Further, detailed analyses have included how emotions, the history of interactions, the quality of friendship and peer relationships, the nature of social groups, group identity, and group functioning have an effect on the emergence of morality in the child. Before discussing how children's social interactions bear on moral development, further discussion of the traditional theories about children's moral development will be described, followed by current formulations and findings.

Morality as Justice

Extending Piaget's theory, Kohlberg (1984) theorized that moral development could be characterized as a set of six stages throughout life, not just early and middle childhood, and that moral reasoning reflected increasingly sophisticated notions of justice, based on philosophical criteria. Using more elaborated dilemmas, which were designed to probe individuals about complex societal issues involving stealing, saving a life, property rights, social obligations, and relationships, Kohlberg provided a basis for extending the range of concepts within the moral domain. In addition to focusing on fair distribution of resources, Kohlberg included issues such as the value of human life, rights, others' welfare, and social equity. Moreover, Kohlberg demonstrated how complex social interactions are related to morality by studying how schools that were established on theories of democracy and rights (Just Community Schools, see Colby & Kohlberg, 1987) were related to the development of moral judgment.

Like Piaget, Kohlberg (1971) contested the notion that morality involved children's compliance to adult rules. Instead, morality involved an understanding about what makes rule transgressions wrong, and how an underlying concept about justice emerges and changes over the lifespan. Kohlberg debated with behaviorist researchers by arguing for a cognitive theory of morality. Very generally, Kohlberg found that young children were premoral (referred to as pre-conventional), and relied on selfish desires to avoid punishment (rather than authority mandates as Piaget had predicted) to determine whether acts were right or wrong. Subsequently, adolescents acquired an understanding about groups and cultures and evaluated acts as right or wrong based on societal laws, rules, and social relational obligations (referred to as conventional reasoning). By adulthood, individuals evaluated acts in terms of principles of justice, and not from a selfish or group perspective (referred to as post-conventional). This approach involved assessing an individual's general scheme (organizing principle) for evaluating social problems and dilemmas across a range of contexts. Kohlberg's formulation was expansive and involved detailed coding and analyses of children's, adolescents', and adults' reasoning about a range of dilemmas.

Most centrally, Kohlberg (Colby & Kohlberg, 1987) focused on reasoning and judgment, and the ways that nonmoral social considerations such as personal desires and group conformity exerted negative pressures on individuals to subordinate morality to these types of concerns. His specific analyses, however, were limited to responses to a complex adult-oriented dilemma regarding the value of life pitted against property rights, marital relationships, and legal consequences (referred to as the Heinz dilemma in which a man steals a drug to save his wife's life).

These concepts were not part of the child's world but were adult-focused and adult-defined. Importantly, though, the theory provided a framework to examine moral reasoning throughout the lifespan.

Social Domain Model of Social and Moral Judgment

By the mid-1980s, though, studies of contextual variation in judgments provided extensive evidence contesting domain-general approaches to moral development, which were identified as broad stages of moral judgment (Smetana, 2006; Turiel, 1998). Instead, Turiel and colleagues formulated a domain-specific model, referred to as the Social Domain model for understanding morality as a distinct conceptual system from other forms of social judgment such as concepts about conventions as well as psychological knowledge. The research program demonstrated the coexistence of different forms of social reasoning from childhood to adulthood. For example, young children's evaluations of transgressions and social events reflected considerations of the self (pre-conventional level in Kohlberg's terminology), the group (conventional level in Kohlberg's system), and justice (post-conventional level, Kohlberg's highest level); these three forms of judgments coexisted in early development (Table 2.1). Moreover these constructs provided categories to analyze social interactions as well as social judgments. This theory was a direct challenge to Kohlberg's theory which proposed that his levels were hierarchically organized in that one came after the other. Thus, in Kohlberg's system, young children are self-oriented, adolescents and adults are group-oriented, and adults with heightened moral awareness are justice-oriented; passing through each stage is necessary before reaching the next stage.

The Social Domain model demonstrated that these constructs do not emerge successively but simultaneously in development, each with its own separate developmental trajectory (e.g., self-knowledge, conventional (group) knowledge, and moral knowledge). Thus, multiple forms of reasoning are applied to the evaluations of social dilemmas and interactions.

Consistent with Kohlberg's theory, though, these findings demonstrated that morality is not strict rule-following behavior as not all rules are the same, nor do all rules have moral underpinnings. As discussed at the beginning of the chapter, the findings revealed, further, that children do not conceptualize all rules the same, and that different justifications and

Table 2.1   Domain-general and domain-specific models. (© 2010 Melanie Killen)

Domain-specific theory	*Domain-general stage theory*
Social Domain theory	*Moral judgment*
• Psychological domain: individual prerogatives; self, autonomy, Theory of Mind	• Preconventional (self): children
	• Conventional (group): adolescents and adults
• Societal domain: behavioral uniformities for making groups work well; societal rules, group traditions, customs, group functioning	• Post-conventional (justice): philosophers, ethicists
• Moral domain: principles of how individuals ought to treat others; justice, fairness, equality, rights, others' welfare	*Cognitive development* (Piaget, 1952)
	• Sensori-motor: pre-representational (infancy)
	• Preoperational: intuitive (early childhood)
	• Concrete: reversible operations (childhood)
	• Formal: abstract (adolescence)

reasons were given for the evaluation of rules. Rules with a moral basis, such as those involving harm or unfairness, are treated differently from rules with a conventional basis, such as those involving customs, traditions, and etiquette. Research over the past 25 years, with over 100 empirical studies published, has provided an extensive research program with many generative applications of the model to different areas of social life (Smetana, 2006)

Social judgments do not reflect one broad template or stage, such as Kohlberg's pre-conventional level to characterize childhood morality. Instead, children, adolescents, and adults use different forms of reasoning – moral, conventional, and psychological – simultaneously when evaluating transgressions and social events. The change in formulation of morality reflected a movement away from a global stage model towards domain-specific models of development and is consistent with changes towards domain specificity in other areas of development such as cognitive development (Kiel, 2006; Kuhn & Siegler, 2006), neuroscience (Blakemore, Winston, & Frith, 2004), and other fields of child development. This is because domain-specific approaches provide for a contextual approach that enables researchers to understand how children's judgment and behavior vary as a function of the context. From a Kohlbergian view, young children evaluate rules from a selfish perspective and then from a group perspective, only holding a justice viewpoint with the emergence of abstract reasoning in adulthood. In other words, a child at the first stage of moral development in Kohlberg's system should judge that rules should not be broken *unless* you "will not get in trouble" (avoid punishment or evade an authority's awareness of the rule violation).

Social Domain studies with children have shown, however, that children differentiate rules along a range of criteria. Rules about the moral domain are evaluated differently from rules about the societal domain because rules about avoiding harm and fair distribution, for example, are evaluated based on the intrinsic negative consequences, and are interpreted as generalizable (not culturally or contextually specific), unalterable (the rules should not be changed), and not subject to authority jurisdiction (the teacher cannot change the rules about it). In contrast societal rules about conventions, customs, and etiquette are evaluated as contextual and culturally specific as well as alterable and within authority jurisdiction. Further, the evaluation of issues within the psychological domain indicates that children view issues such as choice of friends, bodily appearance, and personal correspondence as matters that should not be regulated with rules and are up to individuals to decide (individual discretion and personal prerogatives) (Nucci, 2001).

Several implications of this approach are that children's social understanding and social knowledge are not characterized as "moral or selfish" but as multidimensional, that is, moral, self-oriented, group-oriented, and societally-oriented. Nonmoral, social understanding, for example, includes a concern with group functioning or group identity (societal domain) as well as a concern with autonomy and personal goals (psychological domain). Thus, what may appear as "selfish" from the viewpoint of the adult observing children's interactions, may, in fact, pertain to personal goals and autonomy. This is not to assert that young children are not selfish; it is to assert that adults can also be selfish, and that "selfishness" is not a uniquely age-related phenomenon found only in early childhood. That children may refrain from sharing toys may have to do with their interpretation of the objects in terms of ownership, and when this information is incorrect their behavior appears to be selfish, when, in fact, it is within their ownership priority (Hay, 2006; Ross, et al., 2006). This domain-specific model provides an alternative approach to Kohlberg's (1971) and Piaget's (1952) domain-general models.

As an illustration, research on children's differentiation of social domains has interviewed children about rule transgressions and found that different sets of criteria are used to evaluate the legitimacy or wrongness of a rule violation. For example, two transgressions, hitting someone in an unprovoked encounter, and wearing pajamas to school, are viewed as wrong by children. As shown in Table 2.2, these two transgressions are depicted with the criteria that are used to assess children's criteria for evaluating these transgressions.

Children evaluate the first transgression, hitting, as wrong because of the negative intrinsic consequences to another person (which involve a victim) in contrast to the second transgression, wearing pajamas to school, which children view as wrong because it is disruptive to expectations about modes of dress and traditions. A set of criterion assessments have been applied to children's judgments to determine their differentiation of concepts. These are: (1) *rule alterability* (Can you change the rule about X?); (2) *generalizability* (Does the rule about X apply in other schools or cultures?); (3) *punishment avoidance* (Is it all right to do X if you do not get in trouble for doing it?); (4) *authority jurisdiction* (Is it up to the teacher to decide whether the act X is all right or not all right?); and (5) *rule contingency* (Is the legitimacy of the act X contingent on the

Table 2.2   Children's criteria for social rules. (© 2010 Melanie Killen)

Joe *hits Sarah* for no reason (Rule violation: do not hit someone)
- "What if the *teacher* says it's okay?" ("It's still wrong")
- "What if you don't *get in trouble*?" ("It's still wrong")
- "What if there is no *rule* about it?" ("It's still wrong")
- "What if you could *change the rule* about it? ("It's still wrong")
- "What if there is *another school/culture* where it would be all right to hit?" ("It's still wrong")

Alice *wears pajamas to school* (Rule violation: do not wear pajamas to school)
- "What if the *teacher* says it's okay?" ("It's okay"): Authority jurisdiction
- "What if you don't *get in trouble*?" ("It's okay"): Punishment avoidance
- "What if there is no *rule* about it?" ("It's okay"): Rule contingency
- "What if you could *change the rule* about it?" ("It's still wrong"): Rule alterability
- "What if there is *another school/culture* where it would be all right?" ("It's okay"): Generalizability

---

existence of a rule?). In the case of hitting and wearing pajamas to school, in children as young as 4 and 5 years of age (some studies have shown the distinction as young as 2.5 years of age), the rule about hitting is viewed as not alterable, generalizable, still wrong if you do not get in trouble, not a matter of authority jurisdiction (if the teacher says it is okay then it is still wrong), and not rule contingent (it is wrong even if there is no rule about it). In contrast, the rule about wearing pajamas is alterable (you can change it), not generalizable (it is okay if people in other contexts wear pajamas to school), not wrong if you do not get in trouble, a matter of authority jurisdiction (okay if the teacher says it is okay) and rule contingent (see Nucci, 2001; Smetana, 2006; Tisak, 1986; Turiel, 1998).

These findings demonstrate that young children have underlying criteria that they use to evaluate social events, interactions and relationships in their social world. Children are often unaware of these dimensions, and only through systematic empirical investigation are these capabilities and competencies made explicit.

Reviews of this research have shown that children use these criteria beginning at an early age up through adulthood. Yet, with age, children begin to use more than one criterion to differentiate different types of rules. For example, very young children may recognize that rules about conventions are alterable (the rule can be changed) but not yet recognize that conventional rules are contingent on authority (that authority can deem the act to be legitimate). In general, children use a range of justifications, including moral, conventional, psychological, and pragmatic reasons to evaluate acts, events, and transgressions. Thus, children use a mixture of reasons when evaluating different scenarios, not just one type of reasoning as would reflect a global stage of development.

To a large extent, the foundational research on moral judgment from the Social Domain model concentrated on documenting the universality of conceptual categories and distinctions, such as the extent to which children differentiate moral rules from social-conventional ones (Nucci & Turiel, 1978), evaluate parental jurisdiction about moral rules (Tisak, 1986), evaluate victimizers' emotional states (Arsenio & Kramer, 1992), differentiate rights and freedoms (Helwig, 1995a; Ruck, Abramovitch, & Keating, 1998), determine preschoolers' criteria for evaluating rules and differentiating hypothetical and actual transgressions (Smetana, 1981; Smetana, Schlagman, & Adams, 1993), differentiate teacher responses to transgressions (Killen, Breton, Ferguson, & Handler, 1994), and differentiate the personal domain from the moral and conventional domains (Killen & Smetana, 1999; Nucci, 2001; Nucci & Weber, 1995).

As an example, Killen et al. (1994) showed preschool-aged children different pictures of teachers responding to two different encounters: (1) one child hitting another child in the sandbox; and (2) one child who played with lego in the sandbox. Both acts were rule violations at the school ("Do not hit others", "Do not play with Lego in the sandbox"). Children were asked to evaluate whether the act was all right and why. These two acts were viewed as "moral" and "social conventional" transgressions. Then, children were asked to choose which of two forms of teacher interventions they thought would be best. The first one was "domain appropriate," in which a teacher used language that matched the domain of the act, and the second one was "domain inappropriate," following on Nucci's (2001) distinctions. In Figure 2.2, the "moral" transgression is displayed with the teacher using each response in card 1 (moral) and card 2 (social conventional). With age, from 3–5 years old, children preferred teachers to talk about the negative intrinsic consequences of the act to another person (causing pain) rather than the social disruption, reflecting a preference for teachers to be "domain appropriate" (using moral language for a moral transgression) rather than "domain inappropriate" (using social-conventional language for a moral transgression).

Moral Generalizability

Research on the universality of these principles has demonstrated that children and adolescents in a wide range of cultures believe that equality, justice, and fairness apply to all individuals. This is measured in childhood and adolescence by administering assessments about the generalizability of the act. Thus, this method of examining universality or generalizability reflects whether individuals in a given culture believe that rules about fairness, harm, and rights should be upheld by members of another culture or whether these values are culturally specific. For example, cross-cultural studies in India and the United States have investigated whether individuals in the United States and in India believe that "fair distribution of resources" should be upheld by people in different countries. Answers to this question address theories about moral universalism and moral relativism, that is, whether morality is generalizabile or culturally specific. Another way to address the question of universality of principles, however, is to ask whether individuals include members of other groups (defined by culture, race, ethnicity, or gender) when making judgments about equality and fairness. Do individuals

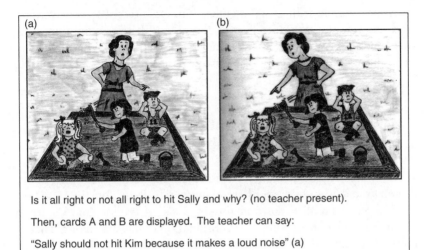

Is it all right or not all right to hit Sally and why? (no teacher present).

Then, cards A and B are displayed. The teacher can say:

"Sally should not hit Kim because it makes a loud noise" (a)

OR

"Sally should not hit Kim because it makes Kim cry" (b)

Which would be better for the teacher to say and why?

Figure 2.2 Cards used in a preschool study on moral judgment. (© 2010 Melanie Killen.)

believe that resources should be divided equitably among individuals regardless of group membership? Does the fair distribution of resources depend on one's majority/minority status, and is this judgment applied similarly to members of the ingroup and the outgroup? What are the contexts in which this judgment is clearly answered in the affirmative, and when do stereotypes about the other influence these types of judgments? These questions concern intergroup relationships, which bear on the universality of morality from the viewpoint of the individual.

Most of the research in moral development has examined how children apply their moral principles to members of their own cultural, ethnic, or gender group. In fact, most research by design involves interviewing children and adolescents about others who are just like them, typically to increase the "comfort" level of the interviewee (e.g., children are shown picture cards that match the gender and race/ethnicity of the participant). Nonetheless, there is an underlying assumption about intergroup relationships in moral developmental theories to the extent that morality is about being impartial and applying concepts of justice and rights to everyone, regardless of group membership. Only recently, however, has moral development research *directly* tested these assumptions and have moral developmental hypotheses included considerations about the influence of intergroup attitudes on moral judgments, as discussed in Chapters 3 and 4.

Morality in the Context of Other Social Concepts: Multifaceted Events

While the early Social Domain studies (in the late 1970s and 1980s) demonstrated how children differentiate rules by these domains, and how children conceptualize the domains by a set of criteria, more current research has examined children's coordination of these domains. That is, given that most issues in social life are multifaceted, how do children weigh different considerations? What happens when a moral rule about not harming others is in conflict with a conventional rule about fulfilling a role as group leader or team captain? In these situations children have to coordinate different concerns and give priority to the types of issues created in an actual situation. Research has examined the multitude ways in which coordination is required with a set of age-related findings. In fact, what changes with development is the way that children coordinate these reasons, and the priority that they give to different reasons when making decisions and evaluating social exchanges.

For example, social problems can be straightforward, where one type of issue is predominant (e.g., hitting someone for no reason is viewed as wrong from a moral viewpoint with few competing considerations), or social issues can be complex with more than one consideration (e.g., excluding someone from a group can be viewed as legitimate to make the group function well or as wrong when the reason for exclusion is arbitrary). While most issues in social life are multidimensional, understanding the fundamental "components" of social issues is essential, and this knowledge begins in early development. The basic components of morality, conventions, and the psychological self provide the foundations for constructing knowledge about complex issues, and for decision-making in social life.

Research from Social Domain theory, then, has shown that children develop three coexisting domains of knowledge early in development: the moral domain (justice, others' welfare, fairness), the societal domain (conventions, traditions, customs, group norms), and the psychological domain (self, personal discretion, individual prerogatives).

The methodology used to investigate children's social and moral judg-ments involves evaluating familiar everyday social exchanges (different from Kohlberg's adult-oriented complex dilemmas and similar to Piaget's focus) and systematic probes to determine children's judgments, justifica-tions, and the underlying criteria by which they differentiate moral, social-conventional, and psychological concepts (which is different from Piaget's global approach).

These domains reflect rich, complex, and dynamic issues for children (and constructs to study in research) that reflect conflict and change, negotiation and resistance, judgments and emotions, the individual and the group, hierarchies and status. The strengths of this model, which has provided a striking contrast to the stage theories of moral development, are that: (1) it provides a way of analyzing the multiple forms of reasoning present in children's and adolescents' judgments rather than solely focusing on moral reasoning; (2) it moves the analysis away from how children and adolescents reason about unfamiliar hypothetical scenarios (sometimes once-in-a-lifetime events) to one that studies reasoning about everyday, familiar issues; (3) it examines how an individual's reasoning varies across a wide range of social contexts rather than reflecting general, global stages, which are theorized to apply across diverse social contexts; (4) it shifts the focus of the study of morality away from the test of a hierarchical, primitive-to-advanced theory and towards an examination of how individuals coordinate different forms of reasoning, moral and nonmoral, at different points in development; and (5) it allows for an examination of cultural variation in moral and nonmoral social reasoning that does not compare individuals from different cultures on one scale or "standard."

Over the past decade, much of the social-cognitive domain research has focused on investigating how individuals evaluate complex issues, those that typically involve multiple domains of reasoning. Complex issues are in contrast to straightforward ones in that more than one form of reasoning is used to evaluate the nature of the act. This has included investigating how individuals evaluate issues such as religion (Nucci & Turiel, 1993), parent–adolescent conflict (Smetana & Asquith, 1994), mixed emotions (Lemerise & Arsenio, 2000; Malti, Gummerum et al., 2009), prejudice and intergroup attitudes (Killen, Margie, & Sinno, 2006), interpersonal responsibilities (Miller, 2001), autonomy (Nucci & Weber, 1995), Theory of Mind (Killen, Mulvey, Richardson, Jampol, & Woodward, in press; Lagattuta, 2005), and cultural expectations of social norms (Turiel, 2002; Wainryb, 1993). In general, age-related changes within the moral domain are that young children first understand the concrete moral principles pertaining to others' welfare (not inflicting physical harm) and distribution of resources (sharing, turn-taking), followed by an understanding of more abstract moral issues, such as psychological harm (teasing), rights, and exclusion (in the context of negative intentions towards others).

Age-related changes from childhood to adolescence regarding moral reasoning are reflected by an increasing ability to coordinate multiple issues and to weigh different points of view when making morally relevant decisions. What also becomes complex is that age-related changes within each domain – the moral, societal, and psychological – occur, and thus weighing multiple considerations in adolescence is quite different from early childhood. Moreover, individuals have the capacity to weigh a wealth of contextual information about persons (intentionality, motivations, emotions, mindreading), groups (power, status, hierarchies), and societies (traditions, customs, rituals) when making moral judgments.

Morality and Theory of Mind

Recent research on the intersection of morality and Theory of Mind has revealed a number of important findings. Researchers have studied whether Theory of Mind competence is related to understanding morally relevant actions (Chandler, Sokol, & Wainryb, 2000; Leslie, Knobe, & Cohen, 2006; Zelazo, Helwig, & Lau, 1996). The focus of studies differs but the overall pattern indicates that these abilities are interrelated; for both abilities it is necessary to understand intentionality. For example, Lagattuta, Nucci, and Boascaki (2010) have shown that from 4 to 7 years of age, children's feelings about compliance with rules increases but only for moral rules, not issues associated with the personal domain, such as choice of friends or activities. Participants predicted that children would feel positive emotions about noncompliance within the the personal domain, such as being happy when asserting autonomy, but negative emotions about noncompliance within the moral domain, such as being sad when someone is a victim. Thus, domain specificity was revealed regarding expectations about others' intentions.

In the area of judgments and decision-making about peer encounters, a recent study was completed in which children from 3.5 to 7.5 years of age were asked to make attributions about an "accidental transgressor" (Killen et al., in press). Three tasks were administered to children: (1) prototypic moral transgression (pushing someone off a swing); (2) prototypic false belief Theory of Mind (ToM) task (false contents and location change); and (3) morally relevant Theory of Mind (MoToM) tasks. The MoToM task involved a story in which a child accidentally threw away a special cupcake while cleaning the classroom when the cupcake owner was outside. The participant was asked where the cupcake owner would look when he/she returned to the room, and how he/she would feel about the classroom helper.

Children who did not pass the false belief ToM task were more likely to attribute negative intentions to an accidental transgressor than children who passed the false belief ToM task, and to use moral reasons when blaming the accidental transgressor. In addition, children who did not pass false belief ToM viewed it as more acceptable to punish the accidental transgressor than did participants who passed false belief ToM. Thus, this study revealed that a child's ability to understand that others have different intentions from the self is related to their attributions of intentional wrong-doing of peers. An implication is that children who do not have false belief knowledge may be more likely to accuse their friends of wrong-doing unfairly (when the act is accidental). These findings provide insights into the domain specificity of social knowledge (moral knowledge being different from psychological knowledge of others' minds) and provide essential information that helps to explain children's interpersonal interactions and social exchanges.

Morality and Social-Cognitive Development

New cross-cutting areas for investigating children's social and moral understanding is in the field of children's cognitive development, particularly in the area of executive control (Carlson, 2005; Zelazo, Carlson, & Kesek, in press) as well as in developmental neuroscience (Blair, 1995; Eisenberger & Lieberman, 2004; Lieberman, 2007). This is because new research on cognitive and brain mechanisms has revealed ways in which the brain can (or cannot) weigh and coordinate different variables when the individual is making decisions, which helps explain coordination between different domains. As will be discussed in other chapters, domain-specific approaches to social and moral development have led to new, interdisciplinary approaches to understanding child development.

Summary

In summary, this chapter demonstrated how morality emerges early in development. Studies in infancy have shown that infants prefer "helpers" to "hinders" and that toddlers engage in spontaneous helping behavior towards others that does not benefit themselves (thus is not about personal gain). Research with preschoolers, children, and adolescents has shown how children have an underlying category system for conceptualizing rules, events, and transgressions that reflects different domains of knowledge, with morality being differentiated from conventions and issues of autonomy.

As early evidence, preschool children spontaneously discuss and negotiate issues about fairness during peer interactions differently from those involving regulations and traditions, and adults discuss these types of interactions in distinct ways. During childhood and adolescence, morality becomes complex, reflecting issues of fairness, rights, and the wrongfulness of discrimination, which have to be coordinated with the context of social events that reflect different types of relationships, emotions, expectations about mental states, and general knowledge about how the world works.

How morality is related to prejudice, group identity, and intergroup attitudes is a more recent focus for research. In the next chapter, we will describe research on categorization and prejudice that has drawn from cognitive psychology as well as social psychology and has guided much of the recent developmental research in this area.

Chapter 3

Emergence of Social Categorization and Prejudice

We know from chapter 2 that children develop morality at an early age. This is clearly a positive aspect of social development which can result in inclusion and positive relationships between children. Yet, there are many contexts in children's lives in which it becomes difficult to apply their moral judgments to situations, when other aspects of children's social development also become important. In such situations the social exclusion of children who are perceived as different may occur. To fully understand social exclusion and inclusion in childhood we need to consider, in addition to moral reasoning, the development of social categorization (i.e., awareness of social categories that divide people into different groups) and prejudice (i.e., the negative evaluation of somebody because they belong to a certain social group). These aspects of children's social development challenge children's moral orientations and provide a basis, at times, for exclusion of others based on gender, race, and ethnicity.

In this chapter we will start by describing how an awareness of social categories develops early in life. Children soon realize through their early experiences that the social world is divided up into social categories (e.g., boys, girls). Then we describe how this can lead to rigid thinking, such as the view that all individuals from a social category share key character-istics (e.g., "*all* boys are aggressive and fearless" and "*all* girls are passive and cautious"). This knowledge of stereotypes if unchallenged by critical reasoning can lead to the emergence in childhood of explicit biases (e.g., girls are associated with positive qualities and boys are associated with

Children and Social Exclusion: Morality, Prejudice, and Group Identity. Melanie Killen and Adam Rutland. © 2011 Melanie Killen and Adam Rutland. Published 2011 by Blackwell Publishing Ltd.

negative qualities). Developmental psychologists have suggested that such rigid thinking and biases are purely a product of a young child's cognitive endowments and become less likely as children develop the ability to think flexibly using multiple social categories (i.e., a boy can see another child as both a girl and a friendly or warm child). Recently, researchers have begun to question this account of prejudice development, in part because of evidence that implicit biases continue throughout childhood and into adolescence.

Social and developmental psychologists have defined stereotypes (generally) as traits that are assigned to individuals based solely on group membership without consideration of intragroup variables (see Mulvey, Hitti, & Killen, 2010). From this viewpoint, we will argue that stereotype beliefs and prejudices are highly dependent on the cultural milieu and do not follow a simple developmental path related solely to a child's cognitive development. Importantly, we think the appearance of these biases and prejudices depend on how children develop complex social reasoning in their everyday lives and weigh concerns about both morality and group identity simultaneously.

Social Categorization as a Precursor of Prejudice

We begin by discussing children's early awareness of social categories, which suggests that categorization plays an important role in the emergence of biases during infancy. Most psychologists believe that awareness of social categories is necessary for a child to fully understand their social world. Moreover, they have for a long time suggested that prejudice may originate from the ability to categorize the social world (e.g., Allport, 1954; Tajfel, 1978). It has been proposed that showing bias or prejudice first requires children to categorize individuals as coming from different social groups. Social categorization makes the world more focused and creates an environment that is less ambiguous by imposing structure. As Allport (1954) stated "The human mind must think with the aid of categories ... Once formed, categories are the basis for normal prejudgment. We cannot possibility avoid this process. Orderly living depends on it" (p. 20). It is a fundamental and universal process as it allows humans to function in complex environments. Yet, what are the parameters that can be used when defining a category? In the world of biology and inanimate objects, as we discuss below, the taxonomy takes a different form than it does for the social world. Why a chair is a piece of furniture or a dog is a mammal reflects a set of well-established criteria that do not exist in the same way for how individuals categorize humans. We will return to this issue later in this chapter.

Research on early categorization in infants and children

Children from infancy develop the ability to recognize characteristic features of people from their own group and other groups, and use this information to begin to cluster individuals together into social categories. The question is to what extent is social categorization a necessary and fundamental process of early development, and what categories are relevant for infants and children. The child's social environment makes categories more or less salient, with some social categories being universal, such as gender, and other categories being more culturally specific, such as those associated with skin tones or facial features. For example, in recent history, race has typically been a highly salient social category in many parts of the world, yet nationality, religion, caste, and political affiliations are more salient in some regions than others. Moreover, the categories children use often vary over time as the cultural salience of the categories changes through history. For example, the category 'British' was used extensively and had more meaning to children in Scotland in the 1960s and 1970s (Tajfel, Jahoda, Nemeth, Rim, & Johnson, 1972) compared to recent times with the rise of a strong Scottish identity and evidence of preference for Scottish identity over British identity in children (Bennett, Lyons, Sani, & Barrett, 1998; Rutland, 2004).

Once infants become aware of social categories, research suggests this leads to visual preferences for members of the infant's own social category rather than others from a different social category. Again, such biases appear to be dependent on the diversity of the infant's visual environment. Developmental psychologists have investigated infants' early racial biases in studies using a visual preference task (e.g., Langlois, Ritter, Roggman, & Vaughn, 1991). In this task infants are presented with examples of faces from two racial categories simultaneously and how long they look at each example is used to indicate preference. Research using this task showed that by 3 months infants living in a predominately racially homogenous (i.e., non-racially mixed) environment preferred to look at faces of their own rather than other racial groups (Kelly et al., 2005). Importantly, this bias was not shown amongst newborn infants suggesting that preferential looking based upon racial categories is learnt and probably originates from differences in exposure to own versus other race faces during early development.

This conclusion is also supported by recent research conducted in Israel and Ethiopia, also using the visual preference task (Bar-Haim, Ziv, Lamy, & Hodes, 2006). Bar-Haim and colleagues found own-race preference amongst Caucasian-Israeli and African-Ethiopian infants living in racially homogenous settings, but failed to find own-race preference amongst African-Israeli infants who were born in Israel of Ethiopian origin and who experienced considerable cross-race exposure (i.e., with White Israelis). These findings suggest that the early development of own-race preference is dependent upon exposure to a homogenous own-race environment.

The influence of selective exposure to different environments also lies behind gender-based looking preferences amongst young infants. Quinn, Yahr, Kuhn, Slater, and Pascalis, (2002), also using the visual preference task, showed that 3- to 4-month-old infants looked after primarily by female caregivers demonstrated a visual preference for female over male faces. In contrast, when they tested the visual preference of infants raised primarily by male caregivers a bias in favor of male over female faces appeared. These findings suggest that social categories (e.g., race and gender) are made salient by the visual environment infants are exposed to from a young age. This has been of interest because most societies continue to reflect racially segregated living patterns for political, economic, and sociological reasons (Graves, 2001).

Rigid thinking about categories in young children

There is a substantial body of research that has examined how children think about categories once they become aware categories exist. This research began with a focus on what is known as psychological essentialism and the development of children's understanding of *natural* categories (e.g., animal species). Psychological essentialism involves thinking that all members of certain categories have an underlying, unchanging attribute or essence that determines that they belong to the category (Gelman, 2009). Despite the fact an individual will change in appearance over their lifetime (e.g., from infant to adult) and despite variation in appearance among individuals within a category (e.g., from typical to atypical individuals), psychological essentialism involves a way of thinking that says there are immutable features (i.e., essences) that define members of the category and determine what they will do. For example, "birds" are physically variable (starlings, seagulls, eagles, etc.) and change substantially through life (i.e., egg to chick to fully grown bird), yet people tend to believe that all birds have an "essence" that makes them what they are and determines how they behave (e.g., a shared DNA). This thinking exists despite changes in appearance over the lifetime of an individual and outward variation in appearances across members of a category. Therefore, when asked to predict what a particular bird will do in the future children tend to rely on the category label (i.e., bird) rather than any obvious physical characteristic.

Psychological essentialism is most evident when children think that properties are fixed at birth, that is, an organism displays innate potential. The "switched-at-birth" task has been used to examine this phenomenon. For example, this task might involve children learning about a newborn kangaroo that went to live with goats, and then being asked whether it would be good at hopping or good at climbing, and whether it would have a pouch or no pouch (Gelman & Wellman, 1991). Children by approximately 4–6 years typically report that it would be good at hopping and have a pouch, despite the fact it is too weak to hop at birth, is raised by goats that cannot hop, and never sees another kangaroo hop. Hopping is seen as inherent or the "essence" of a kangaroo.

To what extent does children's thinking about social categories (e.g., gender and race) reflect essentialist thinking and is this related to decisions about exclusion and inclusion? Some researchers have claimed that psychological essentialism is a core feature of children's cognitive architecture that pervades the way they think about all categories including social categories (Gelman, Heyman, & Legare, 2007). Yet, children's cognitions about social categories (rather than natural or physical categories) are likely to reflect the fact that they themselves also belong to social categories, and thus notions of identity or self are likely to color these cognitions in ways not seen with non-social categories. Researchers have claimed that psychological essentialism contributes to the development of stereotyping and prejudice in childhood (see Arthur, Bigler, Liben, Gelman, & Ruble, 2008). This is significant because, if true, it suggests that children's cognitive systems that promote psychological essentialism may contribute to attitudes that result in social exclusion.

Research on psychological essentialism and social categories has shown that preschool children essentialize gender. They readily expect members of the same gender to share novel physical and behavioral properties based on their category membership (e.g., all girls are passive), misremember or refute gender anomalies (e.g., forget girls who behave in masculine ways), and assume gender-stereotyped traits are innate (e.g., girls are born to be naturally caring). For example, Gelman, Collman, and Maccoby (1986) conducted a study in which 4-year-old children saw pictures of a typical boy, a typical girl, and a boy with long hair (i.e., an atypical boy). Then they were told the gender category of each picture ("boy," "girl," and "boy"). Next they learned that the typical boy played with "trucks and does boy things" and the typical girl played with "dolls and does girl things." Importantly, the child was then asked what does the third child (i.e., the boy with long hair) like to play with. Results showed that preschool children used gender category information (i.e., "he is a boy") 81% of the time to make inferences about the third child, whereas perpetual similarity (i.e., the girl's and atypical boy's similar length of hair) was only used 19% of the time. Children were significantly more likely to say the boy with long hair does masculine rather than feminine things even though there was conflicting information available about his outward appearance (i.e., long hair).

Is this evidence that young children are showing gender stereotyping and prejudice? Would young children showing such psychological essentialism express negative gender attitudes and socially exclude other children because of their gender? In answering these questions one should consider an important distinction between stereotype knowledge (i.e., awareness that certain stereotypes are held by others) and personal beliefs (i.e., personal endorsement of stereotypes and attitudes held by others) made within the social and developmental psychology literature. Devine (1989; Devine, Plant, Amodio, Harmon-Jones, & Vance, 2002), in accordance with her model of automatic and controlled prejudice regulation, defined stereotype knowledge and personal beliefs as distinct cognitive structures. This model views stereotype knowledge as a stable and widely shared cognitive structure that is learnt very early in life via socialization. At a young age, children typically become aware of stereotype knowledge, which may be distinct from their personal beliefs.

For example, children may know that girls are typically perceived as "gentle" or "not good with numbers" by others within their social environment, but they personally may not support these attitudes. In contrast, personal beliefs represent conscious and controllable attitudes towards individuals from different social categories, which are not necessarily shared with others and have been formed after deliberative reasoning rather than being automatic. If one accepts this model, and there is some developmental research that provides support (see Augoustinos & Rosewarne, 2001), then high and low prejudiced individuals should not differ in their knowledge of social stereotypes, rather they should diverge with respect to their personal beliefs.

Thus, one interpretation of the findings by Gelman and colleagues (1986) is that they were measuring preschool children's gender stereotypic knowledge rather than their endorsement of these expectations about boys or girls. Research shows that preschool children are highly aware of gender as a social category and stereotype knowledge about boys and girls (see Bigler & Liben, 2006; Durkin, 1995; Martin, 1995). When asked to make inferences about an unknown child's play preference, and knowing no other information than their hair length (which does not always indicate gender) and their actual gender label (i.e., a boy), it is unsurprising that they draw on their gender stereotype knowledge. Gelman and colleagues showed that preschool children have gender stereotype knowledge but they did not demonstrate that these children show negative attitudes or beliefs towards the opposite gender that might result in social exclusion.

There has been other research into psychological essentialism and social categories among children. The "switched-at-birth" task described above has also been used to examine thinking about the immutability of the gender category (Taylor, 1996; Taylor, Rhodes, & Gelman, 2009). In this task, children and adults are told stories in which a baby is born a member of certain category (e.g., boy) and then raised entirely by members of another category (e.g., females). Preschool children, but not 10-year-old children or adults, allowed little environmental influence since they predicted that babies would develop the physical and behavioral characteristics associated with their birth gender category even if they were brought up completely by members from the opposite gender category. Young children were likely to say that a boy raised among females would still prefer to play with trucks (a stereotypically masculine toy).

Again, here the distinction between stereotype knowledge and personal beliefs is important. Clearly the preschool children had gender stereotype knowledge (e.g., "boys are likely to play with trucks") which they used to inform their inferences about future characteristics of the baby. It is not clear, however, if preschool children endorsed these stereotypes and held negative personal beliefs about the other gender. Do they think that no matter what, all boys *should* play with trucks? Or do they simply think that boys typically play with trucks? It appears older children and adults did not rely solely on stereotype knowledge when making their inferences, which suggests they may have developed distinctive personal gender beliefs (e.g., "boys *should* be allowed to play with dolls and are likely to if brought up by females") that allowed them to consciously evaluate and challenge the automatic stereotype knowledge they most likely learnt from an early age.

The key question seems to be, why do some older children develop personal beliefs that are inconsistent with their early learning of pervasive gender stereotypes? We think the answer to this important question involves an understanding of when and how children begin to give priority to moral reasoning (e.g., fairness and equality), which we showed in chapter 2 is acquired early in life, over stereotype knowledge. This type of reasoning seems more likely if children begin to identify with groups that espouse moral norms of fairness or equality and do not tolerate rigid thinking about social categories. We will return to these points in later chapters, when we propose an integrative perspective on prejudice development that recognizes the importance of both morality and group identity.

Explicit Biases in Young Children

Evidence of rigid thinking or stereotype knowledge in a young child is not necessarily symptomatic of biased attitudes in favor of the child's group over other groups or prejudices involving negative evaluations of other groups. However, there is a substantial body of research in developmental and social psychology that has shown young children exhibit many types of bias or prejudice at an early age (Aboud, 1988; Levy & Killen, 2008). These can be based, for example, upon gender, race, ethnicity, nationality, and body type. Children begin to show bias by favoring those from their own social group over those from another social group and sometimes show negative evaluations of those from a different social group (i.e., prejudice).

Explicit racial bias was first shown in early work by Kenneth and Mamie Clark using the classic "doll test" (Clark & Clark, 1947; Goodman, 1952). These studies were conducted in the United States in the south during the height of racial segregation, when race was an organizing factor in children's home life as well as school life and there were very clear status hierarchies in terms of racial groups. Young children were asked to express their attitudes by pointing to which doll (Black or White) was most like them, which would they play with, and which doll looked "nice/bad," and so on. Clark and Clark (1947) found that over 95% of the European-American children preferred the lighter doll, whereas only about two-thirds of the African-American children preferred the darker doll. This lack of preference for the darker doll was most evident amongst younger African-American children, with over 60% of the 3-year-old African-American children identifying with the lighter doll; whereas 87% of the 8-year-old African-American children self-identified with the darker doll. These findings were used by Thurgood Marshall in his argument to the US Supreme Court to describe one of the many negative outcomes of school segregation in the United States. This case led to the famous decision referred to as Brown v. Board of Education, which resulted in school desegregation laws in the United States (Frankenberg & Orfield, 2007).

From a scientific viewpoint, the Clark and Clark (1947) studies generated an entire field of social science research, in developmental psychology, social psychology, and educational psychology, regarding children's social identity, self-esteem, social experiences in schools, and the developmental emergence of prejudice and bias. The Clark and Clark (1947) studies demonstrated how Black children in the 1950s in the United States recognized the status difference associated with skin color, and how it entered into their self-concept and social desires. What remained less clear was how the findings explained the acquisition of prejudice or bias in White children. The acquisition theory used to explain the differences documented by Clark and Clark (1947) were often socialization explanations, that is, children become aware of the status differences in society and choose to identify with the high-status ethnic group irrespective of their own ethnic group. In the mid-20th century, psychologists mostly characterized children as prejudiced due to direct socialization by parents and other sources of social influence (e.g., mass media). For example, Allport (1954) argued that "the home influence has priority, and that the child has excellent reasons for adopting his ethnic attitudes ready-made from his parents" (p. 297). This approach matched the social learning theories in psychology, dominate in the 1970s (e.g., Bandura, 1977). Yet, the acquisition of identity and prejudice, which has received closer examination over the past few decades, has been shown to be broader and to extend beyond, and sometimes to be at odds with, parental values and beliefs.

Moreover, the details of the "doll test" upon which the socialization approach was based have been closely examined by developmental and social psychology researchers, who have suggested that the ethnic majority child's perspective may involve more than a preference for a same-race doll. One issue has to do with the forced choice nature of selecting between two dolls. This forced choice creates uncertainty over whether the test is a measure of prejudice or, more directly, a measure of preference for the child's own group relative to other groups, whatever that other group might be (Nesdale, 2001a). Others also re-examined this measure since it does not provide an assessment of how strongly children hold their intergroup attitudes and whether other factors than race would be relevant for the decision (Aboud, 1988; Nesdale, 2001a).

Recent studies using methods that do not increase the salience of race to the same extent have found quite different results, with young racial minority children in the United States, Australia and South Africa typically showing equal preference for both their ingroup and the ethnic majority group (Griffiths & Nesdale, 2006; Kelly & Duckitt, 1995; Pfeifer et al., 2007). For example, in the United States, Pfeifer and colleagues (2007) found that 7- to 8-year-old and 9- to 10-year-old Black American children allocated positive and negative traits equally to other ethnic groups (i.e., White, Chinese, Dominican, and Russian). This study also found ethnic minority immigrant children (i.e., Chinese and Dominican) expressed more negative attitudes towards another ethnic minority group (i.e., Black American) than their own ethnic group. Similar findings were shown by Griffiths and Nesdale (2006), who assessed the ethnic attitudes of 5- to 12-year-old children from an ethnic minority status Pacific Islander group in Australia. They found that the Pacific Islander children rated their ingroup and the Anglo-Australian (high-status majority) group equally positively, while the Aboriginal outgroup (low-status minority) was rated least positively. The Pacific Islander children also showed a preference for ingroup neighbors; again with the Aboriginal outgroup being the least desirable as neighbors.

Given these limitations of the "doll test," psychologists in the 1970s and 1980s began to measure explicit ethnic prejudice by asking children to attribute positive (e.g., "clean," "smart") and negative (e.g., "mean," "dirty") traits to a White child or a Black child or to both children. Two of these well-known measures are the Preschool Racial Attitudes Measure (PRAM: Williams, Best, Boswell, Mattson, & Graves, 1975) and the Multiple-response Racial Attitudes Measure (MRA: Doyle, Beaudet, & Aboud, 1988). Research in North America suggests that explicit forms of racial prejudice based on these preference- or trait-attribution tasks develop from 4 to 5 years of age amongst ethnic majority children and typically decline from approximately 7 years of age (Aboud, 1988; Doyle & Aboud, 1995). Like the "doll test," the PRAM and MRA are explicit measures of prejudice. When children complete the tests they are conscious that their attitudes are being measured since the procedures make the social categories (e.g., Black and White) salient and the measures are not rooted in everyday contexts (Killen, McGlothlin, & Henning, 2008).

The issue of whether children control their explicit attitudes through self-presentation will be examined further in chapter 4.

Research since the 1970s using explicit measures has questioned the view that prejudice results from the transmission of values directly from parents to children. The findings have lead psychologists to reject the *direct* relationship between parents' attitudes and the development of prejudice in children. The findings do not support a view that children passively soak up the attitudes in the home environment. This is also true in many areas of child development, including moral development, language, imitation, cognition, and social cognition. Studies have failed to find significant correlations between parental levels of prejudice and child manifestations of prejudice (e.g., Aboud & Doyle, 1996). It appears that while young children may incorporate negative words into their descriptions of minority groups (see Nesdale, 2001b) these attributions do not reflect stable or internalized attitudes amongst children. The conclusion one is forced to face when considering this evidence is that the effects of simple socialization on children's prejudice are seldom constant; the unidirectional characterization of socialization has not been supported in many areas of child development, and not in the area of prejudice acquisition.

Psychologists moved away from simple socialization models of prejudice development to a focus on the social-cognitive basis of childhood prejudice. This reflected a challenge to behaviorist accounts generally within psychology and a realization that children actively construct their understanding of the social world in everyday interaction utilizing their emerging cognitive and social-cognitive abilities.

Cognitive Developmental Approach to Prejudice Development

The cognitive developmental approach to prejudice development contends that a young child's cognitive limitations lead them to show biases. These biases become less likely as children develop the ability to think flexibly, though, and to use multiple social categories (i.e., a boy can see another child as both a girl and a brave child). Cognitive developmental stage theories propose that a child's ability to solve problems could be characterized by broad structural changes in thinking, from one-way functions in early childhood to the concrete operations of reversibility in middle childhood to abstract hypothetical principles in adolescence.

Prior to 7–8 years of age, children are unable to weigh multiple variables simultaneously, such as those involved in the logical classification of objects or an understanding of the conservation of liquids.

Children play a more active and constructive role in the development of prejudice than socialization models suggest, according to the cognitive developmental model. Aboud (1988) stated that the decline in children's prejudice from middle childhood results from their active classification of the world in multiple ways using their developing ability to categorize inanimate objects. As children become capable of weighing two or more categories simultaneously (e.g., concrete operations in Piaget's theory by age 7 or 8 years), children understand that multiple categories could be assigned to the same person (e.g., French, nice, friendly, likes books, shy) and, therefore, focusing on a single category (e.g., French) declines with age, making prejudice less likely. For example, instead of viewing another child merely as "foreign," that child may be viewed as a person who has brown hair, is quite tall, good at sport, and friendly. This is a stage-related account of prejudice development that draws heavily on Piaget's stage model of children's classification of inanimate objects. Young children with rigid schematic processing (Bigler & Liben, 2006, p. 61) and poor multiple classification ability forget or distort their representation of this individual because they cannot recognize subtypes within the broader classification (e.g., "housewives" and "career women" within the schema for women).

While the cognitive developmental approach has been ground-breaking in terms of focusing on the child's cognitive interpretations of prejudice, rather than the child's passive absorption of adult messages, recent research has expanded the focus to include social-cognitive, as well as cognitive, capacities of the child. This is because the relation between children's classification abilities of physical objects and their prejudicial attitudes towards people has mixed results. Moreover, research in social psychology shows that prejudice continues into adulthood and there is ample evidence that adults show strong intergroup biases across a range of groups and situations. Racial outgroup attitudes either remain stable through middle childhood into adolescence or actually become more negative (see Nesdale, 2008). Further, ethnic prejudice based upon nationality does not decrease with age and can in some cases increase in strength amongst older children (e.g., Abrams, Rutland, & Cameron, 2003; Rutland, 1999). In addition, studies indicate that gender bias often appears early and continues unchecked into early adolescence (e.g., Yee & Brown, 1994).

More recently, Bigler and Liben (2006) extended the cognitive developmental model to incorporate intergroup theories. They proposed a domain-general developmental intergroup theory that focuses on the mechanisms that drive the formation of stereotypes and prejudice. Four processes are identified, which include: (1) the establishment of the psychological salience of person attributes, such as explicit labeling of individuals in terms of gender and race; (2) the categorization of individuals who fit salient dimensions, such as classification skill; (3) the development of stereotyping, such as ingroup bias; and (4) the application of stereotyping to individuals. Their research has focused on the type of labeling that individuals use when identifying persons on the basis of group membership, such as perceptually salient features that contribute to gender, for example, and how that contributes to stereotyping by children. They also propose that when adults verbally label groups this has a strong effect on children's conceptualization of people as categories. Thus, this model differs from traditional cognitive developmental ones because it acknowledges that prejudice and stereotyping continues into adulthood. Further, analyses of children's cognition is not focused as much on their classification of inanimate objects but on their stereotyping of persons into rigid categories, similar to some extent to the essentialist perspective, described earlier.

Together these studies counter the contention that prejudice development follows a unidimensional, age-related pattern (i.e., it does not appear to emerge in the preschool years, peaking around 7–8 years, and then declining after middle childhood). Up until the late 1970s such a focus on general age trends was also evident in other areas of developmental science, for example, morality, social perspective-taking, and logical reasoning (Kohlberg, 1984; Piaget, 1952; Selman, 1980). As discussed in chapter 2, the notion was that children have one global scheme which they use to evaluate a range of situations in many different contexts (e.g., a selfish-punishment avoidance orientation does not reflect children's thinking across all contexts). Yet, as discussed already, research on social cognition from the late 1970s onwards has shown that children use multiple forms of reasoning, attributions, and judgments throughout childhood and adolescence. Recent research on children's implicit or indirect biases has also shown that early biases may exist prior to the preschool period. Further, there appear to exist biases of which children may not be consciously aware, which develop early in life and generally do not decline with age. These biases may be related to features within the child's cultural milieu.

Development of Implicit Biases

Implicit biases exist regarding the links between categories of people and negative attributions, emotions, and experiences. In the last 5 years there has been considerable interest in the development of implicit preferences in young children (Baron & Banaji, 2006; Rutland, Cameron, Milne, & McGeorge, 2005). This has resulted from extensive research with adults, which has shown implicit biases leading to the question of how early these biases manifest in development.

There are multiple ways of assessing implicit biases. Implicit biases have typically been defined as unconscious, automatic, uncontrolled processes. Using the Implicit Associations Test (IAT) with adults, researchers have shown that European-American adults hold biases, which they are not aware they have, towards others based solely on race (e.g., Greenwald, McGhee, & Schwartz, 1998). The IAT is a computer screen test that measures the latency (how fast) a participant will associate a negative word ("bad") with a White or Black face. In the case of ethnic majority adults, the response time is quicker when associating negative words with outgroup (Black) faces than with ingroup (White) faces. These findings have spawned an array of IAT studies, with much debate about the extent to which such "associations" reflect prejudice or bear on behavior, such as discrimination towards others.

Some recent developmental studies have examined implicit bias in childhood using IAT-type methodologies. For example, Rutland et al. (2005) conducted two studies using a child-friendly, pictorial-based IAT, and found implicit racial and national biases were present amongst 6- to 16-year-old White British children. This child version of the IAT measured the relative strength of association between concepts (e.g., "White British" or "Black British") and attributes (e.g., "happy" or "sad" cartoon figures) that were presented on a computer screen in a number of trials. Implicit bias was present when children showed faster reaction times in stereotypic (e.g. "White British" and "happy") trails than counter-stereotypic (e.g. "Black British" and "happy") trials. For example, Figure 3.1 shows racial implicit bias was present amongst all age groups in Study 1 conducted by Rutland and colleagues.

Figure 3.1 also shows that implicit racial biases remained in older children who showed reduced explicit racial bias. A decrease in explicit racial bias was evident because the older children consciously attributed more positive and less negative traits (e.g., "friendly" and "nasty" respectively) to the outgroup relative to the ingroup. Baron and Banaji (2006) found converging evidence suggesting the early appearance of

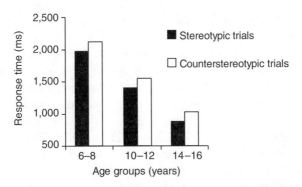

Figure 3.1 Mean median response time for stereotypic and counter-stereotypic trials among 6- to 16-year-old children and adolescents. (Created by Adam Rutland. Source: Rutland et al., 2005.)

implicit racial bias in 6-year-old European-American children which was also present in 10-year-olds and adults. This study also found an asymmetry in the development of implicit and explicit racial attitudes, with 6-year-old children's explicit racial attitudes being consonant with their implicit attitudes (i.e., they showed both implicit and explicit bias). Whereas amongst the 10-year-olds and adults there was a disjunction between their explicit and implicit attitudes (i.e., they showed implicit but not explicit bias).

An asymmetry in the development of implicit and explicit racial bias amongst these ethnic majority children suggests they were engaging in self-presentation and controlling their expression of explicit racial bias. This conclusion is supported by the finding that in the domain of national intergroup bias (i.e., favoritism for one's own national group over a foreign group) there was no asymmetry in the development of implicit and explicit attitudes (Rutland et al., 2005). Rutland and colleagues' second study, using the same measures of implicit and explicit bias as used in Study 1 and described above, found that 10- to 16-year-old British children showed both implicit *and* explicit bias in favor of the British over the Germans. This finding is compatible with previous research that has shown in a European context that children are sometimes willing to show explicit biases in favor of their national group over another (e.g., Bennett et al., 2004; Rutland, 1999; Verkuyten, 2001). The absence of a strong norm against showing national bias in favor of their own country in part seems to explain why the British children continued to show explicit bias in addition to implicit bias.

Others studies have shown the importance of the cultural context in the development of implicit racial biases. There is evidence that implicit racial biases can be reduced by changing the social context, especially frequent and meaningful exposure to members of the outgroup that challenge the stereotypical perception of the group (e.g., ethnic minority status individuals who have been well educated and followed a professional career) (e.g., Dasgupta & Asgari, 2004; Turner, Voci, & Hewstone, 2007). For example, Turner and colleagues (2007) found that 8- to 11-year-old White British children who reported more cross-race friendships with Asian-British children also showed more positive implicit racial attitudes measured using a version of the IAT.

Studies also using the IAT have shown that children from ethnic minority status groups do not always reveal implicit own-group preference. For example, research in the United States found that 5-year-old children from the ethnic minority status Latino-American group showed implicit bias against African-Americans (low status) but failed to do so against European-Americans (high status) (Dunham, Baron, & Banaji, 2007). These data suggest that young children from ethnic minority status groups are sensitive to status differences within their culture and this understanding influences their expression of implicit biases. Collectively these studies suggest that children's implicit attitudes are not entirely dependent on automatic social categorization and preference for the ingroup, rather they are closely influenced by inter-ethnic contact and the relative status of different social groups within the cultural milieu.

Further, there remain a number of unanswered concerns with the IAT measure. Degner and Wentura (2010) point to several limitations, and recommend the use of other indirect measures of prejudicial attitudes to complement the IAT assessment. The concerns with the IAT include the fact that it is a comparative measure, which does not allow for differentiating ingroup bias from outgroup negativity, a point raised with respect to the MRA measure with children (Nesdale, 2004). When children are asked to associate a negative attribute to one of two faces, an ingroup or an outgroup member (e.g., in the case of a White participant asked to associate the "sad" cartoon face with a White or Black face), the association of a negative attribute to an outgroup member could be the result of avoiding assigning the label to an ingroup ("I don't want to associate negative attributes with my own group") or it could be the result of attributing a negative label to an outgroup ("That person is negative or bad").

This confound is of particular concern when measuring implicit bias in children, given the evidence for group identity in early development, which may manifest as ingroup bias ("I like my own group"). This judgment is conceptually different from outgroup dislike ("I don't like the other group") and has implications for understanding the origins of prejudice. There have been no reported age differences with the IAT suggesting that there is a stable ingroup positivity or a stable outgroup negativity, or both, which cannot be determined with the IAT measurement (see Degner & Wentura, 2010). In addition, the attributes presented to participants are forced choice (the target has to be categorized as "negative" or "positive") and it is not clear if these would be the actual categories used by adults or children in everyday interactions. Finally, researchers have shown that there are demand effects for the IAT which means that individuals can control their responses based on what they expect the experimenters to be asking, and the IAT score may reflect this bias, especially if children think that they should comply with what they might assume are adult expectations about stereotypic associations (Olson & Fazio, 2004). These limitations call for additional measures of ingroup and outgroup bias in childhood.

Relation of Implicit Bias to Judgment and Behavior: Is it Prejudice?

For individuals who assert that "discrimination" is part of the past, or is no longer relevant in a global society, implicit bias data are a reminder that negative associations with ethnic minority groups, for example, are still quite pervasive. While explicit stereotypes and biases have greatly diminished over the past 50 years in the United States, implicit biases remain pervasive (Dovidio & Gaertner, 1991).

To this end, a main discussion point about the findings with the IAT measures of implicit bias has to do with the connections between implicit associations and behavior as well as judgment. To date, there is little evidence to indicate that implicit associations are directly related to how racial biases are expressed during interactions with others in everyday contexts. Images from the media in most cultures are filled with negative stereotypes of individuals from ethnic minority groups, for example. Responding to the IAT indicates that these associations are often recognized by individuals. However, this does not mean that one acts on such biases, nor does it mean that it translates into discriminatory behavior towards others. Individuals control, modify, and monitor their own behavior towards others on an array of issues, such as restraining negative impulses or aggressive tendencies or making rude comments to others.

Thus, the question is to what extent do children hold these biases, and if so, do they monitor and self-correct their behavior in the context of actual interactions with others?

Instead, implicit and explicit measures must be considered jointly when predicting future behavior and judgment (Greenwald, Poehlman, Uhlmann, & Banaji, 2009). Indeed, as mentioned, there is evidence that automatic associations can often be controlled if an adult is motivated to do so, and research also suggests that children can inhibit their implicit biases when they express them explicitly (Devine, 1989; FitzRoy & Rutland, 2010; Rutland et al., 2005). In chapter 4 we discuss in more depth children's self-presentation of their attitudes towards different groups and how this process is related to moral reasoning, social norms, and group identity. Here we wish to argue that children's motivation to self-present and control their implicit associations is based upon their conscious beliefs and values, which can be evaluated directly through an examination of their social reasoning. While children evidently show implicit biases at a young age, a focus on social reasoning is necessary if we are to fully understand when and how they control their biases when interacting with others in everyday settings.

Development of indirect biases

Studies using indirect measures of attributional bias have examined how children and adolescents actively reason and interpret possible implicit associations within everyday interactions. Such indirect measures are arguably more conscious and less automatic than measures like the IAT that rely on reaction times. The use of such indirect measures has provided a broader portrayal of the forms of bias in childhood, that is, forms that reflect children's lack of awareness about using race to make judgments, particularly about peer relationships. Drawing on previous methodologies (e.g., Sagar & Schofield, 1980), McGlothlin and colleagues (2005) used ambiguous situations to determine whether children used race to attribute intentions when evaluating familiar, everyday peer encounters. McGlothlin and colleagues presented 6- to 9-year-old European-American children with pictures of children from different racial groups in potential "pushing off a swing" and "stealing money off the ground" ambiguous peer en-counters in the playground. The race of the potential "victim" and "perpetrator" in each situation was systematically varied. For example, Figure 3.2 shows a potential "pushing off a swing" ambiguous situation and lists the five questions the children were asked.

Q1: What did X do? (Intentions)

Q2: How good or bad is it? (Saliene of intentions)

Q3: What will happen next? (Next action)

Q4: Do you think they were friends? (Friendship)

Q5: Can they be friends now? (Friendship)

Figure 3.2 Picture cards and sample questions for the attributions of intentions in ambiguous contexts task. (© 2010 Melanie Killen.)

The results showed that children attributed more negative intentions to a Black child than to a White child in potential ambiguous peer encounters. They also rated a Black child's next action and friendship potential more negatively than that of a White child. While these findings initially appeared to reflect a pervasive racial bias, there was an important qualification. This bias was only revealed by European-American children in racially homogeneous (i.e., racially non-mixed) schools. European-American children of the same age, in the same school district, and enrolled in heterogeneous (i.e., racially mixed) schools did not attribute more positive intentions to their ingroup than the outgroup; in fact, race was not used to attribute negative intentions, as shown in Figure 3.3.

These findings contribute to our general thesis that the cultural context experienced by children significantly contributes to the manifestation of indirect or implicit bias and racially based judgments. While school composition and intergroup contact was related to children's attributions of negative intentions in intergroup contexts, other findings from the same studies indicated that European-American children enrolled in both heterogeneous and homogeneous schools were less likely to view interracial dyad peers as likely to be friends than were ethnic minority children. This

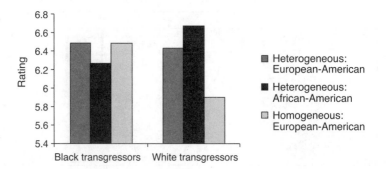

Figure 3.3 Positive ratings of potential transgressors by race of the transgressor for school composition. $N = 302$; 1 = very, very good, to 9 = very, very bad. (Source: McGlothlin & Killen, 2010.)

suggests that European-American children used race to attribute the potential for friendship, and more so than did ethnic minority children in heterogeneous schools. Thus, race was not used by ethnic majority children in heterogeneous schools to attribute negative intentions but it was used in their judgments about interracial friendship potential.

A study that followed this pattern into adolescence found that, surprisingly, ethnic majority and minority adolescents did not use the race of the perpetrator (Killen, Kelly, Richardson, & Jampol, 2010). Instead, using ambiguous pictures similar to prior studies but modified to depict adolescents in the picture cards, adolescents were asked what happened in the picture. Adolescents were also asked whether a prior record for the potential transgressor was relevant for making an accusation, and whether teacher accusations were fair in an ambiguous peer encounter. There were significant differences for the age, gender, and ethnicity of the participant. Younger participants were more likely to attribute negative intentions to ambiguous interracial peer encounters than were older adolescents; boys were more likely to attribute negative intentions; and ethnic majority participants were more likely to attribute negative intentions in ambiguous interracial encounters than were ethnic minority participants.

While all participants viewed peer and teacher accusations of wrongdoing in ambiguous situations as unfair, ethnic minority students as well as females were more likely to view peer and teacher accusations of wrongdoing as unfair, and 11th graders (i.e., 16–17 years old) were more likely to view accusations of wrongdoing for protagonists with a prior history of transgression as fair than were 8th graders (i.e., 13–14 years old) (Figure 3.4). These findings reveal the ways that contextual

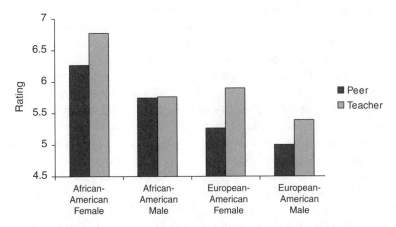

Figure 3.4 Fairness of peer and teacher accusations of negative intentions as a function of the ethnicity and gender of the participants. 1 = very, very fair, to 9 = very, very unfair. (© Melanie Killen. Source: Killen, Kelly, Richardson, & Jampol, 2010.)

information is interpreted by adolescents, and why it is that ethnic majority and minority students may attribute different meaning to interracial peer encounters. Cross-race friendships and opportunities for contact are important factors regarding the types of social experiences that reduce prejudice, as will be discussed in chapter 8.

Adolescents do not passively adopt implicit biases within their everyday interactions, rather they consciously interpret and reason about them and form judgments. These judgments, we think, are likely to have a significant impact of how children and adolescents behave towards others from different groups. Implicit associations formed early in life may establish the potential for biases, but whether these biases turn into prejudices and behavior that excludes others is dependent on how children learn to reason about and judge issues of morality and group identity in everyday encounters.

Summary

Awareness of social categories develops early in life, due to social experience, as children understand that the social world is divided up into categories (e.g., boys, girls). Young children possess rigid thinking about social categories or stereotype knowledge. When the knowledge of stereotypes is unchallenged by critical social and moral reasoning then this can lead to the emergence in childhood of explicit biases (e.g., girls are associated with positive qualities and boys are associated with negative qualities). Recent research has shown the continuation of implicit biases throughout childhood and into adulthood. We pointed out that these biases are dependent on the social context and are not purely a product of the child's inherent cognitive architecture. The appearance of these biases and prejudices depends on how children develop complex social reasoning in their everyday interactions and simultaneously consider both issues of morality and group identity.

Most moral theories have focused on the classic conflict between the self and others, with the implication that not giving priority to morality means acting selfishly. However, Social Domain theory and Social Identity theory provide a more complex formulation. There are times when not acting morally conflicts with the good of your group, or because of stereotypes shared with members of your group, which cannot always be equated with acting selfishly. Conflicts arise from the decision to "do the right thing" from a moral viewpoint when the result will be disloyalty to the group (or conscientiously rejecting stereotypic expectations about others).

For example, young children understand that refusing to share communal resources, such as toys at school, is unfair. Yet, in contexts in which a group identity has been established then members of the group may recognize the fairness rule for the ingroup but not for a member of the outgroup. For example, two school soccer teams are practicing before a game and there are only two balls available belonging to the home team. Here group identity (i.e., "my school") may be so salient that the home team is unwilling to share the balls in the practice session with the away team before the game. This type of exclusion behavior is not for purely selfish reasons, rather it is an expression of group identity and an act that might advantage all children within the home team.

In the next chapter we describe social identity theories of children's prejudice development. The aim is to demonstrate how this approach, with its focus on the importance of group identity, complements Social Domain theory described in chapter 2 to provide a new integrative perspective on children's prejudice.

Chapter 4

Group Identity and Prejudice

In this chapter we will consider how the development of group identity – that is, identifying with social groups – challenges children's moral orientation (which we addressed in chapter 2) and plays a key role in the emergence of prejudicial attitudes. The integrative perspective on prejudice development we outlined in chapter 3 recognizes that children are social beings, with desires and needs to form attachments, and a strong sense of morality towards others (see Rutland, Killen, & Abrams, 2010). We also acknowledge that as children become aware of social categories (e.g., gender, race, ethnicity), forming attachments to and identification with social groups becomes as important as forming attachments to and identification with parents and family. These group identities soon become a key part of a child's life and are relevant for how individuals think, act, and make judgments.

When the salience of a group identity overpowers a child's moral focus then it becomes difficult to apply moral reasoning towards a peer situation. Social decisions become strongly influenced by group concerns (e.g., "What does my group normally do?" "What are the beliefs of my group?" "How can I be accepted by my group?"). In such circumstances children have the potential to show prejudice and, consequently, socially exclude other children who do not belong to their group or threaten the values or norms of their group. In this chapter we consider recent psychological research that has examined the relationship between group identity and development of prejudice. This research suggests that early in development, children identify with social categories and that this identification has the potential to result in favoritism towards their group (i.e., the ingroup) or even prejudice towards those from other groups (i.e., the outgroup). There are also many contexts in which children's

Children and Social Exclusion: Morality, Prejudice, and Group Identity. Melanie Killen and Adam Rutland. © 2011 Melanie Killen and Adam Rutland. Published 2011 by Blackwell Publishing Ltd.

identification with social categories are socially positive, leading to affiliation with groups that provide social support, as we discuss below. Thus, determining when group identity leads to prejudice or when it is related to social support is important.

This research has drawn extensively on approaches in social psychology that have examined how adult identification with different types of groups (e.g., gender, race, or randomly formed groups) is related to bias in favor of the individual's own group. Social psychologists have generally paid little attention to how different types of group identification (e.g., gender or ethnic) impact on adults' attitudes and tendency to show social exclusion. Rather, they have typically assumed that adults' identification with each group is relatively similar and stable within the individual. This is due largely to the reliance on the minimal group paradigm in social psychology research in which participants are affiliated with an artificially created group in a laboratory setting to investigate ingroup–outgroup relationships. While these studies provide insight into basic group processes, the connection to actual groups and to differences between actual groups is often not well understood (or analyzed).

Moreover, the assumption that group processes are the same regardless of the type of group (gender, race, ethnicity, nationality) is problematic when addressing children and adolescents. The developmental literature we reviewed in chapter 3 shows that their identification with different groups varies in terms of its timing (i.e., when it emerges) and appearance (i.e., what the group identity means to the child). This is because there are different developmental phases in which groups become salient and meaningful to children. Children's awareness of social categories that are perceptually salient (i.e., there are discernable physical differences) like gender and race appears early, whereas less physically obvious social categories like nationality, religion, or culture are less apparent to young children. Moreover, children's associations and evaluations of these categories vary extensively such that for some categories, children use explicit stereotypes when making exclusion decisions, for example, and for other categories, biases are mostly implicit. Therefore, throughout this chapter we will refer to "group identity" but acknowledge that the form this identification takes depends on the specific group in question.

Is Group Identity Good or Bad?

The extent to which group identity is a positive or negative aspect of children's social development and social relationships depends on many factors, including the context in which it is salient, sources of influences, group goals, types of identification, and personality characteristics. For example, negative aspects emerge when a strong group identity is used by children to create levels of status and group norms promoting exclusion that result in bullying and victimization, which reflect forms of social inequality in childhood. At the same time, there are many benefits of children forming strong attachments to social groups and developing group identities. Children develop a strong sense of self-worth, academic achievement, and improved social competence to navigate the social world in which social exclusion exists with its many negative consequences (Fuligni, Witkow, & Garcia, 2005; Killen, Rutland, & Jampol, 2008; Ruble et al., 2004).

When children from groups that experience social exclusion have a positive association with their group, and are supported by peers and parents, then their experience of social exclusion may be overcome. Thus, there are contexts in which being part of an excluded group can have the positive effect of empowering children and adolescents to challenge social inequalities and take action to address social exclusion. Research shows that group identity becomes particularly important to excluded minorities (e.g., ethnic minorities or immigrant groups) who think that status differences between groups are impermeable and stable. In such situations, a high group identity may have the positive effect of motivating them to take positive collective action to challenge inequality and discrimination (Ellemers, 1993; Simon et al., 1998). Further, minority status children who have parents who prepare them for the likelihood that they will experience discrimination in the future, as another example, are better adjusted and demonstrate positive social outcomes (Hughes et al., 2006).

In chapter 3 we discussed research showing developmental changes in the way that children evaluate and prefer their own group over other groups. What is the implication of children's developing social identities for the way they react towards individuals of their own and other groups? Research suggests that as children develop a sense of social identification with a group they are motivated to defend this group and support its distinctiveness by showing bias in favor of this group. This bias also creates a disliking of individuals from within this group who do not conform to the expectations of the group (Abrams & Rutland, 2008; Rutland, 2004; Verkuyten, 2002a, 2000b). These attitudes can form the basis of prejudice under certain conditions and at different developmental periods, often resulting in the onset of social exclusion. For example, children typically identify with their ethnic or racial group (e.g., European-American or White Latino) in early to middle childhood. This group identification can result in these children wanting to make their group feel unique, different, and superior to other ethnic or racial groups; so they subscribe to negative stereotypes of these other groups and begin to reject other children within their ethnic or racial group who do not show loyalty to the group. Yet, as children identify with multiple groups, this process becomes complicated. Does a child identify with their ethnic or gender group when categories cross, that is, which category becomes more important? Research on social identity has shown that identification is highly contingent on the context.

Social Identity Theory

To understand better how group identity might impact upon children's prejudiced judgments, developmental psychologists have focused upon Social Identity theory (SIT) (Tajfel & Turner, 1979). Initially we will outline some key tenants of Social Identity theory developed from research conducted with adults. Then we will discuss later in this chapter how developmental psychologists have built upon and adapted Social Identity theory to examine the development of children's group identity and prejudice.

Social Identity theory contends that once an individual identifies with a social group (i.e., forms a group identity) then this group identity becomes an integral part of their self-concept and how that individual perceives him- or herself within the social world. It also proposes that individuals are motivated to sustain a positive group identity, given its importance to their sense of self, by establishing that their own group is positive and distinctive relative to other comparison groups, which are judged negatively. Thus, group identity, while important and necessary for psychological well-being and the effective functioning of society, according to Social Identity theory has the potential to contribute to prejudice through negative judgments of those from other groups. For example, strong identification with being a boy can lead to the uncritical acceptance of overgeneralized negative attitudes towards females, such as "girls are weak." Social identity theorists argue that adults who identify with groups have a stronger motivation to discriminate in favor of their group, support negative stereotypes of other groups, and socially exclude individuals who belong to these groups. As another illustration, an adult living in Northern Ireland who identifies highly with being a

British-Protestant, compared to an adult who does not, is more likely to show bias in favor of their group and socially exclude adults from the Irish-Catholic community in their everyday life.

Social Identity theory's "self-esteem hypothesis" assumes this bias is motivated either to gain or to restore self-esteem. Namely, an individual feels better about him- or herself when their group is perceived as superior to and separate from other relevant groups in any context. This idea has not been without critics, since research suggests that those with high self-esteem often show the most discrimination between groups. Some have suggested an additional motivation, namely the desire to establish coherence and meaning for the self (Abrams & Hogg, 2001; Hogg, 2001; McGarty, 1999). The argument here is that since adults develop attachments to groups and form group identities, they have to justify this by interpreting and giving meaning to their context (i.e., giving legitimacy to the relations between groups) and this often, though not always, involves bias or prejudice through the construction of differentiation between social groups. Individuals may show bias against others from different social groups for a variety of different motives. They may simply evaluate the ingroup more positively than the outgroup (i.e., ingroup bias), they may derogate the outgroup (i.e., prejudice), or they may do both (Brewer, 1979).

Researchers have extended Social Identity theory by noting that an individual's identification with different groups will vary over time and situation because it is highly responsive to what other groups are present in a situation and whether a group category is highly accessible or meaningful (see Rutland & Cinnirella, 2000; Turner, Hogg, Oakes, Reicher, & Wetherell, 1987). An individual's sense of who they are during any social interaction will depend on which of their group identities is most salient at the time and what other groups are available for comparison. For example, a woman working on an engineering project within a group of men is mostly likely to define herself according to her gender identity, but if she was doing that same thing among a group of women from mixed ethnicity then most likely she would use her ethnic identity to define herself. Whether she socially feels included or excluded, these situations will in part depend on which of her group identities is most salient.

Research supporting Social Identity theory has shown that bias and discrimination tend to be elevated to the extent that adults identify (both in terms of self-categorization and feeling an emotional attachment) with an exclusive ingroup (Abrams & Hogg, 2001; Brewer & Brown, 1998). Recent developmental studies have also found that children showing increased identification with their ethnic group tend to show stronger preferences for their group over other groups and favor children within their group that show loyalty to the group (Abrams & Rutland, 2008; Bennett, Lyons, Sani, & Barrett, 1998; Pfeifer et al., 2007). For example, Pfeifer and colleagues (2007) found that bias in favor of the ethnic ingroup was strongest amongst ethnic minority children who identified more with their ethnic rather than their national (e.g., American) ingroup. In contrast, developmental research has shown the promotion of a common inclusive group identity (e.g., a shared nationality or school identity) rather than singular exclusive group identity (e.g., only identification with being either an ethnic majority or minority) can reduce children's bias against those from another ethnic group (e.g., Cameron, Rutland, Brown, & Douch, 2006). In chapter 8 we will discuss further how the latter research can inform attempts to encourage positive attitudes towards other groups and challenge social exclusion in children's lives.

Social Identity Development Theory

Developmental psychologists have recognized that Social Identity theory cannot be applied directly to the study of children, and indeed, the theory does not countenance that children's social cognition, social knowledge, and social reasoning develop and such developments might differentially influence children's group identities and attitudes at different ages. Therefore, researchers have built upon and adapted Social Identity theory to examine the development of children's group identity and prejudice.

One of the first attempts to do this was the Social Identity Development theory (Nesdale, 2004, 2007, 2008), which has built upon the underlying principles of Social Identity theory and its emphasis on group identity, but also provides an account of developmental changes in children's prejudice. This approach is a general model of prejudice development, though it has been primarily founded on research examining children's ethnic or racial attitudes. Nesdale proposes that bias in favor of a child's own group (i.e., ingroup bias) and negative attitudes towards other groups (i.e., outgroup prejudice) follow different developmental trajectories, with ingroup bias generally being established prior to outgroup prejudice.

Social Identity Development theory proposes that there are four sequential developmental phases in the emergence of ethnic prejudice in children (Table 4.1). Initially, in the 'undifferentiated' phase before 2–3 years of age, Social Identity Development theory contends children are not responsive to ethnic categories in the environment. Research

Table 4.1 Social Identity Developmental theory: Phases in the development of ethnic preference and prejudice. (Source: Nesdale, 2004)

Phase	Age	Characteristics
Undifferentiated	Before 2–3 years	Children do not selectively discriminate between objects and people in the social world
Ethnic awareness	From 3 years	Children attend to ethnicity as a social category and begin to show ethnic identification
Ethnic preference	Before 7 years	Strong need for positive ethnic identity leads children to prefer ingroup over outgroup
Ethnic prejudice	Beyond 7 years	The development of negative evaluations of the outgroup is dependent on children's strength of ethnic identification, how much the outgroup is perceived as a threat, and whether the ingroup norm is to show prejudice

described in chapter 3, however, suggests that very young children are aware of social categories (like ethnicity). The key point here might be that 2- to 3-year-old children may be aware of ethnicity as a social category but they do not seem to use these social categories selectively and deliberately to discriminate against others who are not in their group. Then, around 3 years of age, Social Identity Development theory contends that children enter an "ethnic awareness" phase as they show attentiveness to and begin to use social categories (e.g., ethnicity) that have social significance in their community and are emphasized in adult verbal or nonverbal communication, not just to those social categories that are strange and unfamiliar (c.f., Aboud, 1988). Soon after children show ethnic awareness they realize they are a member of a particular ethnic group and begin to identify with this group. In line with Social Identity theory, this means children enter the "ethnic preference" phase around 4–5 years of age and their need for a positive ethnic identity means they develop a strong preference for their own ethnic group over any other group; though other groups will not be disliked or derogated, just evaluated less positively.

According to Social Identity Development theory when and under what circumstances do children show ethnic prejudice and negatively evaluate groups which are not their own? Unlike Cognitive Developmental theory (which we discussed in chapter 3), Social Identity Development theory does not contend that prejudice declines during middle childhood due to cognitive developmental factors. In fact, Social Identity Development theory argues that children can enter the "ethnic prejudice" phase around 7 years and from this moment prejudice has the potential to become established. Research drawing on Social Identity Development theory has shown that this process is dependent on three main factors, which determine whether or not other ethnic groups are seen negatively after the "ethnic preference" phase.

Three key factors in Social Identity Development theory

There are three key factors in social identity development. First, the stronger children identify with their own group the more they will assimilate or use the norms and stereotypes of their group in forming their attitudes towards other groups; if these are negative norms and stereotypes (which is typical amongst ethnic majority and high-status groups) then children are more likely to show ethnic prejudice (Nesdale, Durkin, Maass, & Griffiths, 2005; Nesdale, Maass, Durkin, & Griffiths, 2005).

Second, Social Identity Development theory contends that if other ethnic groups are seen as a threat to the child's own ethnic group this should promote ethnic prejudice. If the context involves conflict between ethnic groups and other ethnic groups are perceived to be threatening to the status or value of the child's own group, then the child is likely to react negatively in defence of their own group with which they strongly identify. Nesdale and colleagues manipulated threat towards a child's group by placing them in a drawing group and then telling them that another drawing group believed they were better artists and that they wished to beat the child's ingroup in a drawing competition. They found that the Anglo-Australian young children turned preference for their own group into explicit ethnic prejudice towards the outgroup (i.e., Pacific Islanders) when they thought the status of their own group was threatened (Nesdale, Maass, et al., 2005).

In addition, consistent with Social Identity Development theory, Nesdale and colleagues have also showed that children with high identification with their own ethnic group were more likely to express explicit dislike (i.e., prejudice) toward other ethnic groups (Nesdale, Durkin, et al., 2005). Other research, which supports Social Identity Developmental theory (Nesdale, 2007), in contexts involving "hot" intergroup conflict in which children perceive very high levels of threat from other ethnic groups, such as in Northern Ireland and the Middle East, has also shown that ethnic prejudice is often shown before 6 or 7 years old (Bar-Tal & Teichman, 2005; Cairns, 1989; Teichman, 2001).

Third, Nesdale and colleagues argue that children's expression of ethnic prejudice will, in part, depend on whether children believe that showing such prejudice is consistent with an expectation held by members of their group concerning the attitudes, beliefs, and behaviors that are considered appropriate to be displayed by children within the group (i.e., a group norm). Children are more likely to show prejudice and socially exclude those from a different group if they think their own group condones such actions and it is seen as typical behavior for those coming from the group. Nesdale and colleagues have shown that children's attitudes towards bullying within a story were significantly more positive when such behaviour was seen as consistent with norms held by their own group (Ojala & Nesdale, 2004). In addition, they have shown that ethnic prejudice was most evident when children thought their own group had an explicit norm of excluding rather than including others from a different group (e.g. Nesdale, Maass, et al., 2005).

Interestingly, one study conducted by Nesdale and colleagues found a significant age effect not predicted by Social Identity Development theory (Nesdale, Maass, et al., 2005). This study used "minimal" groups which were formed by giving children bogus feedback on their drawing ability to create groups of "excellent" drawers and "good" drawers. These groups meet the criterion of "minimal" in the sense that there is no interaction among members, members are completely anonymous to one another, and there is no direct connection between outcomes for the participants and outcomes for the other members. Nesdale and colleagues found that at 7 years of age, when the ingroup had a norm of inclusion, the children liked the outgroup when there was no outgroup threat, but disliked the outgroup when threat was present. When the ingroup had a norm of exclusion, the 7-year-old children disliked the outgroup regardless of whether the outgroup comprised a threat or not. In contrast, at 9 years of age, when the ingroup had a norm of inclusion, the children were more neutral towards the outgroup regardless of whether it was a threat or not. When the ingroup had a norm of exclusion, the 9-year-old children were neutral when the outgroup was not a threat but disliked the outgroup when it was a threat. Thus, at both ages, the children actually most disliked the outgroup when their group had a norm of exclusion and the outgroup comprised a threat to their group. However, the 9-year-old compared with the 7-year-old children were more diffident or undecided concerning the outgroup, except when their group held an exclusion norm and they perceived the outgroup as a threat.

Nesdale and colleagues argued the most plausible explanation for these findings was older children's increasing tendency to self-present and control their explicit ethnic prejudice, which was only set aside when the context became uniquely hostile (i.e., the ingroup promoted a norm of excluding the outgroup and the outgroup challenged the status of the ingroup). They also acknowledged that "social identity development theory needs to be modified to take such interactive effects, particularly those involving age, into account" (Nesdale, Maass, et al., 2005, p. 660), a task which has now been undertaken in a more recent statement of the theory. This has given greater emphasis to the possibility of age effects that reflect both children's increasing awareness that adults typically disapprove of negative intergroup attitudes and behavior and that children have an increasing need to present themselves in the best possible light, particularly when under the surveillance of adults (Nesdale, 2007).

Theory of Social Mind and the Control of Prejudice

Another way to interpret children's desires to be inclusive is to propose that children's control of their prejudice requires an understanding of social or moral norms about expressing bias towards different types of groups (e.g. FitzRoy & Rutland, 2010; Rutland, 2004; Rutland, Cameron, Milne, & McGeorge, 2005). In turn, developing this understanding involves children acquiring social knowledge and social-cognitive abilities, in particular the ability to understand other people's mental states and their attitudes or beliefs about social relationships (see Abrams & Rutland, 2008; Abrams, Rutland, Pelletier, & Ferrell, 2009; Killen et al., 2008). The control of explicit ethnic bias by attending to norms of your group that condemn prejudice is likely to involve recursive reasoning about mental states, since the child is concerned about the way he or she is seen in the mind of others.

This ability initially involves what developmental psychologists refer to as Theory of Mind (ToM), namely the capacity to impute mental states or understand that others have beliefs, desires, and intentions that are different from one's own, as described in chapter 2 of this book. Developmental research shows children from approximately 5 years of age engage in such recursive mental state reasoning about false beliefs (i.e., understand that one person may have a false belief about another person's belief). This second-order false belief understanding, however, is known to develop well into middle childhood (Baron-Cohen, O'Riordan, Stone, Jones, & Plaisted, 1999). From around 6–7 years of age children can understand false beliefs about social, not just physical, stimuli and begin to understand about false emotions as well as false beliefs (Harris, Johnson, Hutton, Andrews, & Cooke, 1989).

From approximately 7 years of age children develop an understanding of other people's minds and emotions that arise in *social relationships* (i.e., Theory of Social Mind – ToSM). Given these findings it is not surprising that older children are better able than younger children to anticipate group members' perspectives on expressing prejudice towards other groups or peers within their own group (Abrams, Rutland, & Cameron, 2003; Abrams, Rutland, Ferrell, & Pelletier, 2008; Abrams et al., 2009). Abrams et al. (2009) measured children's ToSM by examining children's ability to distinguish their own feelings about a character from the feelings of a peer who does not share the same information about that character. This requires an ability to use information about the prior social relationship between two peers to make an inference about their feelings toward one another, independently of the child's own knowledge and feelings about that peer. Children's ToSM is measured by presenting children with a scenario involving a friendship and asking them questions (Figure 4.1). The ToSM task is based in the interpersonal domain, allowing one to be confident that it does not simply measure a child's learning of a particular social norm for a specific group. Abrams and colleagues (2009) found that an understanding of group dynamics and norms (i.e., who will be accepted and rejected by the group) was related to the development of better social perspective-taking ability as measured by the ToSM task. Moreover, children with advanced ToSM were able to use this information to inform their prejudiced exclusion judgments of individual group members.

This finding suggests that ToSM may be important to children's understanding of group norms about showing explicit bias and their self-presentation of explicit bias (Rutland, 2004; Rutland et al., 2005). Such self-presentations are more than the ability to produce and inhibit certain behaviors in accordance with external rules (Bandura, 1986); rather they are a mechanism by which children actively regulate their social attitudes in order to manipulate the impressions of them held by valued others in their group (Leary, 1996; Schlenker, 1980). In support of this argument, developmental research indicates that school-age children,

Steve and Kevin have just met for the first time. Steve is playing a game with Kevin. Steve is having fun and is enjoying playing the game a lot.

Then Steve leaves the room to get a drink. While Steve is gone, Kevin steals some of Steve's toys and hides the toys in his pocket.

Before Steve goes back in the room to play again, Steve's mum asks Steve if he likes Kevin or not.

Q1. Does Steve know that Kevin took his toys?
Q2. What do you think Steve says to his mum about Kevin? Does he say that he likes him *OR* that he doesn't like him?
Q3. Why do you think he says that?

Figure 4.1 Theory of Social Mind task card. (© 2010 Adam Rutland and Dominic Abrams.)

with advanced mental state understanding, have the ability to understand self-presentational motives, and by approximately 8 years of age can provide spontaneous explanations for complex self-presentational behavior (Banerjee & Yuill, 1999a, 1999b; Bennett & Yeeles, 1990).

Moral or Group Norms and the Control of Prejudice

Self-presentation of prejudice in childhood requires more than just advanced mental state understanding. The process is also likely to depend on whether a child understands that their group normally acts according to moral principles (e.g., fairness). Developmental psychologists have recently begun to demonstrate that group norms about showing prejudice affect the self-presentation of young children's explicit ethnic prejudice and their exclusion judgments of individual children within their peer group (Abrams, Rutland, Cameron, & Ferrell, 2007; Rutland et al., 2005). For example, Abrams and colleagues (2007) manipulated children's *accountability* to their own group (i.e., a summer school), in the sense that their actions were visible and may have had to be defended or could be criticized. They were told that other children and adults in their summer school would see their answers to all the questions at the end of the study, thus making salient their own group's norm about whether to exclude or include individuals.

The context of the study was summer schools in England, which are not comparable to a North American sleep-away summer camp since they are non-residential schemes that provide sports and other activities for children drawn from a variety of schools in the local area. Typically, children attend for 1 or 2 weeks, or a few days each week during the 6-week summer vacation period. The mix of children changes daily and according to the activities they pursue. These schools therefore provide a relatively "minimal" group membership with no particular history of close interpersonal relationships but with sufficient meaning and value that children evaluate their own summer school positively relative to others. In this context, then, showing bias in favor of your own group and excluding individuals because they contravene the norms of your group was understood as legitimate and tolerated. Increasing accountability to the peer group in this context promoted children's desires to defend their group norms, increased their exclusion of other disloyal children within their own group, and resulted in bias in favor of their group over other groups.

In contrast, another study by Rutland et al. (2005, Study 1) was conducted in the very different and sensitive context of inter-ethnic relations in Britain. This study assessed 5- to 16-year-old White British majority status children's personal moral norms about ethnic exclusion, by describing to them an imaginary situation involving a group of ethnic majority status children excluding a minority status child and asking them how right or wrong was this social exclusion. Rutland and colleagues found that children who showed a strong moral norm against social exclusion showed lower explicit prejudice towards those from a different racial group. In contrast, children with a weak moral norm about social exclusion (i.e., they thought the social exclusion was

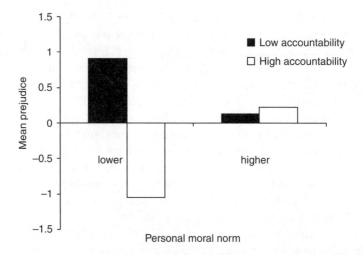

Figure 4.2 Mean racial prejudice under high or low public accountability for children with either higher or lower personal moral norms about social exclusion. (Created by Adam Rutland. Source: Rutland et al., 2005.)

relatively less wrong) only inhibited their prejudice when the contrary social norm of their own ethnic group was made highly salient by increasing their accountability to this group (Figure 4.2). An increase in accountability was achieved by making the children think their answers were being recorded on video and could be shown to other children and adults from their own ethnic group.

Here what we seem to be finding is that when White majority children who have the potential to show ethnic prejudice, because they have relatively weak moral norms, are made accountable to their own group they "put the brakes upon their prejudices. They do not act them out – or they act them out only up to a certain point. Something stops the logical progression somewhere" (Allport, 1954, p.332). Writing in the United States during the 1950s, Allport described a few examples of situations when adults attempted to control their ethnic prejudice. The study described above by Rutland and colleagues (2005) suggests that children also at times show such prejudice control. Nonetheless little is known about the "something" that Allport said helps stop the development of prejudice, especially amongst children who are known to show explicit ethnic bias at an early age.

Processes Underlying the Control of Prejudice

To address this concern other research has examined affective and social-cognitive processes important in White majority status 6- to 9-year-old British children learning to control their ethnic intergroup bias (FitzRoy & Rutland, 2010). This research revealed that *both* children's ToSM (as described above) *and* their understanding of their group's social norm about showing explicit bias moderated how their explicit ethnic bias changed when they were made accountable (in a similar way to the previous study by Abrams et al., 2007). ToSM was assessed using the task first developed by Abrams and colleagues (2009; see above).

In contrast to previous studies (e.g., Rutland et al., 2005) that have assessed children's moral norms about showing ethnic exclusion, FitzRoy and Rutland (2010) examined their awareness of their own group's social norm about showing ethnic prejudice. Children were presented with a pictorial, ambiguous money scenario adapted from the Ambiguous Situations Task (McGlothlin & Killen, 2006). In this money situation picture, two children (one White and one Black) are standing outside in a playground. The White child has her/his pockets pulled out with a distressed expression on their face. A £5 note or bill is on the ground behind them. The Black child is bending down picking up the £5 note. Children were first presented with this picture, then asked to imagine that another White child or White teacher in their class had seen the picture. Then they were presented with 12 different statements that could be said about this picture (six positive and six negative). Finally, children were asked to rate how many children and teachers in their class would say each of the positive and negative statements if they saw the picture. Their responses were used to calculate a social norm score showing how much they were aware that their own group held a norm about not showing explicit racial bias (i.e., an anti-prejudice norm).

FitzRoy and Rutland (2010) manipulated children's accountability to their own ethnic group so it was either relatively low (i.e., only a researcher from the child's own ethnic group was present) or it was relatively high (i.e., a researcher from the child's own ethnic group was present and the children thought their answers would be shown to classmates and teachers from the child's ethnic group). In Study 2, FitzRoy and Rutland (2010) found children with high ToSM scores showed little ethnic bias irrespective of the level of public accountability. They also found that when children were not aware their own group held an anti-prejudice norm their ethnic bias was unaffected by manipulating public accountability. However, when children understood their group

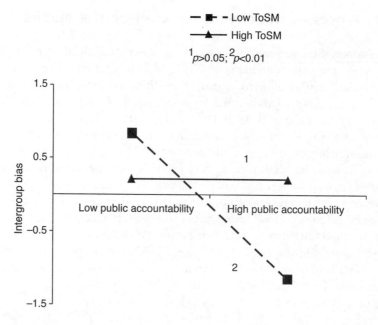

Figure 4.3 The effect of public accountability on high and low Theory of Social Mind (ToSM) scoring on children's intergroup bias when they understand their ingroup holds an anti-prejudice norm. (Source: FitzRoy & Rutland, 2010.)

held an anti-prejudice norm), children with low ToSM scores significantly decreased their ethnic bias when public accountability was made relatively higher (Figure 4.3).

The key finding here is that children with low ToSM scores, who were not able to readily or easily attend to a moral norm or the social norm of their group about not showing ethnic bias, only controlled their bias when they had some awareness that their own group would not show ethnic bias and this norm was made salient by increasing their accountability to their group. This study for the first time revealed that children's ToSM and awareness of their own group's norm together are important processes in how they learn to control their ethnic bias. These findings go beyond previous research showing that children control their prejudice by highlighting how social-cognitive and normative processes combine during the process of ethnic bias control in childhood (Abrams & Rutland, 2008; Nesdale, 2004; Rutland, 2004; Rutland et al., 2005).

Given recent research in the adult literature has suggested that social emotions (e.g., guilt, embarrassment) encourage people to control their explicit ethnic attitudes, FitzRoy and Rutland (2010, Study 1) also considered whether children's propensity to show embarrassment influenced their level of explicit ethnic bias when being made accountable to their own ethnic group. They measured children's self-attribution of embarrassment by presenting a child with a hypothetical scenario involving a rule violation which included the child being responsible for a younger friend. This context of having the child taking care of a younger friend when violating a rule or convention was included because it accentuated the potential for social emotions in the situation. The children with high social emotions were more likely to say they would feel embarrassed in this situation.

This study found that 8- to 9-year-old children's propensity to show embarrassment moderates their ability to control explicit ethnic bias. The ethnic attitudes of the younger children (6–7 years old), who overall showed little tendency to attribute social emotions, were, as expected, unaffected by the public accountability manipulation. Also as predicted, FitzRoy and Rutland found that 8- to 9-year-old children with a higher individual propensity to attribute embarrassment, were unaffected by the public accountability manipulation. In contrast, 8- to 9-year-olds with a low individual propensity to show social emotions controlled their ethnic intergroup bias when public accountability was increased. Arguably, these children did not establish under low accountability conditions that they and their group would feel social emotions (e.g., embarrassment) when expressing ethnic bias and only did so when made highly accountable to their own group.

Children's social emotions (i.e., their ability to show embarrassment) acted in a similar way as ToSM, within FitzRoy and Rutland's Study 2, in the process of controlling the children's ethnic bias, with children low in these abilities suppressing their bias when made accountable to their group. This finding suggests that children's understanding of social emotions and ToSM are interrelated. Namely children who show the ability to understand others' mental states about emotions within social relationships are more likely to feel social emotions like embarrassment. Indeed, previous developmental research has suggested that the attribution of social emotions such as embarrassment is associated with recursive cognitions about others' mental states and second-order mental state understanding (Banerjee, 2002). The studies conducted by FitzRoy and Rutland (2010) suggest a child's developing capacity to understand their social emotions and beliefs, and how they might be different or the same as others' social emotions and beliefs, is important if they are to control their bias in favor of their group over other groups. This type of recursive reasoning about emotions and mental states in group contexts arguably offers the child the potential to frame their group attitudes to create a positive image amongst members of their own group (i.e., engage in self-presentation).

Such recursive social reasoning may not always result in low explicit bias, however, since children's control of their attitudes towards social groups appears to depend on the specific norms children perceive to be held by their own group to which they are most often accountable (especially in highly homogenous or non-mixed environments). Prejudice control also appears to depend on when children develop enough social knowledge, to the extent that they know whether their group will or will not tolerate explicit bias against an outgroup.

Typically, when group norms condemn explicit ethnic prejudice, children's self-presentation of these attitudes results in the control of prejudice. In contrast, the story can be very different when considering social norms and explicit attitudes towards social groups based upon categories other than ethnicity. For example, take prejudice based upon the social category of nationality: pro-bias norms regarding other na-tionalities have been found before in studies with White European children in either the United Kingdom (e.g., Abrams et al., 2003; Rutland, 1999) or the Netherlands (e.g., Verkuyten, 2001). Therefore, unsurpris-ingly, Rutland et al. (2005, Study 2) found that 10- to 12-year-old White British children's *increased* their national bias when they thought they were accountable to their own group, presumably because they thought their group held a norm that such bias was tolerable. These studies show that the self-presentation process can also operate to promote bias or prejudice in attitude domains other than ethnicity (e.g., nationality or school group).

Do children readily apply moral principles (e.g., fairness) when judging others from all the different kinds of groups in the social world (e.g., nationality, gender)? Killen and colleagues demonstrated that gender bias can be reduced when the principle of fairness is introduced by peers (Killen, Pisacane, Lee-Kim, & Ardila-Rey, 2001). They found that young children who made stereotypic decisions in peer play contexts (e.g., excluding a girl from playing with trucks, or excluding a boy from playing with dolls) were more inclusive and used moral reasoning after hearing fairness probes from a peer (e.g., "What if she likes trucks and wants to play, too?"). Later on in this chapter and in chapter 8 we consider children's application of moral principles (e.g., fairness) across different group contexts (e.g., nationality, gender, ethnicity) when we consider research that has examined both morality and group identity.

Developmental Subjective Group Dynamics

Another recent theoretical perspective on children's group attitudes has also built on Social Identity theory, adapted it to study children, and offered a more social and contextual model of attitude development. This is the Developmental Subjective Group Dynamics (DSGD) model (see Abrams & Rutland, 2008). So far the focus of this chapter has been understanding when and why children show bias or prejudice against children from different social groups. In contrast, the DSGD model focuses on how group identity can also result in social exclusion *within* groups (i.e., intragroup bias), with children within a group being excluded because they challenge the norms of the group. This should be of particular interest to those concerned with the increasingly common situation of social exclusion *within* peer groups when group memberships are salient (e.g., in ethnically heterogeneous schools). Here the issue is how children make sense of a situation where identities are salient because the context is multicultural but particular peers differ from their fellow group members.

Cognitive developmental theory (Aboud, 1988; Katz, 1976; Lambert & Klineberg, 1967), described earlier in chapter 3, suggests a given relationship between bias against individuals within your group and bias against those from another group. This theory holds that initially a child's social perception is focused on the self. Children cannot relate to another individual's point of view and they dislike anything that is different from them. Then, with age, children begin to attend to groups, focusing on group differences, and start to show a preference for their own group over other groups. Finally, they cease to focus on group characteristics as they become capable of making social judgments on the basis of the unique characteristics of an individual. Consequently, with age, the availability of information about individuals' characteristics should help to reduce group biases. Specifically, Aboud's (1988) theory of cognitive development holds that there is a developmental sequence in which the child's focus of attention shifts from the self to the group (i.e., intergroup) and finally to the individual's characteristics (i.e., intragroup). At this final stage, children may still express more positive evaluations of some individuals over others, but the criterion for judgment will not be solely that of group membership (see Aboud, 1988, pp. 23–25).

In contrast, the DSGD model (see Abrams & Rutland, 2008) holds that children develop a *dynamic* relationship between their judgments about individuals *within* groups (i.e., intragroup attitudes) and about groups as a whole (i.e., intergroup attitudes). At the same time that children's advanced mental state understanding develops (i.e., ToSM) they experience belonging to more social groups. As this occurs, they are more likely to integrate their preferences for different groups with their evaluations of individuals within groups based on particular characteristics or behaviors. Specifically, the DSGD model proposes that children shift from evaluations of members of their own group and other groups based solely on preference for members of their own group (Tajfel & Turner, 1979) to judgments that both differentiate between groups and amongst individuals within groups, and they do this at a fairly young age (by 8 years of age).

For example, a group of children identifying with a sports team should prefer their team over another team but they should also begin to show more negative attitudes towards peers within their own team, who act like, or prefer, members of a rival team (i.e., disloyal peers). This would include peers who keep praising a "star" sportsperson on another team rather than anyone on their own team. This change in children's social cognition means they can often both exclude peers because they are from a different social group (i.e., intergroup bias) and also exclude peers from *within* their group who deviate from their group's social-conventional norms (e.g., by being disloyal).

This model contends that during childhood and adolescence peers within a group who are deviant because they contravene an ingroup norm (e.g., loyalty) are judged negatively compared to similarly deviant peers from another group who are also deviant because they do not conform to their ingroup's norm (i.e., the "black sheep effect": Marques, Yzerbyt, & Leyens, 1988). For example, imagine there was a clique of adolescents who dressed as "goths" (e.g., body piercings and black clothes) and there was another clique who dressed like "jocks" (e.g., sportswear and neat hair) and these two groups were continually in conflict. Then one day some members from the "goths" clique were fighting with some members of the "jocks" clique and one of the "jocks" appears with a pierced nose and says they should not fight the "Goths" because they have some really "cool" clothes and fashions. To members of the "jocks" clique this adolescent is a deviant within their group (i.e., a "black sheep") and should be judged negatively compared to a deviant from the other group, an adolescent from the "goths" clique who wore sports trainers and said the same thing (i.e., "goths" should not fight with the "jocks" because they have some really "cool" clothes and fashions).

This can be a *subjective* phenomenon, because it is not necessary to have all the members from each gang objectively present for this effect to occur. This is akin to what occurs during the dynamics of real-life face-to-face small groups when everyone is present, with efforts to exclude and differentiate between peers so constraining deviants in order to reinforce the boundaries of group norms (e.g., Levine, 1989; Schachter, 1951). If these dynamics occur when social identities are salient, however, then exclusion between peers within groups (i.e., "differential evaluation") occurs simultaneously with the motivation to sustain a positive group identity and distinctiveness between groups, which is known to result in group bias (Tajfel & Turner, 1979). The former process involves attention to individual peer group members to identify and devalue deviant peers (i.e., intragroup exclusion) so upholding group norms, and the latter process implies general exclusion of those peers from other groups. These two processes combined are considered subjective group dynamics.

The DSGD model contends that during middle childhood, as children gain more experience of interacting within groups, they begin to show advanced mental state understanding or ToSM (Abrams et al., 2009). Therefore they begin to recognize that deviant peer group members constitute a departure from norms that other group members would want to preserve (i.e., deviance here is a variation between individuals that is relevant to their group membership). Children in middle childhood sustain their social identity and the distinctiveness of their group by excluding deviant peers within their group in favor of those who provide stronger support for the norms of the group (Abrams & Rutland, 2008). Children's developing social-cognitive capacity to focus on differences within groups therefore sustains rather than diminishes bias because exclusion becomes targeted on particular deviant peers within their group.

Research on developmental subjective group dynamics

Research following the DSGD model has investigated children's group biases alongside constructing an experimental paradigm to examine how children would evaluate peers from their own group and other groups who either show "normative" (loyal) behavior or "deviant" (disloyal) behavior. In Europe there has been a long history of rivalry or even conflict between nations off the sports field (e.g., World War II or struggles for colonial reach around the world) and on the sports field (especially in the European and World Soccer Championships). This has arguably resulted in well-established and often rigid national group boundaries, despite attempts to promote the European Union and European integration, making it interesting and timely to investigate when and how children socially exclude and include others from different national groups.

Abrams and colleagues when studying British children have often used competition between national teams as the intergroup context (e.g., English soccer team vs. German soccer team). In their experiments children were first asked to rate how they felt towards their group as a whole and another group as a whole (i.e., national bias) (Abrams et al., 2007; Abrams, Rutland, Cameron, & Marques, 2003). Then the children heard descriptions of normative and deviant peers who were either in the same or a different national group. Normative peers made two positive statements about the group, while deviant peers made one positive statement about the group, but also one positive statement about the other group. Initially, children were asked to evaluate the normative and deviant peers (i.e., intragroup exclusion). This indicated whether the children were excluding peers *within* each social group. Importantly, then the children were also asked to judge whether other peers from their group and the other group would exclude or include the normative and deviant peers. This measured children's expectations about the way others will exclude or include peers. Subjective group dynamics should be evident in children who have correct expectations and, therefore, provide positive evaluations of peers who are acceptable to *their group* rather than peers who are more acceptable to the other group.

In addition to studies that have used national groups, other studies have also examined summer school groups and minimal or "arbitrary" groups (Abrams, Rutland, Cameron, et al., 2003; Abrams et al., 2007, 2008). They have all shown that the relationship between exclusion between groups and exclusion within peer groups tends to be reliable after the age of around 7 years. At this age children can simultaneously exclude those from other social groups and exclude those within their peer group that threaten the social conventional norms central to their group (e.g. loyalty). In addition, these different forms of social exclusion are more strongly linked when older children are more motivated to support their own group (i.e., show high intergroup bias or identify more strongly with their own group) (Abrams, Rutland, & Cameron, 2003; Abrams et al., 2009).

Research also suggests that the development of exclusion judgments between peers within groups is sensitive to the normative aspects of the group context (i.e., what is acceptable behavior for peers from a child's own group and another group). Thus, increasing children's *accountability* makes the norms of a child's own group more salient. The DSGD model predicts that this should encourage self-presentational concerns among children and variations in their exclusion judgments. In support of this prediction, research in a non-competitive summer school context has found increased accountability results in more peer exclusion within groups and subjective group dynamics (Abrams et al., 2007). Together these findings indicate that social exclusion within groups is related to the children's sense of group identity, their desire to maintain differences between their group and other groups, and their motivation to defend group norms about legitimate peer group behavior.

Morality and Group Identity

Children's evaluations of peer behavior in any context, however, reflect a multitude of interrelated factors, relating to considerations of the self (e.g., individual autonomy), group (e.g., norms or social conventions), and morality (e.g., fairness or justice) (Bukowski & Sippola, 2001; Killen, 2007; Turiel, 1998). The dynamic relationship between morality and group identity was examined directly in recent developmental research on age-related increases in social exclusion judgments, in which older children excluded peers who challenged their own group's norms (Abrams & Rutland, 2008; Abrams et al., 2008). New studies have considered how deviance from an individual that threatens the group may arise not in the social-conventional but in the moral domain. The focus was on how children weigh their concerns about group identity (i.e., maintaining the group norms) with moral beliefs about fairness and justice. Which aspect of the situation do children consider most important, the favorability of peers who preserve the group norms (i.e., the individual who supports their group) or their knowledge about the basis for exclusion (i.e., whether the act is unfair)?

Abrams and colleagues (2008) conducted studies using the paradigm familiar to DSGD research but with the addition in one study of a moral norm variation, drawn from the Social Domain model (Killen, 2007). This research employed a minimal group paradigm to eliminate the possibility that previous findings reported above reflect behavior that applies only to particular intergroup relationships (Tajfel, 1970; Tajfel & Turner, 1979). Specifically, children were assigned ostensibly randomly to "star" and "diamond" groups (all were actually in the diamond group), and were asked to evaluate pairs of anonymous normative and deviant peers from those groups.

This research investigated how children judged peers in minimal groups whose behavior was loyal versus disloyal (Study 1) or morally acceptable versus unacceptable (Study 2). Consistent with the DSGD model and previous research (Abrams et al., 2007), in Study 1 children used their understanding of loyalty norms as a basis for their own evaluations of peers. In addition, higher commitment to their own group increased children's use of group-based criteria for judging peers. Study 2 is most relevant here since it analyzed how children employ both moral and group-based criteria when evaluating peers from their own group and other groups who deviate according to moral principles.

In Study 2, 5- to 7-year-old (i.e., younger) and 10- to 11-year-old (i.e., older) children were asked to judge peers from a minimal ingroup and outgroup who either adhered to (i.e., normative) or transgressed (i.e., deviant) moral principles. They were also asked how others from their group and the other group would judge these peers. The moral principle used was fairness. For example, an unfair peer was described as someone who "doesn't take turns and pushes people to get ahead in the queue" or was someone who "is very selfish with toys and games." It was found that older children had a better understanding of whether groups would exclude or include different peers (i.e., differential inclusion) and were willing to exclude peers themselves on the basis of the peer's group membership (i.e., group-based bias). At the same time, however, older children also invoked principles of morality (e.g., behaving according to the fairness principle) when making exclusion decisions. Thus, children favored members of their own group over members from the other group but also favored peers from either group who behaved according to a moral principle over morally deviant individuals from each group.

In addition, when considering group-based judgments, Study 2 also showed children's understanding of how other group members will respond to deviance (i.e., differential inclusion) and their own evaluations of peers (i.e., group-based evaluations or bias) were more strongly linked the more the children identified with their own group. The relationship between inclusion and bias was only marginally significant when identification was low, but was larger and highly significant when identification was high. In contrast, with moral-based judgments children who believed their peers would more strongly favor fair over unfair members made similar judgments themselves. Most importantly, their judgments were not affected by how strongly they identified with the group or their beliefs about how peers judge members from their group and other groups.

So the more strongly children identified with their own group, the more closely related were their judgments of group-based (but not moral-based) inclusion and their own group-based (but not moral-based) differential bias toward members. These findings tell us that children's social identity is relevant to the group-based and not the moral-based domain of discrimination within groups.

It does not appear that children's responses to peers from their own group and other groups requires a trade-off between favoring peers because of their group membership versus favoring them because of their morality. Instead, Abrams and colleagues showed that when moral breaches are objectively uncorrelated with group membership, children use both morality *and* group memberships as independent bases of judgment. This study supports our new integrative perspective, outlined at the end of chapter 3 and at the beginning of this chapter, by showing that morality and group-based judgments are not opposites. Rather, children employ *both* when engaging in bias and social exclusion of peers.

Other recent studies have also investigated how children coordinate moral concerns of fairness with group identity. For example, in a study on exclusion from social cliques, Horn (2006) showed that both social identity and group status influence adolescents' judgments about inclusion and exclusion within adolescent cliques. Adolescents who identified themselves as members of high-status groups (e.g., cheerleaders, jocks) exhibited more bias in favor of their own group in their exclusion decisions. They were also more likely to use conventional rather than moral reasoning in justifying their judgments, and were more likely to invoke stereotypes than were adolescents who identified as members of low-status groups.

Adolescents typically view exclusion from a valued resource, such as a scholarship, as morally wrong (e.g., it would be wrong to deny a "jock" the chance of an academic scholarship) independent of which group of adolescents are being excluded (Horn, 2003). However, Horn still found the adolescents' stereotypes about groups significantly influenced their evaluation of exclusion from group participation (e.g., it is all right to exclude a "goth" from joining the cheerleaders). Here the adolescents were more likely to condone acts of exclusion when individuals did not fit the stereotypic expectations of the group and, therefore, challenged the functioning of the group. These findings show that adolescents are more likely to use stereotypes to condone exclusion when group-based criteria are relevant (i.e., a need to maintain group norms for effective group functioning).

Important new findings have demonstrated the coexistence of different forms of social and moral reasoning regarding group exclusion between Dutch and Muslim adolescents (Verkuyten & Slooter, 2008). This research involved an experimental questionnaire study with Muslim minority and non-Muslim majority Dutch adolescents, which found that their social and moral reasoning about civic liberties and tolerance of others was dependent on their group membership. For example, Muslims compared to non-Muslims were less tolerant of free speech by others when it involved offending God and religion. In contrast non-Muslims compared to Muslims were less tolerant of minority rights (e.g., the idea of separate religious schools, the wearing of a headscarf, and the right to burn the national flag in demonstrations). In the "hot" context of Muslim and non-Muslim relations in Europe, an adolescent's group membership influences their social reasoning about moral issues and level of tolerance towards others. Verkuyten (2005) also found that the more Dutch participants endorsed multiculturalism the more likely they were to evaluate other ethnic groups positively, indicating that a multicultural identity (i.e., a willingness to value multiple group identities) was related to positive attitudes towards other ethnic groups.

The relationship between group-based and moral-based reasoning suggest that with age children are able to simultaneously make exclusion judgments involving group-based and morality-based reasoning. They also show that children's propensities to engage in group-based exclusion will depend on the strength and salience of their group identity, which will be related to the specifics of the group context. For example, which groups are available for social comparison? Is the child's own group seen as under threat from other groups? Is there conflict (real or imagined) between the groups within the environment?

Summary

In this chapter we have examined how social motivations relating to children's group identities challenge their moral reasoning and can result in prejudice development. In line with our new integrative theory, which draws from both the Social Domain model and Social Identity theory, we have shown how children's moral focus is often overpowered by their strong attachment to social groups, and their desire to favor their group over other groups and defend the norms of their group (see Rutland et al., 2010). We have detailed, in this chapter, how Social Identity theory contends individuals are often motivated to sustain a positive social identity given its centrality to their self-concept, by showing a preference for their group and forming negative attitudes towards other groups.

Social Identity Development theory (Nesdale, Durkin, et al., 2005) was the first attempt to extend the social identity approach to provide a social motivational account of developmental changes in children's group attitudes. This theory stated that bias in favor of a child's own group and bias against other groups follow different developmental paths, with the former generally being established prior to the latter. The theory also proposed that three main factors determine whether children show ethnic prejudice: strength of a child's ethnic identification, perceived threat to the child's own ethnic group from other groups, and norms about the legitimacy of expressing prejudice held by the child's own group. In this chapter we have also described research that has shown that children's recursive social reasoning about emotions and mental states in group contexts enables them to control their explicit biases and frame their group attitudes to create a positive image amongst members of their own group (i.e., engage in self-presentation). Specifically, this research suggests that children learn to control their explicit prejudice through their developing advanced mental state understanding (i.e., Theory of Social Mind), attribution of social emotions (e.g., embarrassment), and understanding of norms held by their group about legitimate attitudes and behaviors.

Finally, in this chapter we discussed the Developmental Subjective Group Dynamics model which has shown how group identity can also motivate social exclusion *within* and not just between groups. This approach proposes that children shift from evaluations of groups based solely on preference for members of their own group to judgments that also differentiate among peers within groups. The result is that children will exclude a peer either because they are from a different group or because they deviate from the group's social-conventional norms. Research suggests this phenomenon is most evident when children have more advanced mental state understanding, are highly aware of their group's norms about legitimate behavior, and strongly identify with their own group. Research that has drawn on both Social Domain theory and social identity approaches research shows that children do not abandon moral reasoning when judging whether to socially exclude somebody; rather they consider both group and moral factors simultaneously. In the next chapter we will review different forms of social exclusion within peer groups, and show that to fully understand social exclusion morality, group identity and prejudice all play a role.

Chapter 5

What We Know about Peer Relations and Exclusion

In this chapter, we will provide a brief overview of different theoretical approaches to peer exclusion and then review findings on inclusion and exclusion in children's lives. To fully understand problems that occur as a result of experiences of exclusion, it is also necessary to understand children's experiences with inclusion. In our previous chapters we focused on morality, which is reflected in children's orientations to be fair, children's prejudice, bias, and group identity, which are often revealed in their decisions to exclude others. Focusing on only one or the other is often necessary, and yet, to understand the "whole child" it is important to capture both the positive and negative aspects of social development. In this chapter, and the next chapter on peer exclusion and group dynamics, we explain the interweaving of these two aspects of social development.

The consequences of peer rejection and exclusion bear on children's healthy social development. Excluded children can experience hurt feelings and anxiety; in more extreme cases, excluded children can experience depression, social withdrawal, and disengagement. As has been mentioned there are many different types of exclusion. As explained by Abrams, Hogg, and Marques (2005), the study of exclusion can focus on individual personality traits that lead to exclusion (intrapersonal), the psychological dynamics when one person excludes another person (interpersonal), the group dynamics that occur when an individual excludes someone from their own group (intragroup), and the group dynamics that occur when a group excludes someone from another group (an outgroup).

Children and Social Exclusion: Morality, Prejudice, and Group Identity. Melanie Killen and Adam Rutland. © 2011 Melanie Killen and Adam Rutland. Published 2011 by Blackwell Publishing Ltd.

Identifying these different sources of exclusion is important because intrapersonal and interpersonal exclusion focus on the personality traits of the individual, whereas intragroup and intergroup exclusion focus on the role of the group, both in terms of group norms as well as group identity. Perhaps the most distinguishing feature of these sources of exclusion has to do with the focus on personality traits and individual differences that lead to peer rejection (interpersonal), on the one hand, in contrast to the focus on normative expectations that lead to prejudice, bias, and exclusion (intergroup), on the other hand. While there are psychopathological dimensions to the extreme cases for both types of exclusion, such as "ethnic cleansing" for group exclusion (Opotow, 1990; Staub, 1990) and victimization in the form of bully–victim relationships that result from extreme personality traits, the conceptualization of exclusion and the implications for intervention are quite different. As well, the source of the problems associated with exclusion based on personality (intrapersonal and interpersonal) and based on group identity (intragroup and intergroup) are different. Because not all forms of exclusion are detrimental or negative, it is essential to define, examine, and describe the multitude of ways in which children engage in exclusion at different levels in social interactions, relationships, and groups. Thus, in the next section of this chapter, each form of exclusion will be briefly discussed.

Intrapersonal and Interpersonal Exclusion: Social Traits and Individual Differences

As mentioned, intrapersonal and interpersonal exclusion refer to exclusion based upon the individual psychological dispositions of children that make them vulnerable to the negative consequences of being excluded or excluding others, as well as the cost that they incur as a result of being excluded, such as depression, anxiety, or loneliness (Boivin, Hymel, & Bukowski, 1995). Individual psychological dispositions of children have been studied by researchers who have used sociometric techniques to identify children's places in the group as a function of their popularity status (Rubin, Bukowski, & Parker, 2006). Sociometric techniques involve asking children in a group or classroom to nominate who they view as their friends or their "nonfriends" (in various studies the "nonfriend" category includes acquaintances or enemies) and then combining the information from all children to determine which children have friendship nominations, and which children do not.

Peer nominations show how multiple profiles exist in classrooms (and schools), including those children who are deemed as popular (nominated by a lot of children) in contrast to those children who are rejected or neglected (nominated by very few children). There are also children who are referred to as "controversial" (nominated as high friendship and high "antagonist"). Not surprisingly, the majority of children are referred to as "average" (who receive some friendship nominations) and constitute 70% of the children in a classroom or school, leaving about 15% who are classified as rejected, neglected, or controversial, as well as 15% who are ranked as popular. Rejected status, even amongst children as young as 5 years of age, is negatively related to engagement and participation in classroom interactions as well as motivation to achieve in school (Buhs & Ladd, 2001). Thus, this type of analysis identifies the children who are the outliers and who have significant problems with peer relationships.

There are different approaches for understanding the personality and social characteristics of individual children that contribute to identifying which children are vulnerable to being excluded or rejected. Examples of social skills that appear to be lacking in excluded or rejected children include the ability to read communication cues from peers, resolve conflicts constructively, or enter peer groups effectively (Crick & Dodge, 1994; Lemerise & Arsenio, 2000). Social information processing models (Bierman, 2004; Crick & Dodge, 1994; Lemerise & Arsenio, 2000) outline the steps that are necessary for children to encode and interpret social cues, clarify social goals and responses, and make a decision to act. For example, children might encode others' behaviors as negative, which influences their goals and decision to act, in contrast to encoding cues as positive, which leads to a different line of thinking and social outcomes (Rubin et al., 2006).

Social cognitive processing research on rejected children has shown that these children are more likely than "non-rejected" children to have negative goals of "revenge" and to interpret others' cues as negatively motivated (a benign or neutral expression by a peer is viewed as hostile by a rejected child). Further research has shown that rejected children reflect two different types of psychological patterns of social interaction, rejected-withdrawn and rejected-aggressive (Hymel, Bowker, & Woody, 1993). Rejected-withdrawn children are more likely than rejected-aggressive children to have problems with social skills, interpreting others' intentions, and clarifying their social goals. Recently, research has show that, in fact, aggressive children figure out how to manipulate others and wield power in ways that brings them high status, even when they are not well liked (Garandeau & Cillessen, 2006). The major behavioral correlate of peer rejection is aggression, however, and thus rejected children are at risk for aggression towards others (Dodge et al., 2003), which has also been referred to as externalizing behaviors. Some children who are rejected are shy and withdrawn, and are at risk for what has been termed internalizing behaviors, such as depression. Overall, these children reflect between 10% and 15% of the total population of children, and are targeted for special treatment programs and intervention.

Temperament is one of the intrapersonal factors that has received the most attention in the literature. Temperament refers to a person's emotional, reactive, and attentional disposition, measured in infancy, which is related to social behaviors in childhood and even adulthood (Rothbart, Ellis, & Posner, 2004). Research has shown that reticence and social withdrawal in infancy predict peer rejection in childhood, indicating that there are individual differences regarding dispositions that account for why a child is rejected by his or her peers (Gazelle & Ladd, 2003). Negative emotionality has been documented as a behavioral profile in infancy that is viewed as relatively stable throughout childhood, and related to being rejected and victimized by one's peers (Rubin et al., 2006). These analyses focus primarily on the individual given that these traits are measured in infancy and measured in relation to social relationships and interactions throughout childhood. Further, the focus remains on individual differences, and, particularly, on children at risk.

Recently, there has been more attention to the interaction between peers within the broader context of a group, and how rejection serves a social function of the group (Juvonen & Gross, 2005). Juvonen and Gross (2005), along with other peer relations researchers, assert that it is important not to rely solely on a developmental psychopathology model for understanding patterns of exclusion and rejection. Children often become social outcasts for reasons that have to do with group processes, not just the intrapersonal deficiencies of the child. Patterns of bullying and victimization are relational and can continue for reasons due to the interpersonal dimensions of social exchanges with peers, in addition to intrapersonal dispositions.

Group processes, from this perspective, refers to the ways in which groups react to children with different social interactional profiles, and how these profiles have implications for interactions in group contexts. As an example, Chang (2004) asserts that it is essential to study classroom norms in order to contexualize children's peer acceptance and rejection. Chang (2004) measured social norms in classrooms about prosocial leadership, aggression, and social withdrawal and then compared these norms to peer nominations and found that contextual norms affected children's behavior by reinforcing social acceptance of peers. For classes in which there was a high level of social withdrawal this behavior was more accepted among peers than in classrooms with a low level of social withdrawal (Chang, 2004). This study was conducted in China, which also provided a context with varying social norms about classroom expectations. Thus, in this case, the source of exclusion was related to classroom norms in addition to an intrapersonal dimension, like temperament. What makes these analyses important is that a diagnosis of individual personality deficits may be incomplete without consideration of how group expectations are a contributing factor to why children are rejected.

If classroom norms vary regarding expectations that contribute to sociometric status then it follows that societal norms may be related to patterns of rejection and exclusion as well. Research on intragroup and intergroup exclusion focus on forms of exclusion that reflect group identity and social identity, processes in childhood that stem beyond the level of the classroom to societal norms and categories that reflect ingroup and outgroup attitudes.

As an example of how intrapersonal and interpersonal forms of exclusion are related to group forms (intragroup and intergroup), research by Nesdale has shown that children who are rejected by peers are often at risk for displaying prejudicial behavior towards others, which is a form of intergroup exclusion (Nesdale et al., 2007). Using a variant of the minimal group paradigm from social psychology (as discussed in chapter 3), Nesdale suggests that peer rejection increases anxiety and negative affect rather than decreases self-esteem, per se. Thus, Nesdale's research on peer group rejection emphasizes the significance of groups, namely how shifting group memberships result in shifts in social attitudes. Children who are rejected by others often display aggressive tendencies towards others, and these tendencies may manifest in negative attitudes towards others based on group membership. Yet, the process of exclusion that reflects intergroup dynamics is quite different from rejection that stems from individual personality traits.

Intragroup and Intergroup Exclusion: Ingroup/ Outgroup Identity

Intragroup and intergroup exclusion refer to exclusion based on group membership. As discussed in chapter 4, studying group membership requires understanding Social Identity theory, and how children's social identities are related to ingroup favoritism, the categorization of members of who are perceived to be the "outgroup," and the stereotypic expectations and attitudes that result from ingroup/outgroup distinctions. Thus, this notion of "group" is different from that studied in intrapersonal and interpersonal exclusion in which the individual–group relationship is discussed in terms of the child in the classroom, where the classroom is the group. In the studies on how peer rejection is a function of the classroom environment, however, "classroom" does not form an ingroup or outgroup identification for the child. While peer relation studies examined the individual in the context of groups, the focus is on the relations of the individual within the group, and not the social identity of individuals in one group towards another group, which would reflect group identity processes.

In general, there are many different forms of group identity in childhood and many different ways of measuring identity. While much of the social identity literature has examined children's behavior in groups created by experiments (e.g., "yellow" and "blue" groups (see Bigler & Liben, 2006) or art drawing groups (see Nesdale, 2004)), studies using actual categories, such as gender, race, ethnicity, culture, nationality, and religion, have also provided significant findings regarding group processes and group identity. Actual groups have complex societal histories that create hierarchies and status among individuals in cultures, which has to be factored in to studies on group identity. Determining and measuring group identity based on race, ethnicity, or culture is a complex task, though, given that these categories often overlap and are related to other indices such as socioeconomic status as well as culture.

Bennett and colleagues have examined children's subjective identification with groups and make the important point that categorizing oneself into a group is quite different from how one subjectively identifies with a group (Bennett & Sani, 2004). If I categorize myself as a girl this does not mean that my gender identity has the same salience in different situations. In some contexts it is important to me, perhaps when I am the only girl in a group setting; in other contexts, it may be less important than my cultural identity or identity based on age, nationality, or ethnicity.

Research has distinguished "given" groups, such as gender, race, ethnicity, or culture, as described in earlier chapters, from "chosen" groups, such as cliques, political affiliations, or religion (which is sometimes viewed as a "given" identity). Some group identities fall into both of these categories, depending upon the individual's perspective (e.g., sexual orientation may be viewed as "given" or "chosen," and research has been conducted on how individuals view this group identity from this vantage point; see Horn, 2008). Intragroup and intergroup exclusion focuses both on evaluations of exclusion based on group membership, as well as on group identity and ingroup/outgroup relations.

As we discussed in chapter 1, exclusion is complicated because there are many instances in children's and adults' lives in which exclusion is viewed as legitimate and necessary to make groups work. Most of these examples of "legitimate" forms of exclusion in children's worlds stem from adult decisions about how to structure children's everyday lives, including home events, sports, and school rules. Exclusion also occurs for legitimate reasons among children. Social groups share common goals, and children will exclude someone who may disrupt the group for reasons such as being too aggressive or displaying bullying behaviors. Even for forms of exclusion that most individuals view as legitimate, there are emotional and psychological consequences to the recipient, who may or may not view him/herself as a victim. Thus, understanding the motivations and intentions of exclusion in childhood is important both for individual psychological development as well as for addressing pertinent societal issues and conflicts.

Social Reasoning and Exclusion

Before discussing more complex aspects of group identity, such as the relationship between exclusion and inclusion, or intragroup and intergroup dynamics, it will be helpful to discuss what we know about children's evaluations of intergroup exclusion, and the reasons that they use for justifying exclusionary decisions in peer groups. Research on social reasoning from the Social Domain model, described in chapter 2, has examined how children evaluate exclusion and has revealed that concerns with group functioning are significantly related to decisions that justify exclusion based on gender, race, and ethnicity. Individuals use three forms of reasoning to evaluate social issues, the moral (unfairness, equality), the societal (customs, traditions, and group norms), and the psychological (autonomy, personal discretion), as reviewed in Chapter 2.

This model has been applied to the topic of intergroup exclusion (Killen, Margie, & Sinno, 2006; Killen, Sinno, & Margie, 2007). For example, one could view a decision to exclude as "unfair" (moral), or as legitimate to make the group work well (conventional), or as a personal choice (psychological), as shown in Table 5.1. What makes the application of a social domain model to the topic of exclusion novel is that exclusion, from this view, is conceptualized as multifaceted, rather than

Table 5.1 Social reasoning about exclusion: Social exclusion domain categories.
(© 2010 Melanie Killen)

Moral: Fairness, justice, others' welfare, and rights. Exclusion involves considerations relating to the negative intrinsic consequences to another with wrongful intentions:

- *Fairness*: "It's not fair to exclude others for that type of reason;" "It's okay to exclude her because this is not about fairness but about who is better at the game"
- *Discrimination*: "It's treating him differently because of his race and that's a form of discrimination;" "Sometimes it might feel like discrimination which would be wrong but this is about something else"
- *Equal treatment*: "They are not being treated equally because girls and boys are the same and both should get to try out for the music club"
- *Psychological distress and others' welfare*: "How will he feel if he knows that he has been rejected by the group for that reason? You have to understand what it would feel like and how painful it would be to know it's wrong"

Social-conventional: Customs, traditions, and group regulations. Exclusion involves considerations about the group and making the group function well:

- *Group identity*: "It's okay to exclude her because the group needs people in it who are the same and who have the same goals;" "You should include her because she will make it a better group and she fits the identity of the group"
- *Group functioning*: "Sometimes you have to exclude others because the group won't work well with someone new and different;" "I would include her because then the team will win"
- *Traditions*: "It's always been that way, and it should stay the same. My parents didn't date people from other backgrounds so why should we start doing that now?"
- *Conventions*: "The game is for boys and they know how to play it and everyone agreed to do it this way so it's okay to tell her she can't join"

Psychological: Personal prerogatives, autonomy, identity, knowledge of others' minds, and individuality. Exclusion involves considerations about the individual perspective and individual goals:

- *Personal choice*: "It's a personal choice who to be with;" "It's just up to her who she wants to be friends with;" "It's not a good reason to not be friends with someone because of their race but it's her decision and she has to be happy"
- *Theory of Mind*: "She isn't thinking about what they are thinking about in this situation"
- *Autonomy*: "It's her life and she can do what she wants"

---

strictly moral or nonmoral (selfish or negative intentions), and empirical research findings have verified this approach.

Gender Exclusion in Early Childhood: Okay or Unfair?

In a series of studies on children's reasoning about exclusion, children were interviewed about how they evaluated gender and racial exclusion from peer groups. The studies were designed to determine how children balance evaluations of exclusion in which issues of fairness, group identity, and stereotypic expectations were made salient. The goal was to examine when children give priority to fairness in the context of intergroup interactions when making decisions about inclusion and exclusion of peers from everyday contexts. These studies examined whether children apply their moral concepts about fairness to situations that involve stereotypic expectations that were made explicit, or situations that involve implicit biases. Even though stereotypes about gender are highly salient in early development (Devine, 1989; Liben & Bigler, 2002), this does not mean that young children will use stereotypes to condone exclusion based on gender. Moreover, determining whether young children will use moral or social-conventional reasoning to explain their exclusion and inclusion decisions was tested in these studies.

In the first set of studies, to be described below, children and adolescents evaluated exclusion in contexts that applied stereotypic expectations, such as a boys' group excluding a girl from truck-playing and a girls' group excluding a boy from doll-playing. Assessments were varied and the contextual elements were made more or less salient (such as past experience or talent). In addition, some contexts were straightforward and others were more complex or ambiguous with the expectation that stereotypes might be more readily activated in complex and ambiguous situations. Subsequently, other studies were conducted to minimize stereotypic expectations (e.g., exclusion from a music club) or to maximize the level of intimacy (e.g., exclusion from a birthday party "sleepover"). The studies and findings are described below to provide the set of factors that contribute to understanding children's evaluations of peer exclusion.

In several studies with young children (4.5 and 5.5 years), assessments were administered to evaluate children's exclusion decisions based on group membership (ethnicity reflected the United States' distribution with 71% ethnic majority and 29% ethnic minority for the Killen, Pisacane, Lee-Kim, and Ardila-Rey (2001) study, and an ethnically homogeneous sample for the Theimer, Killen, and Stangor (2001) study). In the standard design, children were interviewed about play activities associated with gender stereotypes (e.g., doll-playing, truck-playing, role playing as firefighters, and role playing as teachers) (Killen et al., 2001; Theimer et al., 2001). In one study, interviewers asked children whether it was all right for a group of boys who were playing with trucks to exclude a girl who wanted to join them, or for a group of girls who were playing with dolls to exclude a boy. Children who viewed exclusion as okay gave conventional and stereotypic reasoning such as "I think they should pick the girl because girls like being with girls" or "Pick the girl because the girls are playing and he will just play the wrong way; he hasn't played dolls before" or "Boys can't play with dolls because they're for girls and boys just look silly playing with dolls." These reasons reflect what would be typically expected; that is, that children would rely on stereotypic knowledge to justify exclusion.

Surprisingly, though, the majority of children viewed it as wrong to exclude someone, even when stereotypic knowledge would suggest that it would be all right. The majority of children gave moral reasons, such as equal opportunity or fairness ("You should give the girl a chance to play trucks because she might like it and doesn't get to play with trucks very much" or "It wouldn't be fair to not let the boy play with the dolls because he should be able to just like the girls can do it"). What was unexpected about this finding was that research on stereotyping has shown how highly associated play activities such as dolls and trucks are with gender identity at this age period. In addition, children attending the ethnically mixed school were more likely to view straightforward exclusion as wrong (87%) than were children in the homogeneous school (65%). One possible reason could be that intergroup contact facilitated an inclusive orientation (Pettigrew & Tropp, 2005), although this hypothesis was not tested for these studies.

In another condition, children were asked to evaluate more complex decisions in which a group had to decide which of two children the group should pick when there was only room for one more child to join – a child who fit the stereotype (the girl for dolls) or a child who did not (the boy for dolls) (Figure 5.1). More than half of the children picked the stereotypic child for the activities and less than half for the roles, but about half across all types of activities.

A third manipulation was conducted in which the interviewer introduced a statement regarding the child's choice, referred to as a counterprobe, which entailed giving a reason for the alternate choice, either equal

Figure 5.1 Picture cards for a gender exclusion task. (© 2010 Melanie Killen. Source: Killen et al., 2001.)

opportunity reasoning (e.g., "Boys don't get a chance") or stereotypic reasoning (e.g., "Dolls are for girls") (Figure 5.2). The results demonstrated that children who initially relied on stereotypic expectations to make a decision about whom to include in a play group were more likely to switch their judgment after hearing a "moral" counterprobe than children who initially relied on moral judgments to make their decision; children who initially used moral judgments were less likely to change their decision after hearing a stereotypic counterprobe ("Even though

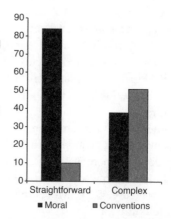

Figure 5.2 Moral and conventional reasons used by children in straightforward and complex exclusion contexts. Complex contexts evoke conventions, group functioning, and stereotypes. (Created by Melanie Killen. Source: Killen et al., 2001.)

dolls are for girls, you should still give the boy a chance to play with them"). Thus, moral judgments were less malleable than social-conventional reasoning and stereotypic judgments. Children who viewed the exclusion situation in moral terms were not easily influenced to change their decision and to agree to exclude the child who did not fit the stereotype. Yet children who viewed the situation in stereotypic terms were more likely to think about it differently, and subsequently view exclusion as wrong.

Overall, younger children relied on stereotypic expectations more than did older children, and there were no differences for gender of the participants, which was somewhat surprising. It might be expected that girls would view boys excluding a girl as more wrong than girls excluding a boy, or the reverse. But instead, girls, overall, viewed exclusion as more wrong than did boys. No ingroup bias was found. This may be because girls have experienced exclusion more than boys from experiences with sports and other types of club activities. It is clear, though, that young children use different forms of reasoning to evaluate exclusion and stereotypes often overwhelm their decisions about fairness.

These findings revealed that young children weigh both moral and conventional judgments to make exclusion decisions. A question raised was whether older children use conventional reasons to justify exclusion and whether stereotypes bear on their decisions about the exclusion of peers. It could be that stereotypes have less of an impact as explicit stereotypes decrease with age. Yet, prejudice continues into adolescence and maybe studies of exclusion will reveal what underlies biased behavior.

Comparing Gender and Racial Exclusion: Group Goals and Qualifications

Determining whether increasing the salience of the group identity by using situations that were associated with stereotypes in older children was tested by Killen and Stangor (2001), who interviewed European-American students in the first, fourth, and seventh grades about excluding children from counter-stereotypic activities based on race/ethnicity or gender. The goal was to determine the cost to group functioning for children's judgments about exclusion by manipulating the qualifications of children who wanted to join the club or group. This study expanded the category of group conventions used in previous studies generated by Social Domain theory. Instead of framing conventions as adult-generated norms for keeping order, such as school regulations about classroom management ("raise your hand before you speak"), conventions were conceptualized as the expectations that establish group identity.

The situations involving race/ethnicity were: (1) excluding a European-American child from an all-Black basketball club; and (2) excluding an African-American child from an all-White math club. The situations involving gender were: (3) excluding a girl from an all-boys baseball card club; and (4) excluding a boy from an all-girls ballet club (gender and race were not mentioned as participants were shown picture cards for all scenarios). Children were asked whether it was all right to exclude and whether someone's qualifications would influence children's evaluations of exclusion.

While most children and adolescents considered it wrong to exclude someone based solely on their group membership, presenting an inclusion situation that varied the qualifications of the peers who wanted to join revealed *stereotypic* responses from children. In this case, a club had to pick either one of two children (for race, a European-American or an African-American to join, and for gender, a boy or girl to join), and participants were told that in one condition the two individuals who wanted to join had "the same level of talent" (equal qualifications condition) and in another condition the participants were told that of the two who wanted to join, the one who fit the stereotype was also "better at it" (unequal qualifications condition).

When children's qualifications to play baseball or ballet (or basketball or math) were the same, the majority of the participants picked the child who did not fit the stereotype. Thus, all things being equal, children picked someone who had not had an opportunity to engage in the activity much, even when this changed the make-up of the group. Yet, when the qualifications were not equal, children were more likely to pick the child who fit the stereotypic expectations. There were gender and age effects as well, such that girls were more likely to chose the nonstereotypic child than were boys across both conditions.

As children got older, they paid more attention to qualifications. Older children, specifically 13-year-olds, were less likely to pick the nonster-eotypic child in the unequal qualifications condition than younger children. Many 6- and 9-year-old children stated that it would be good to include someone who did not conform to the stereotype, even when not as skilled, to provide a new opportunity for the child (e.g., "Boys don't get a chance to take ballet, even if he is not good at it, they should pick him"). With age, stereotypes increased, such as "They should pick the girl for ballet because boys can't do it very well" or "Pick the Black kid for basketball because the White boy might not be able to jump very high." The increase in stereotype use provides another example that stereotyping does not decline after age 7–8 years, as suggested by cognitive-developmental models. Instead, stereotyping to justify exclusion increased with age, and was related to a concern about group functioning.

Adolescents (aged 13 years) were also more likely to rely on talent level for making a decision about who to include than were younger children. Age differences were particularly reflected in the gender exclusion context (Figure 5.3). This may be due to the general greater acceptance of gender stereotypic activities than racial associations with activities, and that explicit gender stereotypes are more readily condoned than racial stereotypes.

When complexity was added to the decision – such as who to include when two new students wanted to join and there was only room for one more to join – adolescents used multiple reasons to explain their evaluation decision, including conventions, traditions, as well as stereotypes. Thus, the situations with stereotypic associations were more likely to be viewed as legitimate contexts for exclusion than were situations that did not invoke stereotypes. Because the Killen and Stangor (2001) study was homogeneous regarding ethnicity, a new, larger study was undertaken to expand the ethnicity sample to four groups and to evaluate exclusion using peer encounters that were not associated with stereotypic activities.

- *Moral reasons*
  - "It's good to pick someone different because sometimes you learn that they can do it and then they'll get a fair chance."
- *Conventional reasons*
  - "It will be weird to have a girl in the baseball club and they're not used to it."

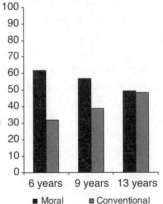

Figure 5.3 Reasons for a decision about who to pick in gender-equal qualification decisions. (Created by Melanie Killen. Source: Killen & Stangor, 2001.)

Interviewing Ethnic Minority and Majority Children and Adolescents about Exclusion

An aim of the study by Killen, Lee-Kim, McGlothlin, and Stangor (2002) was to determine what types of criteria children and adolescents applied to their evaluation of different types of exclusion. In social domain research, researchers such as Smetana (2006) have shown that children use one set of criteria for moral transgressions and a different set of criteria for social-conventional transgressions. For example, as discussed in chapter 2, children view a rule transgression such as hitting someone as wrong, even when teachers say that it is all right; yet a rule transgression such as not raising your hand when talking in class is only wrong if the teacher says it is wrong. The reasons for the hitting violation pertain to the negative intrinsic consequences to a "victim," whereas the reasons for the raising hand violation are due to the group functioning of the group, which is determined by the teacher in the classroom (the rule is contextually based). We were interested to determine whether children view exclusion as a moral transgression (wrong even if parents or friends say that it is okay) or a conventional transgression (wrong depending on what others say) and generalizability. Acts that are evaluated as "moral" are viewed as wrong in other contexts and cultures, whereas acts that are evaluated as "conventional" are contextual and culturally specific. Thus, we also asked children whether the act of exclusion would be wrong in another cultural context.

Using a large sample with boys and girls from four ethnic groups (African-American, European-American, Asian-American, and Latino) participants evaluated exclusion based on race or gender from three contexts: (1) friendship (dyadic exclusion in which one person does not want to be friends with someone else based on gender or race); (2) music club (group exclusion, in which a group does not want to include someone based on gender or race); and (3) school (institutional exclusion, in which a school does not admit children based on gender or race). These contexts were selected because they arose in pilot testing as situations that often involved peer exclusion and were not explicitly associated with stereotypes.

The interview involved a list of semi-structured questions (see Killen et al., 2002 for the complete protocol). Participants were asked for their judgment of the exclusion ("Is it okay or not okay?"), their justifications for their judgment ("Why is it okay or not okay?"), two counterprobes about whether exclusion is all right when parents condone it, or peers condone it, and a generalizability question that referred to whether exclusion would be allowed in another cultural context. The counterprobes involved asking the child whether it would matter if an authority figure (parents) had a different viewpoint from the participant ("What if Jerry's parents said it was okay to not be friends with Damon [the Black child]?") or peers ("What if Tom's friends say that they don't think he should hang out with Sally because she's a girl. Would it be okay then to not hang out with her?").

While the majority of children and adolescents judged exclusion based on race or gender as wrong and focused on the wrongfulness of discrimination and harm to the individual (i.e., moral concerns), there was a range of reasons used depending on the context, the target, and the age and demographics of the participants. We found that, with age, exclusion in the friendship and peer group exclusion contexts was viewed as multifaceted because these acts were evaluated as moral, conventional, *and* personal (whereas younger children more often viewed exclusion in solely moral terms). Overall, adolescents were more likely than were younger children to evaluate exclusion from friendship and a music club as okay.

In addition, the contexts for exclusion reflected different forms of reasoning. In the friendship situation, for example, in which one child did not want to be friends with someone because of their gender or race, adolescents often evaluated it with psychological justifications such as "personal choice" ("It's up to me to decide who I want to play with"). In contrast, exclusion from peer groups was often evaluated with conventional justifications about group functioning ("It might not work to have someone different in the club"). Yet, exclusion from a societal institution (when the school excludes girls or minority children) was viewed almost exclusively with moral reasons ("It's unfair to not let girls go to school").

An example of a reason based on *fairness* for the friendship context is from a 9-year-old (fourth grade) girl who said:

> I don't think it's fair because you can't just have friends who are boys, you have to have some girls that are your friends, and he shouldn't judge her by if it's a boy or a girl, he should judge them by personality and stuff . . . like if they are a meanie or like you give them something and they won't give it back or share.

Typically, friendship choices are viewed as a *personal choice* issue for children (Nucci, 2001). Yet, this 9-year-old girl viewed friendship exclusion based on gender as unfair. While much of the friendship literature focuses on gender as an organizing principle for friendship in the elementary school years, refusing to be friends with someone because of their gender is viewed as wrong. In the friendship literature, the notion of homophily is often invoked, which refers to the tendency of individuals to associate and bond with similar others (Rubin et al., 2006). Yet, what counts as similar requires in-depth examination. While physical features may be the first category used by children (gender, race), developing shared interests and forming psychological compatibility may be a more fundamental basis for friendship as children have more opportunities to interact with children from different backgrounds. While children's friendships are often same-gender this does not mean that all children view friendship choices based solely on gender as legitimate. When children do use gender as a reason for exclusion, it often has to do with personal autonomy. For example, in contrast, a 13-year-old (seventh grade) boy, who evaluated the decision of a boy who did not want to be friends with a girl, used *personal choice* reasoning:

> I think it's okay because boys and girls don't get that much along. Right now, it's like Tom should make his decision about who he wants to hang out with. You pick your friends. It's something you do on your own. It's really up to you to decide.

This is a very different orientation to the same type of exclusion. A 9-year-old girl views friendship exclusion in fairness terms whereas a 13-year-old boy views the same type of exclusion in personal choice terms. In this case, age, not gender, of the participant contributed to these differences. With age, children used personal reasons to discuss the legitimacy of friendship exclusion decisions. Yet, these discrepant views reflect the potential for conflict when these types of situations arise. When children view exclusion differently, such as when one views it as unfair and the other as legitimate (because it is a personal decision) then intervention strategies to reduce potential conflicts need to focus on these divergent viewpoints.

Similarly, in the adolescent literature, Smetana (2006) has shown that parents and adolescents often have conflicts over issues that generate different forms of reasoning. The classic example is the conflict about cleaning one's room. Adolescents view this type of issue as a personal decision ("It's my room and I can do what I want in it") whereas parents often view it in conventional terms ("The house will be messy and look bad to the neighbors"). Overall, children and adolescents were more likely to appeal to personal choice when condoning not being friends with someone because of the person's race or gender than not allowing someone into a club or a school, which were viewed quite differently. A set of children and adolescents reasoned that it is okay for someone to not be friends because of someone else's race due to the personal nature of the decision – it is up to the individual to decide who his or her friends are.

For the music club context, however, exclusion was justified more often on the basis of preserving group identity and group functioning. A 13-year-old (seventh grade) European-American boy viewed exclusion of a girl from the music club in terms of group functioning:

> I think that Mike and his friends are right for not letting her in the club because it's their club and then like if they don't want girls to join and make it an all-boys club that's okay. They like the same kind of music. She might not like it and she might not have any good CDs. If she wanted to make her own group then she can do it and make it so that no boys are allowed.

This type of reason is quite different from using personal choice. The adolescent is not viewing the exclusion decision as okay because it's up to an individual to decide. Instead, the reasons are about shared interests, decisions about membership, and decisions about formulating a club with a set of criteria for the goals of the club.

Interestingly, though, a 13-year-old (seventh grade) European-American girl, viewed this type of exclusion quite differently. She said the following about a boys' club's decision to exclude a girl:

> In a way, yes, and in a way, no, because it's trying to keep her out just because she's a girl. That's discrimination. But boys, they talk about stuff that, you know, girls just don't like or don't like doing. But really, they don't have a good reason not to let her in and I think it's a form of discrimination.

Again, when one child views exclusion as a form of discrimination this is quite different from viewing it as personal choice or group functioning. In this case, the girl who is quoted refers to moral reasons. Overall, boys use more group functioning and personal choice reasons than did girls. This may have to do with many reasons, which have been explored in other studies. As suggested above, it may be that girls, who have experienced more general exclusion than boys (e.g., sports) view it as more wrong due to understanding the perspective of the excluded individual. One argument for attributing moral interpretations of intergroup exclusion to past experience is that there are very few gender differences for ethnic minority students, who also experience exclusion (boys as well as girls). This indicates that, again, discussing different viewpoints could be important for combating forms of exclusion that turn into prejudice and discrimination.

For a small number of participants, appeals were made to stereotypes based on gender and race (e.g., "He [the Black child] listens to hip-hop and they don't, so he wouldn't fit in with the group" or "Girls don't really like being in clubs they just like to do other stuff"). On the whole, justifications supporting exclusion in the friendship and music club contexts were based on social-conventional considerations but stereotypes may also underlie these forms of reasoning. For example, children may state that "he won't fit in the club" and the basis of this "fit" is a stereotypic association. This underlying rationale requires close examination.

While the majority of children and adolescents in the Killen et al. (2002) study judged racial exclusion as wrong across all contexts, there were significant age-related findings. Instead of appealing to explicit stereotypes or negative views of race per se, students appealed to the individual's autonomy in making the friendship decision or the importance of the group to maintain an identity and high level of functioning.

When asked about exclusion from school ("What if a school does not allow Black children/girls to attend?"), adolescents were explicit about what would make that wrong. As an example, a 15-year-old (10th grade) Latin-American female shared her insights on why a Black child should not be excluded from school:

> We have a Constitution now, and it's forming us. We should be able to, we have to stand united, not look at people because of their race. [Interviewer: "What do you mean? Can you explain a little bit more?"] Like, if you see a homeless person, and they're light skinned, and you're Black, and they ask you for a dollar, and they're really hungry, and you know they've been there for many days, you should at least give them something, even if it's like a nickel or something. You don't know what that person's been through. People have been through many things over these years, and every single race, and it's time for us to stand united. We shouldn't just be like "oh, we don't like him because he's Black, or we don't like him because he's White." That's not right, we have to stand united . . . We need to do something about that, and we need everybody to come together. He should be able to go to the same school.

The counterprobe technique used in the interview, which involved discussing an alternative position to the child's original exclusion judgment from both authority members (parents) and peers (friends in the club), revealed that with age, children viewed authority influence fairly critically (rejecting parents' affirmation of exclusion) and viewed peer influence as more significant (adhering to what friends might say). Yet, even with this pattern, there were gender and ethnicity interaction effects. For example, when asked about whether it is all right for peers to exclude a girl from an all-boys music club, a 15-year-old (10th grade) European-American girl explained:

> It doesn't matter what other people say. It is still the same basis. You have to keep your view even if different people's opinions are told to you. Like if a new person comes and is the captain of the club and says that I am not going to let girls in then that is not going to work. It is still against different people and you have to keep it in some order. If there was a good reason that was different from being a girl, okay. But if there isn't then they should let her in.

This explanation indicates that the criterion of "social influence" bears on the categorization of exclusion for this girl, indicating that she views the decision in moral, not conventional terms. In contrast a 15-year-old (10th grade) European-American girl used group functioning to justify why it is okay for the music club to exclude the girl:

> Maybe they don't want to have a club that has girls in it. Sometimes like it was a group of guys and I was a girl and I went rock climbing with them, I might not be as good as all of them. It would be harder for me and they don't want me. [Interviewer: "So it's okay for the boys to not let Jessica join?"] Yeah, she can start her own club.

When asked about whether it is all right to exclude based on gender or race if *parents* (authority) condoned it, children did not view exclusion as strictly a matter of authority mandates because the majority of the participants stated that it would be wrong to do it for intrinsic negative reasons (unfair treatment). However, when asked whether it would be okay if the parents approved of it, some children viewed this as legitimate. The legitimacy was not strictly in terms of viewing the act as okay, the way that teachers can make a conventional transgression permissible (e.g., not raising your hand to talk in class). More often, children were conflicted about it.

An example of a response to the authority permissibility question is from a 9-year-old (fourth grade) European-American boy who said: "Well, it's okay because you should listen to your parents. You should obey them. But he can just tell her that his parents said no so she won't feel bad about it." In contrast, though, an African-American 9-year-old (fourth grade) girl gave priority to fairness: "The parents are teaching their son not to like people like that and like they are just doing wrong things and stuff just only to like White people and not Black people, and that's not right."

Most children used both authority and fairness reasons when asked to consider parents' influence on whether Damon should be friends with a girl. For example, a European-American 9-year-old (fourth grade) girl explained:

> I don't think it's right to do something that your parents don't want you to do, but still you should be friends with everyone. Maybe his parents had a good reason for telling him it was okay to not play with Damon [who is Black].

With age, children were less conflicted about authority expectations and more likely to reject them. An Asian-American 15-year-old (10th grade) student explained why she believed excluding a Black child from a music club would be wrong even if the parents encouraged it:

> I strongly don't like people that are so racist about things. I mean, it's so weird because like when I was growing up as a kid, my parents were always racist against different, I mean, they are not really racist, but they didn't like how I hung out with people from different countries and different cultures. I mean it's just not right to be racist, everyone is created equal and everyone is the same in the inside, it's just, we are unique in the outside. We are alike, there is just no reason for anyone should be eliminated from like anything just because of the way they look or their sex or the color of their skin.

Regarding whether children changed their judgments based on counterprobes, children were more likely to change their judgment upon hearing that friends and peer cohorts were inclusive and encouraged the protagonist to be friends with the target of exclusion or to include the target in the group. However, the reverse was not true. Children who rejected exclusion were unlikely to change their judgment after hearing that friends and peer cohorts encouraged exclusivity and suggested that the protagonist reject the target. As with young children, this finding indicated that the "moral" position was more difficult to change than the nonmoral position.

Guided by the Social Domain model, it was shown that children's evaluations of exclusion depended on the context and the target of exclusion, as well as the gender, age, and ethnicity of the individual making the judgment (Killen, 2007). Social Domain theory indicates that social judgments are sensitive to the context of social interactions, and that an analysis of the context is necessary in order to determine patterns of social reasoning (see Helwig, 1995a, 1995b; Smetana, 1995; Turiel, 1983, 2002; Turiel, Killen, & Helwig, 1987).

In fact, children at all ages made clear distinctions between exclusion in the three contexts, friendship, peer groups, and societal institutions, such as school, and they used different forms of reasoning to evaluate exclusion in these contexts. Friendship was also viewed as the most legitimate context in which someone could decide not to be friends with a peer solely on the basis of their gender or race, and this was because friendship was viewed as a personal decision. What requires further examination is what underlies the notion of "group functioning" and group identity.

Even though participants reflected four ethnic backgrounds, European-American, African-American, Latino, and Asian-American, there were surprisingly few differences in children's and adolescents' evaluations of exclusion based on ethnicity. The majority of participants from different ethnic backgrounds evaluated gender exclusion (a boy excluding a girl) or racial exclusion (a European-American "White" student excluding an African-American "Black" student) as wrong. The few differences that arose pertained to the "parental influence" question in which participants were asked whether it was all right (or not all right) for a parent to endorse a viewpoint different from the participant (in most cases this meant a parent who endorsed exclusion). In this condition, more Asian-American and Latino participants than European- or African-Americans were willing to go along with the parents' position. This may have to do with several reasons, which require further examination. Most Asian-American and Latino participants in the study were first- or second-born generation, which means that their parents or grand-parents were immigrants. Immigrant status may be related to the extent to which a child or adolescent will challenge a parent's influence about social relationships involving exclusion. In addition, Asian-American and Latino participants were "third-party" observers to some extent given that the exclusion involved a White– Black interaction. Yet, there were no differences for their evaluations of general exclusion, indicating that other studies need to be conducted to understand the role of ethnicity and exclusion judgments.

Exclusion based on group membership extends to many groups beyond gender and race. Given how important group functioning was for adolescents, Horn (2003) conducted a line of research on how adolescents evaluate exclusion from social groups as defined by cliques and crowds, which will be described in the next section.

Social Reasoning about Exclusion in Adolescence: Crowds, Cliques, and Networks

Horn has focused on adolescent reasoning about exclusion in the context of adolescent groups that are defined by the adolescent social world (Horn, 2003, 2006). In a study on social cliques, Horn (2003) conducted a pilot study to determine the salient cliques in an adolescent sample and used these groups (e.g., "goths," "jocks," "preppies," "druggies," "cheerleaders") to administer surveys regarding their evaluations of excluding or denying resources to another adolescent when the individual did not fit stereotypes (e.g., denial of resources: student council denies a scholarship to a "jock;" exclusion: cheerleaders exclude a "goth" from joining the team). Overall, adolescents evaluated denial of resources to other adolescents as more wrong than exclusion and used moral reasons to justify their judgments. When evaluating exclusion situations in which no individuating information was provided (e.g., the skill level of the excluded individual was not known), adolescents more often relied on stereotypic expectations than when the individuating information was made explicit. Ninth graders and boys more frequently evaluated exclusion and denial of resources as acceptable and used conventional reasoning or stereotypes in justifying their evaluations than 11th graders and girls.

In another line of research, Horn (2006) provided evidence that both social identity and group status influence adolescents' judgments about inclusion and exclusion. Overall, high-status group members were included in school activities more frequently than low-status group members. Adolescents who identified themselves as members of high-status groups, however, exhibited more in-group bias in their choice judgments, were more likely to use conventional rather than moral reasoning in justifying their judgments, and were more likely to invoke stereotypes than other adolescents.

Social Reasoning about Sexual Prejudice

Adolescents' beliefs about personality characteristics associated with gender identity (e.g., sexual orientation) are related to their reasoning regarding harassment as well. Horn and her colleagues (Horn, 2007, 2008; Horn & Nucci, 2003) have studied adolescents' views about the contexts in which it is acceptable or wrong to exclude peers based on their sexual orientation. Prejudice towards lesbian, gay, bisexual, and transgender individuals is prevalent in most societies and yet only in the past 20 years has this topic reflected a body of research in social psychology, and even more recently in developmental psychology and child development. Surveying 14- to 18-year-olds in several large Midwestern high schools, Horn and Nucci (2003) found that while 50% of the students surveyed believed that homosexuality was wrong or somewhat wrong, only 11% evaluated exclusion based on homo-sexuality as all right or somewhat all right, and only 6% viewed teasing as all right or somewhat all right.

One of the novel findings was that gender conformity, that is, the outward appearance of individuals in terms of dress and mannerism is more important for acceptability than self-reported sexual orientation. Thus, individuals who do not appear to be different based on clothes and mannerism but self-report to be homosexual, for example, are more accepted by the majority of adolescents than are individuals who dress in a non-normative manner or act differently, and self-report to be hetero-sexual. Sexuality is often viewed as an intimate and thus personal issue, which is up to the individual to decide. Yet, outward displays of sexual identity are often highly conventional in appearance and this is given high priority, especially in adolescence. Thus, this line of research has implications for the timely and important issue of sexual prejudice, which has become an issue of great concern and discussion, particularly in high schools. One of the issues that has arisen with sexual prejudice has to do with the intimacy that is associated with sexual prejudice. While much of sexuality is about identity, it is also about intimacy, and areas of intimacy in social life are often the last places in which individuals are comfortable crossing the boundaries of group identity. In the area of childhood, this is related to cross-group friendships, as we discuss in the next section.

Exclusion in Interracial Encounters: Lunch Table, Birthday Parties, and Dating

Aboud and her colleagues compared same-race and cross-race friendships and found that the quality was the same with one exception: reported levels of intimacy (Aboud, Mendelson, & Purdy, 2003). While children reported liking both types of friendships, children reported higher levels of intimacy for same-race rather than cross-race friendships. This finding is a concern for many reasons. First, children's experiences of cross-race friendships have been shown to be highly related to the reduction of prejudice (Tropp & Prenovost, 2008). This is presumed to be due to the empathy and perspective-taking that is associated with friendships. In addition, being friends with someone enables an individual to draw on direct experience to challenge stereotypic expectations that are pervasive in cultures. Stereotypes are generalizations about individuals based on group membership and when a friend does not conform to the stereotype then this makes it easier to reject the stereotype ("My friend is not like that"). Second, cross-race friendships decline dramatically with age, and particularly during early adolescence. This is the time when dating begins and thus a lack of comfort or shared intimacy with someone based on group membership may contribute to the decline of intergroup friendships. Third, the finding that children reported a lack of intimacy raises questions about what factors contribute to this deficit. Thus, a new study was undertaken to examine exclusion in interracial contexts which were not identified by an activity associated with stereotypes (such as ballet and baseball for girls and boys, respectively) but rather by increasing levels of intimacy, such as a sleepover birthday party (who you would invite over) or a school dance (who you would invite for a date).

In addition, this research study more closely examined the issue of intergroup "discomfort." In prior studies, children and adolescents often justified intergroup exclusion by stating that the group would be "uncomfortable with someone different." What is not known is the extent to which this "discomfort" is due to an underlying stereotypic expectation about what contributes to comfort or more legitimate bases for establishing group harmony. Social psychology research has shown that stereotypic expectations often involve confusion between competence and group membership (e.g., girls are slow at running; ethnic minority students are bad at math). Thus, children may attribute social incompetence to members of outgroups without actual evidence of social incompetence. Moreover, societal conventions and expectations are often used to justify inequities and allocation of resources in an unfair manner (Levy, Chiu, & Hong, 2006). Thus, in this study, participants were asked "What is it about race that makes people uncomfortable?" This phrasing was used to pose the question in a general manner, to analyze whether stereotypes were used to explain interracial discomfort.

In order to examine how children and adolescents evaluate intergroup exclusion in interracial intimate settings, 9-, 13- and 15-year-old children (fourth, seventh, and 10th grade) ($N = 685$) evaluated different types of peer encounters that reflected multiple levels of intimate relationships in the area of racial/ethnic exclusion (Crystal, Killen, & Ruck, 2008; Killen, Henning, Kelly, Crystal, & Ruck, 2007). Specifically, children and adolescents were asked about racial exclusion in a friendship context (not having lunch with a different-race peer), a dating context (not bringing a different-race peer to a school dance), and a home context (not inviting a different-race peer home for a birthday sleepover party). These contexts were developed from pilot focus groups with children and adolescents of the same age group as those who participated in this study. Children and adolescents were asked to evaluate interracial peer scenarios that included multiple possible reasons for the exclusion. There were two types of reasons: race-based (e.g., "What if X excludes Y because Y is a different race?") and non-race-based (e.g., "What if X excludes Y because Y has different sports interests than X?"). As found in previous studies, the vast majority of all participants judged race-based exclusion as wrong using moral reasons.

What was unique in this study was that the reasons for exclusion, in interracial interactions, such as lack of shared interests, were viewed as more wrong by ethnic minority than by ethnic majority participants. Thus, when told that a White student did not want to have lunch with a Black student because they did not share sports interests, ethnic minority children were more likely to judge it as wrong due to the potential interpretation that underlying this decision there could be a racial bias. In addition, ethnic minority students voiced a more critical viewpoint about the basis for not having lunch with someone due to a lack of shared interests then did ethnic majority students. For example, a seventh grade ethnic minority student said:

> I don't think that she should not have lunch with her just because she doesn't like soccer. After all they can still be friends. It's just lunch. What if she thinks it's because of being Black? Then what? How will she feel?

In contrast, a seventh grade ethnic majority student said:

> It's okay if he doesn't want to have lunch with him. He doesn't like soccer and it's his choice who to be friends with.

It is important to examine more closely the perspective-taking on the part of ethnic minority children and adolescents. In addition, in this study, ethnic minority children were more likely to expect that racial exclusion will occur, perhaps supporting the view that these students are concerned about the implications of using a non-race-based reason to exclude someone in an interracial encounter because they often experience this type of exclusion.

Overall, ethnic background, social experience, and age were significantly related to interpretations of interracial peer motives for exclusion.

Similar to previous studies on race-based exclusion, adolescents were also less likely than younger children to consider non-race-based friendship exclusion wrong. This is because adolescents view decisions about friendship as part of their autonomous decision-making ("It's up to me to decide who I am friends with") (Nucci & Turiel, 2000).

In the context of potential bias and prejudice, however, these types of decisions take on different meaning, especially for individuals who have experienced unfair exclusion. When interracial friendship decisions are explicitly made on the basis of race then the vast majority of adolescents view it as wrong (and this increases from 9 to 15 years of age) and more so then when the stated reasons are due to "lack of shared interests," which are viewed as more legitimate. Yet, when interracial friendship decisions are made due to the "lack of shared interests" then the basis for determining what counts as "shared interests" may be viewed more critically, though, by those who are the recipients of the exclusion, particularly regarding race, which has long reflected segregated patterns in the area of friendships and intimate relationships. Not surprisingly, then, ethnic minority students in the Killen et al. (2007) study viewed reasons such as "lack of shared interests in sports" or "parental dis-comfort" for not having lunch or not inviting someone to a party (respectively) as wrong, and more so than did ethnic majority children.

With age, children thought that it was wrong for a European-American child to decide to not invite an African-American friend for a sleepover party because the parents might be uncomfortable. Yet, with age, children viewed peer disapproval as a legitimate basis for not inviting a different-race friend as a date to a dance. These findings point to ways in which parental discomfort, peer approval, and group functioning are used by children, particularly White majority children, to justify racial exclusion.

What is not clear is the extent to which these considerations are proxies for stereotypic beliefs. As mentioned, Levy et al. (2006), have shown how children invoke lay theories about work ethics (the "Protestant work ethic") to make decisions about the fair allocation of resources (moral decision-making) based on race and ethnicity (Levy et al., 2006). Whether children are aware of the potential ways in which societal traditions, expectations, and group approval reflect underlying stereotypes or prejudicial behavior requires further research. Moreover, these findings provide further evidence for how contextual factors are differentially weighed by children and adolescents when evaluating exclusion.

Regarding interracial discomfort, children's and adolescents' social experiences (and intergroup contact) are related to the extent that they explicitly use stereotypes to explain racial discomfort in these three contexts (Killen, Kelly, Richardson, Crystal, & Ruck, 2010). European-American children and adolescents attending ethnically homogeneous schools were more likely to use stereotypes to explain racial discomfort then were European-American students in ethnically heterogeneous schools (and reporting cross-race friendships). For example, when asked what it is that contributes to "interracial discomfort," in a friendship context, a child stated that "Blacks and Whites just don't get along because Black people like different music." One explanation for the relative absence of these types of statements by children and adolescents reporting cross-race friendships is that they are exposed to the heterogeneity within the "outgroup" and these experiences enable them to reject the stereotypes. Another reason may have to do with the school and class environments that contribute to understanding what it means to pre-judge others. As will be discussed in chapter 8, positive contact with the outgroup reduces prejudice when significant conditions are met, which includes parental support of the goals of inclusion and diversity.

Most of the studies described so far pertain to exclusion in peer encounters at school. What about exclusion in the home context? Studies in social psychology have examined gender exclusion, and specifically exclusion based on social roles in the home. Determining how children evaluate exclusion based on gender in the home provides another window into how children both experience, and evaluate, exclusion.

Gender Exclusion in the Family Context: Children's Views about Parental Expectations

As demonstrated by Dunn (2006), the child's first social milieu in which morality emerges is the family. Yet, as Okin (1989), a political scientist, has written, the family has not always reflected concepts of fairness and equality, which creates complexity for the child. Okin (1989) wonders how it is that children construct concepts of equality when the home environment is often one of inequality, particularly based on gender roles, duties, and division of labor. Researchers studying family dynamics have explored the many ways in which the balance of workload and chores reflects equity and the bearing that these arrangements have on social development (Crouter, Bumpus, Head, & McHale, 2001; Crouter, Head, Bumpus, & McHale, 2001). This is an area ripe for investigations of exclusion as well, and specifically exclusion based on gender. What makes it relevant for understanding peer exclusion is that siblings in the home receive different messages about gender roles, which bear on their interactions with peers in the school setting.

As an example, McHale and Crouter, along with their colleagues, have extensively investigated gender expectations about family workload balance in the home (Crouter, Head, et al., 2001; Durkin, 1995) and found that the division of labor and workload in the home was related to gender differences for boys and girls regarding gender role attitudes, including gender stereotypic expectations in educational and career settings (Crouter, Manke, & McHale, 1995; McHale, Bartko, Crouter, & Perry-Jenkins, 1990; Taylor, 1996). In one study, girls from egalitarian homes (regarding the division of labor) were more likely to have high expectations for academic achievement than were girls in families that were not egalitarian, and this bears on gender stereotypic expectations in the school setting.

Gender stereotyped expectations, particularly about balancing career and child-rearing obligations, are pervasive in most cultures (Biernat, 2003; Fuegan, Biernat, Haines, & Deaux, 2004). Parents who view themselves as more traditional in their family roles often endorse their children's acquisition of gender stereotypic roles and behaviors (Ruble & Martin, 1998). Further, parents convey gender stereotypic expectations to children who then carry these expectations into the school context regarding peer social competencies and abilities (e.g., "Girls are dumb at math" or "Boys are always mean").

To examine children's perceptions of gender expectations at home, Schuette and Killen (2009) interviewed 120 children at 5, 8, and 10 years of age regarding exclusion decisions in the home. Children were asked to evaluate parental decisions to exclude a son or daughter from engaging in chores that do not fit gender stereotypic expectations. Unlike previous studies in which children's use of gender stereotypes to justify peer exclusion *decreased* with age, this study found that children's gender stereotypes about chores in the home *increased* with age, and were used to justify exclusion. Moreover, boys were more likely than girls to condone stereotypic expectations regarding father–son activities (such as changing the oil in the car or mowing the lawn) as well as mother–daughter activities (such as sewing curtains or baking brownies); further, boys' support for excluding children from chores increased with age from half in kindergarten to the vast majority by fifth grade. The reasoning associated with evaluations of exclusion by parents differs from evaluations of exclusion by peers due to the overwhelming support for stereotypic decision-making by parents. This finding indicates that parents and adults play a powerful role in condoning or rejecting inclusion and exclusion decisions based on stereotypic associations in the home; these expectations may carry over into the peer world.

Park, Lee-Kim, Killen, Park, and Kim (2009) examined whether this support for parental use of gender expectations to exclude a son or daughter from chore-related activities in the home generalized to peer activities. They interviewed students in the United States and Korea regarding parents' decisions to prevent children from engaging in peer activities associated with gender expectations, such as ballet and football, as has been studied in past peer-exclusion studies. Interviewing 230 Korean ($N = 128$) and Korean-American ($N = 102$) children at third (8 years) and fifth grades (10 years) about scenarios in which a boy or girl desired to learn ballet or football, the findings revealed that participants were unlikely, overall, to support parental decisions to treat sons and daughters differently based on gender, or to exclude them from participating in an activity, even when the activity did not fit the stereotypic expectations (e.g., a boy learning ballet or a girl learning football). While stereotypes were used to justify same-gender interest in an activity ("She wants to learn ballet because it's what girls do"), the same expectations were not used to constrain interest in an activity ("If he wants to learn ballet he should be able to do it because it's his life").

Sinno and Killen (2009) applied the analysis of social reasoning about exclusion to the topic of parental roles in the home and extended it to career choices. The goal of the research study was to determine the type of social reasoning used by children to evaluate parental decisions to constrain a spouse's decision to take on a role associated with the opposite gender (a father who wants to stay home and take care of the children, or a mother who wants to work outside the home). Interviewing 121 second grade (7-year-old) and fifth grade (10-year-old) American children, the findings revealed that children used personal choice reasoning for mothers' desires to work but applied gender stereotypes to fathers' desires to take care of children. In fact, with age, children were more flexible about gender expectations and were more likely to view it as legitimate and unfair to constrain a father's decision to stay home and take care of the children (Sinno & Killen, 2009).

While children viewed it as acceptable for parents to take on roles typically associated with the other gender, children from traditional family structures (in which a mother stayed home and the father worked outside the home) used more stereotypic expectations than did children from non-traditional homes. Thus, experience with flexible home arrangements was associated with support of fathers in the non-traditional role. Overall, though, children viewed a mother's decision to work as one of autonomy but a father's decision to stay home as going against conventions and reflecting incompetence.

In a related study, Sinno and Killen (in press) surveyed adolescents about "second shift parenting" and the fairness of a mother or father taking on both the work and family obligations. The findings indicated that adolescents viewed it as more unfair for fathers to take on "double duty" than for mothers to do so, reasoning that mothers are familiar and competent at both roles, unlike fathers who are not competent at child-rearing. Again, stereotypic expectations about father involvement in the family contributed to adolescents' inconsistent application of fairness reasoning to the family context. One implication of these findings is that girls may not aspire to demanding careers that would make "double duty" difficult, and boys may not plan for a career that enables them to take on family obligations and duties. Because father involvement in the family has been shown to be related to children's successful academic achievement as well as social development (Palkovitz, 2002; Tamis-LaMonda & Cabrera, 2003), this pattern of judgments about gender expectations in the home warrants further examination

These studies indicate that children are aware of family dynamics, particularly those interactions that involve various forms of exclusion. The findings on exclusion in the home indicate that the underlying categories of reasoning brought to bear on peer exclusion are similar, reflecting moral (fairness), conventional (group functioning), and personal (autonomy) considerations as well as stereotypic expectations.

Summary

To conclude, social exclusion in the context of peer relationships is a fundamental part of social development. All children experience different forms of exclusion, which reflect a range of consequences. For exclusion that occurs in situations in which the criteria are well understood, agreed upon, and fair then the consequences are part of learning how to interact with others, such as when a child is excluded from a club due to lack of talent essential for the club (e.g., sports, music). When the criteria for exclusion are unclear, nonexistent, or unfair, however, then the consequences of exclusion may be severe, resulting in depression, anxiety, or disengagement. Peer rejection that results from individual differences in terms of psychopathology regarding personality traits is one form that has negative consequences.

What has not been examined as often in childhood as exclusion based on personality traits is exclusion that results from being a member of a social group that experiences prejudice and discrimination, such as gender, racial, and ethnic exclusion. These forms of exclusion have severe consequences as well, and are also part of childhood, not restricted to the adult world, as was previously thought. In the next chapter, we discuss new research on how children's group identity and understanding of group dynamics is an essential aspect of how children view exclusion and inclusion. Not only do children think about individuals from other groups but their views about the ingroup are important, and particularly when they view it as legitimate or unfair to exclude someone from their own group. With age, children understand the complexities of group dynamics, which is what we will discuss in more detail.

Chapter 6

Intragroup and Intergroup Exclusion: An In-depth Study

Group Dynamics: Conceptions of Groups in the Context of Exclusion

One of the pervasive findings on how children evaluate exclusion is the reference to group functioning and group identity. What does this mean for children, and how early do children understand group functioning? Peer group dynamics are about how peer groups work and documenting children's spontaneous notions about how to form a group, who stays in the group, and establishing, supporting, and, at times, rejecting group norms. Given the pervasiveness of peer exclusion as well as the way in which it is within children's and adolescents' purview to make changes (unlike parent–child or adult–child contexts), an in-depth focus on group dynamics regarding peer group exclusion is essential. As mentioned in previous chapters, children begin to understand subjective group dynamics in early childhood. Children begin to realize that groups that they highly identify with may have members who do not support the group norms; further their own group may have norms that they do not support. When this happens they may decide to exclude a member of their group who is deviant, or to include a member of another group who supports their norms, as discussed in chapter 4.

Most of the research on this topic has used national groups (Abrams, Rutland, & Cameron, 2003), summer school groups (Abrams, Rutland, Cameron, & Ferrell, 2007; Abrams, Rutland, Cameron, & Marques, 2003), and minimal or "arbitrary" groups (Abrams, Rutland, Pelletier, & Ferrell, 2009). Generally, the findings indicate that from around ages

Children and Social Exclusion: Morality, Prejudice, and Group Identity. Melanie Killen and Adam Rutland. © 2011 Melanie Killen and Adam Rutland. Published 2011 by Blackwell Publishing Ltd.

7–8 years old, children view it as legitimate to exclude those from their own group and from other social groups who threaten the social-conventional norms central to their group. At this age children focus on social-conventional norms of the group, and make decisions to minimize any potential threats to the conventions of the group.

Considering the prior research on social reasoning about exclusion, there are a number of questions that arise regarding children's knowledge about subjective group dynamics. For example, what types of deviance from group norms will children be willing to tolerate in a group? When children highly identify with their group then they will want the members of their group to go along with the norms that contribute to their identity. What types of norms do children care about, and when will they want to reject someone who does not follow the norms? Norms can refer to many different organizing principles from the concrete and basic, like a group name, to the more abstract and complex, such as an explicit expectation about shared interests, or an unstated expectation about attitudes and style.

While subjective group dynamics studies have shown that children will exclude an ingroup team member who roots for an outgroup in a competitive "game" context (e.g., excluding an English peer who roots for the German soccer team), will children reject an ingroup member who supports a positive norm in another context, such as the allocation of resources or a situation that does not involve competition? What if the ingroup norms are negative from a moral viewpoint? Will children continue to exclude an ingroup member who deviates from the "negatively motivated" ingroup norm? These questions raise important issues that involve a close examination of the types of group norms that children use to exclude and include group members.

Group Dynamics: Group Identity, Group-Specific Norms, Domain-Specific Norms

We propose that there are three aspects of group dynamics that children weigh when considering decisions about exclusion. First, there are expectations about group identity. How much do I identify with my group, whether it is a group defined by gender, race, ethnicity, culture, or other categories? Second, there are group-specific norms. What are the norms of my group that I support or reject? Third, how do I categorize my group-specific norms with respect to different domains, such as the moral and conventional? Are the group norms that I support about morally relevant issues, such as fairness or justice, or are the norms of my group about conventions, customs, and traditions?

In general, research has been designed to investigate the importance of various norms to children and adolescents for group cohesion in daily interactions. Clearly, groups have the potential to play both positive and negative roles in children's lives. One the one hand, groups provide children with a sense of community and support; groups such as teams and clubs enable children to engage in organized activities that foster social and cognitive development. On the other hand, groups can create extreme ingroup/outgroup divisions that lead to violence and destruction, as is sometimes associated with gang involvement. Thus, understanding how children evaluate the norms associated with groups and group identity is important for predicting the role that group engagement plays in child development.

We know that children display ingroup favoritism and outgroup bias in interracial dyadic contexts and evaluate exclusion from groups as wrong. One way to address this apparent contradiction is to understand children's judgments about normative and deviant peers in a range of peer contexts that vary by status, social norm, and group membership. For example, would a boys' group be willing to include a girl who supported the norms of the group? What if an ingroup member was less supportive of the norms than an outgroup member? Which takes precedence? The answers to these questions are complex, and depend on a multitude of factors, such as the status of the group, the type of social norm (moral or social-conventional), and the group member (normative or deviant). It also depends on the age, gender, and ethnicity of the individual making the judgments. For example, supporting a deviant peer regarding a moral norm about fairness may be quite different from rejecting a deviant peer who holds an unconventional norm about group membership.

As we have argued, integrating the Developmental Subjective Group Dynamics (DSGD) model with the concepts of social and moral norms reveals the complexity of childhood exclusion. For example, it is not known how the DSGD model is extended to groups that generate everyday prejudice and bias, along the lines of gender, race, and ethnicity. While competition and antagonism exists between nationalities in Europe, the groups chosen in the research to date (e.g., English and German nationality) reflect relatively equal status. This is not true for groups based on gender, race, and ethnicity, which, in most parts of the globe, reflect different status within a cultural hierarchy, often resulting in discrimination, oppression, and prejudicial treatment (Nussbaum, 1999; Turiel, 2002; Wainryb, 2006).

What remains unclear is what underlies group functioning considerations in exclusion situations. When all-male executive boardrooms of the past century were asked to include women, many members balked at the idea and cited the need to preserve the group and maintain "group order." The idea of admitting women was viewed as disruptive and unconventional. Most likely, both forms of group functioning were operative: a concern for a lack of traditions, and an underlying set of stereotypes about women. To some extent, these two dimensions are related in that stereotypic views about women's business knowledge, if true, would be disruptive and prevent the group "working well." Yet, when challenged and shown that the assumptions are false (as a group category label) then the notion of what makes the group function well changes. As change comes about, individuals are differentiated from norms such that women who espouse the norms of the group are preferred over men who espouse the norms of the outgroup. Understanding how these processes operate in childhood helps to clarify the precursors of adult judgments and values. On the one hand, a concern for making groups work well is a legitimate issue regarding social coordination and group cohesiveness; on the other hand, a concern for group functioning could be a proxy for stereotypic assumptions and outgroup bias.

What is the relative weight children place on moral and social-conventional criteria in different intergroup relationships? For example, a perceived outgroup threat may encourage children to base their exclusion judgments more on group membership factors than morality, and exclusion based on social norms may also facilitate the use of social-conventional reasoning over morality when children differentiate within the peer group. In middle childhood, children infer group loyalty norms and consider both the moral and social-conventional domains of knowledge when differentiating amongst peers. As described above, children's evaluations of peer behavior in any context may reflect a multitude of factors relating to considerations of the self (e.g., individual autonomy), group (e.g., norms or social conventions), and morality (e.g., fairness or justice).

The type of norm matters

Children do not seem to trade-off between favoring people because of their group membership versus favoring them because of their morality when evaluating ingroup and outgroup peers. Rather, Abrams and colleagues (2009) showed that when moral violations are objectively uncorrelated with group membership, children use both morality *and* group membership as independent bases to determine who to exclude. This supports Social Domain theory by showing that morality and group-based judgments are not opposite ends of the same continuum. Instead, children employ both when engaging in social exclusion and peer rejection. Older children have an understanding of group dynamics in an intergroup context. Investigating children's perceptions of group dynamics – that is, what makes the group "work well" – provides an in-depth understanding about ingroup and outgroup relationships and the ways in which exclusion decisions manifest for children in peer settings.

Group dynamics, morality, conventions, and group-based exclusion

To study exclusion from this multilevel perspective, we investigated how children and adolescents evaluate deviant group members for groups identified by gender (boys and girls) and school affiliation (Killen, Rutland, Abrams, Mulvey, & Hitti, 2010). This required examining how children evaluate intragroup exclusion, that is, excluding someone from the ingroup who is deviant, and determining the contexts in which children would be willing to include a member of an outgroup into their own group.

In several studies, we set up groups that children identified with, established group norms, and then asked children to make decisions about how much they liked the ingroup members, whether they thought the norms were okay, and how much they would be willing to include someone from another group who did not support the ingroup norm. In addition, this type of assessment involves identifying different types of norms, and rationales for why the groups have the norms that they do, and what it means to be deviant from the group. Further, children's experience in clubs and groups was measured to examine the relation between their own involvement in peer groups and their decision-making about inclusion and exclusion. One goal of these studies was to determine how important ingroup identity is for children when making inclusion and exclusion decisions that involve different types of norms.

Moral and conventional norms within peer groups

As we have discussed in chapter 2, children make conceptual distinctions between moral and conventional rules. Two types of norms, associated with peer groups, were investigated: (1) moral norms about equality (dividing up resources); and (2) conventional norms about dress (wearing club shirts). Including both types of group norms provided a measure of how children and adolescents evaluated exclusion and inclusion of members of groups who supported or rejected norms about the equal or unequal allocation of resources (money) – something fundamental to issues of fairness that emerge early in development – as well as how norms about group traditions, to support or reject a convention about wearing a team t-shirt, central to establishing group identity. The expectations were that children would evaluate exclusion differently as a function of the type of moral or conventional group norm.

Group-Specific Norms

To avoid the confound of using group norms that were both developed by a specific social group and those that reflected larger societal expectations about social interactions, four types of group-specific norm conditions were created. The four possibilities were: (1) the group had a norm that affirmed an equality principle (distribute money equally); (2) the group had a norm that affirmed a convention (wear club t-shirts); (3) the group had a norm that rejected an equality principle (distribute money unequally); and (4) the group had a norm that rejected a convention (do not wear club t-shirts). In this way, it was feasible to examine whether children supported the group norm purely on the basis of what the peer group wants to do or whether norms that were consistent with larger societal norms were more strenuously supported in the context of group identity.

Deviance in Social Groups

What is interesting about measuring children's decisions about rejecting peers who deviate from the norms of the group is that it provides a relative context for what is considered "deviant" in social groups. Deviance has been typically studied as a form of psychopathology – deviant from "normative" development. Particularly in developmental psychology, deviance usually refers to maladjustment or antisocial behavior (Hawker & Boulton, 2000). In social psychology, however, there is a history of examining individuals who are deviant from social groups on the basis of their beliefs and attitudes, not as result of their psychological functioning (Abrams, Hogg, & Marques, 2005). Groups do not always have positive norms and thus there are times when deviance is a positive act. Civil disobedience, for example, involves acts of deviance in which the deviance is conducted to promote fairness or justice. Martin Luther King famously stated that there are times when it is necessary to be maladjusted to the norms of the group if the norms reflect injustice (King, 1957/1986).

In the current research program, deviance was defined in both positive and negative terms. For example, a child who rejects a group norm of equality (sharing with others) would be viewed as deviant in the negative sense. In contrast, a child who rejects a group norm of "selfishness" or inequality (giving more to one's own group than to others) would be viewed as deviant in the positive sense. The deviance is positive because the group member is rejecting the group norm that violates a larger moral norm about fairness. This aspect of deviance was tested in the present research program. The studies were designed to measure whether children would support deviance by an ingroup member when it violated a larger norm. Similarly, how children evaluate deviants from groups with conventional or unconventional norms about a group custom, such as wearing a team shirt, also provides a comparison of different types of deviance, with varying domains of rules (both moral and social-conventional). This creates the possibility of examining forms of deviance that are not reflecting an absolute negative value but values that are relative to the norm associated with a group.

Group Identity

As Bennett and Sani (2008) have demonstrated, identifying and establishing group identity is complex because group identity varies depending on the context. Many studies in social psychology and a handful in developmental psychology have examined individual's identification with artificially created groups ("minimal group paradigm"). As discussed in chapters 3 and 4, the, "minimal group paradigm" involves investigating group identity by using artificial groups, such as teams divided by the color shirt they are wearing (red shirts and blue shirts), and determining that individuals identify with their group to the point in which they prefer the ingroup and reveal dislike for the outgroup.

With adults this has been done in laboratory settings in which students are assigned to groups, with minimal group affiliation, and who are then found to display ingroup bias when distributing resources

(Dovidio, Kawakami, & Beach, 2001). With children this has been done by assigning children to groups, such as the red shirts or the blue shirts, and associating different status to the groups; biases are then displayed as well (Bigler, Brown, & Markell, 2001; Nesdale et al., 2007). These findings have shown the power of group identity. In the present research program, we measured group identity using actual categories that children identity with such as gender, ethnicity, and school affiliation. Gender and ethnicity groups have also been associated with different status in society and we compared these groups to groups based on school affiliation.

Gender identity. In the present program of research, we examined gender identity given how much emphasis is placed on gender in children's lives and particularly regarding intergroup issues (Arthur, Bigler, Liben, Gelman, & Ruble, 2008). Children's lives are often quite gender segregated, leading to high identification as a girl or boy and to being part of girls' or boys' groups (Ruble, Martin, & Berenbaum, 2006). Notwithstanding recent evidence about the early onset of homosexuality and transgender identity (Horn, 2008), most children strongly identify with the same gender. Thus, we assigned children to same-gender groups and identified the outgroup (the other group) as the opposite gender. This enabled us to examine whether gender identity would be a factor in the unwillingness to exclude a deviant member of a group, especially when the norm of the group was to be equal.

Status of groups. Associated with each type of group identity is the "status" of the group. This factor has been studied extensively by researchers studying social identity and peer relations. Children are aware of group status; this is clear from the types of stereotypes that children have about others based on group membership. This awareness contributes to an asymmetry in different types of ingroup and outgroup exclusion. As mentioned earlier, when girls join boys' groups they are "moving up the hierarchy" but when boys join girls' groups they are "moving down the hierarchy." Similarly, this asymmetry exists for many types of groups in terms of race, ethnicity, religion, and nationality. This variable was also examined in the current program of research.

General design and expectations

To investigate these issues, children's favorability towards normative and deviant peers (e.g. possible targets for exclusion), as well as how children evaluate acts of exclusion under different conditions were measured. In the first study, participants included 382 children and adolescents, at two grade levels, elementary school and middle school (fourth and eighth grades, 9 and 13 years of age respectively), and with a range of ethnic backgrounds in a metropolitan region of the United States (Killen et al., 2010). This study, however, is current and ongoing, so we will highlight just a few findings from our study to illustrate our approach, and what we mean by an integrative model for understanding intergroup attitudes in childhood and adolescence.

Method for study: Gender identity, exclusion, deviance, and social norms

In this study, children were asked to join a same-gender group that met together after school and they were told that there was another opposite-gender group at the school as well. The interviewer explained that their group had formed a group norm (moral or social-conventional), and then they were asked to make decisions about inclusion and exclusion of other members.

Instrument. We made the groups salient by asking participants to choose a club name and logo, and to pick what type of special event that they wanted their group to have at the end of the school year (pizza or ice cream party). We identified two groups, the participant's group and the other group (different gender), to establish an ingroup and an outgroup. There were four conditions, two in which moral norms were introduced and two in which conventional norms were introduced. For each condition, participants were asked to make a series of judgments. The moral norms were about allocation of resources. Participants were told that the student council had $100 to give to the two clubs to divide up. In the first condition, the participant's ingroup wanted to divide it up equally ($50 for both groups) and the outgroup wanted to divide it up unequally ($80 for their own group, and $20 for the outgroup). In the second condition, the assignment of the moral norm to group was reversed (the ingroup wanted to divide it unequally and the outgroup wanted to divide it equally).

The conventional norm was about wearing a club shirt (Figure 6.1). Participants were told that the school gives out club t-shirts to wear to county-wide assemblies. Thus, in the third condition, the ingroup wanted to be conventional and wear the t-shirt while the outgroup was unconventional and did not want to wear the t-shirt (because it's "not cool"). In the

In the past, your group

Diana   Clair   Gaby   Sandra

YOUR GROUP

has **not worn** their green and white club shirts because they think it's not "cool."

In the past, the other group

Danny   Erick   Peter   George

THEIR GROUP

has **worn** their red and black club shirts.

Figure 6.1 Picture card for measuring group norms and group identity. (Task: © 2010 Melanie Killen, Adam Rutland, Dominic Abrams, Kelly Lynn Mulvey, & Aline Hitti. Illustrations: © 2010 by Joan M. K. Tycko.)

fourth condition, the norms were reversed and the ingroup wanted to be unconventional while the outgroup wanted to be conventional.

Measures. The children were then asked about excluding a deviant member who does not go along with the norm, as well as the favorability of the normative members and the deviant members. The assessments included: (1) evaluation of the act of exclusion (is it all right to exclude?); (2) favorability of the target (how much does the group like the excluded person?); and (3) ingroup deviant versus outgroup deviant (who should the group pick, the ingroup member who deviates from the norm, or the outgroup member who goes along with the ingroup norm?). There were other assessments as well but for the sake of a brief overview these three assessments will be summarized.

Findings and implications

Ingroup bias and deviance from groups. Children and adolescents weighed many considerations when evaluating group exclusion. Children and adolescents expected that the group would not like the deviant member and this was the case for all four types of deviance. This confirms the notion of ingroup loyalty (Abrams, Rutland, & Cameron, 2003). Interestingly, as shown in Figure 6.2, children and adolescents stated that they would like the deviant more than they expected that the group would like the deviant, suggesting that they viewed the groups to be less tolerant of deviants than they would be. This may reflect a social viewpoint about groups in which groups are viewed as particularly exclusive, which, in turn, might influence their personal decision making in groups.

As shown in Figure 6.3, in cases in which the group norm was to be equal, the deviant who wanted more money for his or her own group (being unequal) was viewed in a negative light. The reason for disliking an unequal member was that it would be selfish or unfair for one group to get more than another group. In contrast, the reason for disliking the unconventional member (who did not wear a t-shirt) was that it would be confusing if he or she did not wear the club shirt; some adolescents also viewed it as disloyal. Other children, though, viewed being unconventional as positive because it demonstrated autonomy and independence, and this reasoning increased with age.

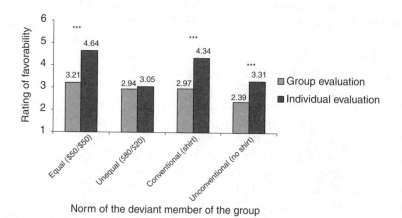

Figure 6.2 Individual and group favorability of deviants (*** $p < 0.001$). $1 =$ not at all, to $6 =$ very favorable. (Source: Killen et al., 2010.)

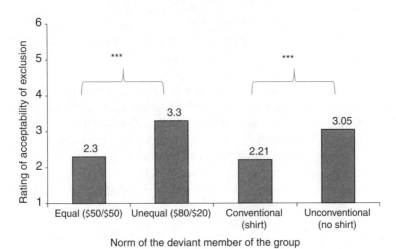

Figure 6.3 Evaluation of deviant members of groups: moral and conventional norms (*** $p < 0.001$). 1 = really not okay, to 6 = really okay. (Source: Killen et al., 2010.)

This was surprising in light of many social psychology studies on the allocation of resources that reveal an ingroup bias. In this study, children were steadfastly strident about the group dividing up resources equally. Children do not start with strong preferences to be biased towards the ingroup, as might be expected by social psychological theories, which often assume that the onset of social categorization "automatically" results in ingroup bias and a desire to support the ingroup (Banaji, Baron, Dunham, & Olson, 2008; Fiedler, Freytag, & Unkelbach, 2007). In fact, young children were more focused on equality than on ingroup loyalty.

Adolescents focused on supporting inequality when it benefited the group but only relatively compared to the younger children; overall, most adolescents did not like an unequal deviant when the group had a clear norm to divide up resources equally. When the norm is explicitly to be fair then children and adolescents dislike an ingroup member who vocalizes an ingroup bias in the allocation. When the norm is explicitly to be unequal then children and adolescents like a deviant who wants equality. With age, though, adolescents were less likely to support a deviant group member who wants to be equal when the group wants to give more resources to itself than to another group. This means that the equal norm takes priority over group identity in childhood but by adolescence both considerations are weighed. What this also means is that even in adolescence when group norms become quite salient and group identity is very important, adolescents give high priority to the moral significance of deviant acts and decisions to exclude members of groups. For adolescents, who are known to care about conforming to social groups, the norm matters. When a deviant member of a group wants to voice equality when the group prefers inequality, the majority of the adolescents view it as wrong to exclude him or her. Moreover, when asked to pick a member of an outgroup over an ingroup member, adolescents are willing to do so when the norm is about being equal. These findings indicate that both group identity and morality are salient aspects of group decision-making even in early adolescence when social cliques and networks peak.

Salience of equality norms

In a recent study on the allocation of resources using the "dictator game," economists in Norway found that inequality acceptance increases during adolescence (Almas, Cappelen, Sorensen, & Tungodden, 2010). The dictator game is often used in economic research and social psychology studies in which individuals are asked to divide up money between themselves and a fictitious "other" player. In the Almas et al. (2010) study, children viewed the allocation of resources in strict equality terms, but adolescents took individual achievements into account when giving out resources and were more supportive of unequal allocations when merit was involved. This finding is similar to what we have found, although a major difference was the absence of an analysis of group identity.

In the current study being discussed, using peer clubs at school, children went beyond the equal allocation of resources from person A to person B to the expression of an equal or unequal allocation of resources by a member of one's own group. While children were more centered on strict equality considerations than were adolescents, both children and adolescents made a distinction between how much they thought the group would like someone who expresses equality when the group does not, and how much they would like that person. Children and adolescents stated that while the group who wants to give more money to themselves than to another group might not like a member who wants to be equal, they would like that person because it is the fair thing to do.

Yet, children were more willing to exclude a group member who voiced inequality of resources than were adolescents, reflecting adolescents' reluctance to disrupt the identity of the group. This reflects the "moral" orientation of children described in chapter 2 that becomes woven in with other considerations by adolescence.

In addition, there was a clear asymmetry to different forms of deviance in the context of exclusion. Children and adolescents supported and liked deviant members who were affirming general equality more than deviant members who were negating general equality. Being deviant and going against an equal norm was potentially grounds for exclusion; being deviant and supporting an equal norm was not regarded as a reason for exclusion. This was the same for the conventional norms. This tells us that children carefully weigh the type of deviance that children voice in groups and that the moral or conventional considerations are quite important in the context of exclusion decisions.

Ingroup or outgroup?

To determine whether children cared more about group identity or group norms, children were asked to make a forced choice decision. They were asked who the group should pick when there was only room for one more member to join, an ingroup member who rejects the group norm, or an outgroup deviant who supports the ingroup norms? Children and adolescents indicated that principles matter more than group identity when the principles were about equality. Both children and adolescents would be willing to include a member of an outgroup (a girl in a boys' group, or a boy in a girls' group) when that member wanted to distribute resources equitably.

When the outgroup member matched the unequal norm of the group, only half of the participants would include that member in the group. For example, if the group had an equality norm, and the deviant voiced an unequal distribution (giving more to the ingroup) then half of the participants picked the ingroup member (a girl for a girls' group or a boy for a boys' group), their reasons being that it would be important to keep the group the "same." The other half of the participants picked the outgroup member (a girl for a boys' group or a boy for a girls' group) who voiced equality, stating that this person might be able to influence the group to be more equal in their allocation decision. What contributes to children and adolescents focusing on ingroup norms or equality norms is not known and requires more investigation. Yet, these findings reveal that children as young as 9 years of age, and up to 13 years of age, weigh many factors when thinking about inclusion and exclusion in groups.

A different pattern of responses was shown for the case when the group norms were about conventions. For conventions, if the club liked to wear the shirt then children picked a girl or boy who did too. If the club did not like to wear the shirt then children picked the girl or boy who also did not like to wear it. Surprisingly, when other information was presented, such as the type of norm and deviance, the gender identity of the group was not a major factor in how children thought about exclusion.

Implications for Group Identity in Childhood

These findings have implications for understanding the emergence of intergroup exclusion as well as morality and prejudice. In many exclusion situations presented to children for their decisions, the most salient factor is group identity as defined by shared interests or activities. When children are asked whether it is all right for the girls' ballet group to pick a girl instead of a boy to join, most children will say that it is all right because ballet is for girls (Killen & Stangor, 2001). What is not presented or measured is whether the girl who is chosen would support the norms of the group. Maybe a girl would not share the same norms and, in fact, the boy would more closely match the norms of the group then the girl. In fact, in everyday interactions children discover this complexity but it is not made explicit.

Without acknowledging the different levels of group norms and values individuals fall back on stereotypic expectations and assume that gender identity, alone, is sufficient for commonality and shared interests. Parents and educators often reinforce these general group identities without recognition for the way that the norms of the group are central to including, as well as excluding, others.

Summary

Children and adolescents weigh a number of complex variables when considering exclusion and inclusion in groups. Some accounts of children's intergroup attitudes focus on ingroup bias and other accounts zero in on stereotypes about members of other groups. What needs to be understood is when children display ingroup bias or use stereotypes to make decisions about peers from different groups. The only way to understand this process is to disentangle the different factors that children weigh and to understand when ingroup bias contributes to exclusion, or when fairness judgments take priority, leading children to be inclusive. In this chapter we looked at exclusion decisions that focused on gender identity, moral and conventional norms, and peer groups with an American sample. What does exclusion look like in a range of cultures, and what are the salient topics that have been investigated? Cultures vary in the importance placed on group membership based on factors such as gender, race, ethnicity, and religion, and these factors will be described in the next chapter, where we discuss how exclusion decisions manifest in different cultural contexts.

Chapter 7

Peer Exclusion and Group Identity Around the World: The Role of Culture

For most of this book, we have described studies that focus on exclusion based on actual groups such as gender, race, and ethnicity, or ad hoc (summer camps) and minimal groups (laboratory-created groups). What has not been discussed is exclusion based on culture. Recently, there has been a focus on social reasoning and group identity in contexts of cultural exclusion, and mostly in the context of immigrant groups. Exclusion based on cultural membership when the culture is a group that has newly immigrated to an existing culture, creates a highly salient context for group identity for both the newly immigrated group as well as the existing dominant group. In several ways, cultural exclusion differs from gender and racial exclusion. Gender exclusion, unlike exclusion based on race and ethnicity, is typically justified on the basis of social roles that are condoned by society as well as segregated organizations (such as all-girl or all-boy schools, clubs, and organizations as well as family arrangements and the workforce). These explicit forms of socially sanctioned exclusion and segregation perpetuate gender exclusion in many parts of the world, and through most of human existence. Racial and ethnic exclusion, while quite pervasive in most cultures, has become less explicitly condoned over the past century and reflects less explicit sanctioning (as an example, one of the most egregious contexts of explicit forms of racial exclusion, apartheid in South Africa, was condemned by much of the world).

Children and Social Exclusion: Morality, Prejudice, and Group Identity. Melanie Killen and Adam Rutland. © 2011 Melanie Killen and Adam Rutland. Published 2011 by Blackwell Publishing Ltd.

Yet, cultural membership continues to reflect common, socially sanctioned forms of exclusion such as the criteria for citizenship as well as team sports (e.g., the Olympics) and other contexts. Thus, group identity for nationality and religion, when salient, has a powerful bearing on children's evaluation of exclusion based on culture (nationality and religion).

Culture is a broad category and it often includes gender, race, and ethnicity. These categories are often not mutually exclusive. For example, Arab culture is quite heterogeneous, reflecting a wide range of secular, Christian, and Islamic cultures, plus reflecting many nationalities on multiple continents (e.g., Jordanian, Saudi Arabian, and Lebanese in the Middle East, and Moroccan and Egyptian in northern Africa). Similarly, Judaism is both a religion and a culture with multiple nationalities reflected in Israel (Jews from Ethiopia, Russia, and other regions in the world). Latinos in the United States come from Cuba, Puerto Rico, and Central and South America. Mexicans in California have different experiences from Cubans living in Florida, or Puerto Ricans in New York City. Yet all experience prejudice as "Latinos." The movement of individuals across the globe has created heterogeneity within cultures that previously were assumed to be homogeneous (Gjerde, 2004). This makes the task of understanding cultural exclusion all the more important, and, at the same time, quite complex. Yet this is also why studying how exclusion emerges in development is all the more timely and essential (for a review, see Hitti, Mulvey, & Killen, in press).

How early do children identify with their nationality and does this identification lead them to justify exclusion based on nationality? In the immigrant contexts, exclusion is often justified in the adult world on the basis of threat to the dominant cultural identity, and status quo. Three questions addressed in this chapter are: (1) how early does nationality/cultural identity emerge; (2) how do children justify exclusion based on nationality/cultural identity, and when do they view this form of exclusion as wrong from a moral viewpoint; and (3) how do majority and minority viewpoints compare? We will review some recent findings on exclusion based on cultural membership in non-North American contexts.

Within each cultural context there are unique regional sources of exclusion, some of them stemming from recent patterns of migration, such as South and Central American children who experience exclusion in Spain (Enesco, Guerrero, Callejas, & Solbes, 2008), Muslim children who are excluded in the Netherlands (Gieling, Thijs, & Verkuyten, 2010) or Eastern European (Albanian, Serbian) immigrant children who experience exclusion in Switzerland (Malti, Killen, & Gasser, in press). At the same time, cultural exclusion also pertains to patterns of migration that are decades old, such as the experiences of Turkish children excluded by mainstream German children (Feddes, Noack, & Rutland, 2009), Moroccan children excluded in Spain (Enesco et al., 2008) and Portugal (Monteiro, de Franca, & Rodriques, 2009), and Gypsies excluded in Spain (Enesco, et al., 2008).

One of the striking aspects about investigating cultural exclusion in childhood around the world is that it is an extremely recent focus for research, unlike the predominant focus on race, and particularly "Black/White" relations, which have served as the focal point for most research in North America and, more recently, Europe (Graves, 2001). Understanding exclusion based on other categories expands the discussion beyond the "Black/White" dichotomy, which no longer adequately reflects the complexity of prejudice and discrimination in most cultures, including North America, given the existence of many ethnic groups as well as groups that identify as biracial, multiracial, and interracial. The focus on cultural exclusion in childhood brings the discussion to a developmental point of view which has been absent in much of the societal discourse about patterns of cultural mobility and immigration.

Cultural Context of Exclusion

Understanding the cultural context of exclusion requires identifying the cultural norms and expectations about intergroup contact, how groups vary by status (high and low status), the history of exclusion, and patterns of immigration (and reasons for immigration). These facets of intergroup relationships are often fluid, changing from one generation to the next. In his review about the factors that reduce prejudice in adulthood, Pettigrew (2010) notes the changing focus of research from being predominantly American based in the 1950s to being European-focused, especially following the publication of Tajfel and Turner's (1979) Social Identity theory. As examples of the non-United States focus of research on exclusion and prejudice, he describes research conducted in Northern Ireland (Hewstone et al., 2005) as well as South Africa (Dixon, Durrheim, & Tredoux, 2005), which have focused on prejudice and exclusion in adults. In the past decade, however, research on prejudice and exclusion has also focused on its developmental origins and emergence, which necessitates a *child-focused* research agenda and perspective, as we will describe here.

As mentioned, unique histories associated with exclusion based on culture need to be understood in order to adequately and appropriately determine patterns of exclusion. For the purpose of this chapter, we are focusing on culture as nationality, ethnicity, and religion given that the rest of the book has focused mostly on gender and race. The reason for the predominant focus of the latter two categories in this book has to do with the preponderance of empirical research, which has been conducted on these categories. It is also a function, however, of where most of the research comes from – North America and Europe.

The research has focused on two types of cultural exclusion contexts, which we will discuss: (1) intergroup cultural contexts that reflect an extended, deeply rooted, intercultural conflict; and (2) intergroup contexts pertaining to recent immigrants. As we have done in other sections of this book, we examine cultural exclusion from the perspective of social judgments. Do children and adolescents view exclusion based on cultural membership as unfair and discriminatory, which would reflect the moral domain? Or, do they view such exclusion as legitimate, reflecting group identity and national pride, which would reflect an aspect of the societal domain? It may also be that youth view exclusion based on cultural membership as a personal choice, with little "regulatory" force, an act that is up to each person to decide. As we chart the findings in this area, all three forms of social reasoning are employed by youth to evaluate cultural exclusion. What is important, though, is the extent to which these forms of reasoning are related to one's identification with the excluder or the excluded, and how this changes with age.

Previous findings for other types of exclusion have shown that with age and experience, adolescents become more aware of the roles of social conventions in maintaining structure and order in society. In middle adolescence, social-conventions are prioritized with a strict acceptance of the importance of social structure (Turiel, 1983), reflecting the increased importance of social identity and group functioning. When evaluating intergroup exclusion between youth from different social cliques and ethnic groups, adolescents rate exclusion as more acceptable in peer and group contexts than younger children, particularly for reasons of autonomy and personal choice in friendship, group identity, norms, and functioning. Previously prosocial and inclusive attitudes towards intergroup interaction are subordinated to group norms. Whether this occurs for exclusion based on culture is another focus of this chapter.

Long-Standing Intergroup Cultural Conflicts

Places that have experienced long-term, deeply rooted intergroup conflict include, for example, the Middle East (Jews and Arabs), Northern Ireland

(Protestants and Catholics), South Africa (White and Black South Africans), and Colombia (Indigenous and Spanish peoples). Multiple categories are reflected in these forms of exclusion: with religion, race, nationality, region, and political categories unique to each context. In general, research on childhood outcomes of violence initially focused on the psychological trauma and psychopathology resulting from living in cultures of high conflict (Brenick et al., 2007; Leavitt & Fox, 1993). More recently, however, researchers from a developmental intergroup perspective have examined the extent to which children living in these cultures have stereotypes of the outgroup, experience exclusion, have a strong identity, and whether intergroup contact is effective at reducing prejudice, even in difficult societal circumstances. The fact that research psychologists have more directly addressed these issues in childhood around the globe helps to provide an explicit focus to the problems that stem from exclusion, and are often ignored in early development. In this first section of the chapter, we will focus on exclusion and intergroup contact, primarily, for the Middle East, Northern Ireland, South Africa, and Colombia.

Cultures with Intractable and Violent Conflict

Middle East

In the Middle East, research has demonstrated that young children have negative stereotypes about the outgoup, and that messages throughout the media reinforce negative attributes about the outgroup. While it is known that children in the Middle East have stereotypes about others (Bar-Tal & Teichman, 2005), recent research (see Brenick et al., 2007; Cole et al., 2003) has also shown that Jewish and Arab young children do not always apply their negative stereotypic expectations to peer encounters involving children from other cultural groups.

In one study, cultural stereotypes and evaluations of peer exclusion were analyzed for three groups of Arab children in addition to a Jewish group, prior to viewing a new *Sesame Street* show that was designed to promote tolerance and mutual respect among children from different cultural groups in Israel, Jordan, and the Palestinian Territories. Children from four groups were interviewed about their stereotypes, and their evaluation of intergroup peer encounters. The children were Palestinian, Jordanian, Israeli-Palestinian, and Israeli-Jewish ($N = 433$; mean age $= 5.7$ years of age). Thus, the goal of the empirical study was to document the "baseline" knowledge of the young children living in the Middle East prior to viewing the *Sesame Street* show. Not surprisingly, the results revealed that one of the negative consequences of living with intergroup tension was the use of negative stereotypes when asked to describe a member of the outgroup in general terms ("What is an Arab/Jew?"), which included negative adjectives for Arabs ("dirty," "rock-throwing," "mean") and violent attributions for Jews ("killer," "destroyer").

At the same time, however, results for evaluations of peer exclusion, based upon a number of different factors, surprisingly showed positive results about children's inclusive views regarding peer interactions. Children were interviewed about three types of peer exclusion: (1) excluding a child from a game because "he/she is from a different country;" (2) excluding a child for having a different custom (wearing a different party hat from everyone else); and (3) excluding a child who speaks a different language (Arabic or Hebrew). As with the previous study, these issues were embedded in the context of playing together; for instance, a group of friends is playing and a child "from a different country" comes to join them, and whether it is all right to exclude the new child from playing.

In this study, all children evaluated excluding a child who spoke a different language as wrong, but there was variation regarding different customs and country of origin, with Israeli-Jewish, Israeli-Palestinian, and Jordanian children viewing it as more wrong than did the Palestinian children. All children explained their decisions about letting someone in the group who dresses differently using inclusive justifications (Taylor, Rhodes, & Gelman, 2009). At the same time, Palestinian children were more likely to reason about this issue in terms of group functioning, that is, that the group will not work well if someone dresses differently. For this context, the findings suggest that the conventional norms about dress may be more salient for Palestinian children than for children in the other groups. Even though the scenarios did not refer specifically to religious or cultural customs (e.g., wearing a party hat is different from wearing a yarmulke), conventions about dress reflect religious and cultural customs that are embedded in cultures and acquire deeply important symbolic dimensions (Turiel, 2002). These types of issues have to be taken into account in cultural exclusion research. Somewhat encouraging was the inclusive orientation of the Palestinian children who have one of the lowest socioeconomic positions in the Middle East, and certainly among the groups interviewed in the *Sesame Street* study.

Thus, even in a cultural context with severe antagonism, dislike, and negative stereotypes, very young children have inclusive orientations towards intergroup encounters. This type of interaction is not typically condoned by adults and yet children evaluating peer encounters focus on the importance of inclusion with less attention to group identity. Many new questions could be examined for this sample, including what changes with age, and how early does group identity become salient and serve as a basis for exclusion? Moreover, studies on children's experience with intergroup contact would provide a basis for determining whether children are inclusive due to actual friendships with members of outgroups or other factors.

Northern Ireland

Turning to another culture that has experienced high conflict, extensive research in Northern Ireland has examined self-identity quite closely, measuring national identity (British or Irish) as well as religious identity (Protestant or Catholic) with a large sample ($N = 261$) of Irish adolescents living on the border between the Irish Republic and Northern Ireland (Muldoon, McLaughlin, & Trew, 2007). In this study, Catholic adolescents living in the Irish Republic as well as Protestants living in Northern Ireland were proud of their nationality, in contrast to adolescents who were a minority in their cultural context (e.g., Catholics living in Northern Ireland or Protestants in the Irish Republic), who were more ambivalent about their national identity and were also more likely to spontaneously derogate the outgroup (Protestant or Catholic). While this study did not explicitly measure judgments about exclusion, the focus on group identity indicates that studying exclusion would be fruitful.

Adolescents were interviewed about what it means to be Irish or British. As examples of group identity, one Protestant male adolescent (age 14 years) stated that: "I live in Northern Ireland and I am proud of our link with Britain. We are in a different country and have different rules which are made by the Queen of England and not the Government of Ireland" (Muldoon et al., 2007, p. 587). In contrast, a Catholic girl in Northern Ireland (age 15 years) stated that: "I would rather be called Irish than English. I don't like English people. I don't like them and they think they rule us ..." (2007, p. 587).

An example of Irish Catholics from the Republic of Ireland who were proud of their identity was from a 13-year-old girl who stated that: "Being Irish makes me proud. I'm proud of my nationality because the Irish are very well liked world-wide. I dislike the way that we are known for pubs and alcohol. I was very proud when Ireland done well in the World cup, but I don't think our government should have let the

Americans re-fuel in Shannon airport and bringing our wee country into the war" (2007, p. 587).

As Trew (2004) notes, children growing up in Northern Ireland today are not exposed to daily violence and thus exposure to violence is less of an immediate concern than are the aftermaths of living in segregated communities. Research on patterns of contact in Northern Ireland have shown extensive segregation, with 97% of children in Northern Ireland attending homogeneous schools (Catholic or Protestant) (Cairns & Hewstone, 2002). The next step for research is to fully examine children's intergroup attitudes about the outgroup and to find ways to foster integrated school environments. As Trew (2004) recommends, research on child development in Northern Ireland could benefit by drawing on social identity and social-cognitive developmental intergroup research (described in chapters 4 and 5).

British identity and nationality

A longitudinal study examined British children's $(N = 329)$ attitudes towards different national cultures each year between 1995 and 1997 (Rutland, 1999, 2004). The national ingroup bias and prejudice amongst children aged 6–16 years was measured using a photograph evaluation task. This task involved the children evaluating 10 "passport" style photographs showing people's heads on two occasions, separated by approximately 1–2 weeks, with or without the national category label applied. The national labels were British, American, German, Australian, and Russian. A difference in the children's ratings of the photographs across the two testing sessions indicated a bias and desire to exclude the national outgroup.

Rutland (1999) found in 1995 that children showed national prejudice only towards the German outgroup, from 12 years onwards; younger children did not display this bias. No evidence of prejudice towards the Americans, Australians, or Russians was found (all allies of Britain in World War II). Again, in 1996, national prejudice was only shown towards the Germans amongst children above 13 years of age. It was also amongst the older children (i.e., 10 years old upwards) that evidence was found of national stereotypes; for example, when children were asked what things made them proud or glad to be "British" they typically said such comments as "we have the best army in the world thanks to Oliver Cromwell. We beat Germany in World War II ..." (10-year-old) or "we are more civilised and friendly compared to the French and Germans ..." (14-year-old). These quotes illustrate the power of cultural history for exclusion given that these children were discussing events that occurred 50 years or more prior to their birth.

Importantly, the Rutland (2004) study also found evidence of temporal variability in national prejudice towards the Germans since in 1997 the data showed no clear sign of outgroup derogation of the Germans. Children's outgroup attitudes are influenced by the context. When the context highlights the relationship or contrast between two groups, then outgroup bias is higher.

Social identity in Europe

Another recent study conducted in Europe also showed the significance of cultural and historical events in shaping children's evaluations of different nations (Bennett et al., 2004). Bennett and colleagues asked 6-year-old children ($N = 594$) from five culturally diverse nations (Azerbaijan, Britain, Georgia, Russia, and Ukraine) to attribute positive and negative traits to their national ingroup and four national outgroups. The British children judged the French, Germans, Italians, and Spanish, while the children from the former states of the Soviet Union judged the Americans, Azeris, Georgians, Russians, and Ukrainians. They found that although children showed overwhelming favoritism for their ingroup over other nations, outgroup derogation was limited to specific nations and reflected the negative cultural stereotypes (arguably resulting from historical political conflict between nations) held by adults in their particular nation.

For example, British children who strongly identified with their nation only expressed negative attitudes to Germans. Similarly, high identifying Azeri children held the least positive attitudes to the Russians and were relatively more favorable to other nations. Bennett and colleagues note that this finding is understandable since the Russians supported the Armenian occupation of Azeri land in 1992, and this historical event was mentioned frequently in public debates about national affairs during the data collection. This study also found that amongst the former states of the Soviet Union only high identifying Georgians and Ukrainians showed significantly favorable attitudes to the Americans. Again, Bennett and colleagues suggest this finding reflects the cultural and political context within the nation at the time, since it was widely known that the United States had supplied aid to Georgia and Ukraine after the recent collapse of the Soviet Union, and America was seen to reflect modernity and affluence which chimed with the aspirations of these relatively new independent nations (Bennett et al., 2004).

These few selected studies about stereotypes and outgroup attitudes in cultures with long-standing conflict provide some hope and optimism. While stereotypes pervade about the outgroup and social identity is quite salient, children show inclusive orientations, as with the Middle East study in which young children were directly asked about exclusion and inclusion. Moreover, social identity is fluid, changing with the cultural norms about outgroups, as shown in the British studies. One of the outcomes of examining research on cultural exclusion is the recognition that the unique political and social factors in a culture need to be taken into consideration when understanding children's inclusions and exclusions (Ruble et al., 2004). Outgroup derogation is not found across the board and it depends on the outgroup. Thus, stereotypes, which contribute to exclusion in childhood, are pervasive for groups in which there is a history of conflict. At the same time, newly immigrated groups to most cultures also experience stereotypic expectations based on issues of status and socioeconomic status, even in the absence of a history of conflict.

Recently Immigrated Groups

Immigrants groups in Spain

Recent research in Spain has demonstrated how different ethnic minority immigrant groups are treated and often excluded by majority White Spanish children (Enesco et al., 2008). Whereas Gypsies have been in Spain for more than 500 years, Moroccans began migrating in the 1960s (50 years ago) and Central/South Americans are recent immigrants (since the 1980s). Yet, each group experiences exclusion. Even with Gypsies having been in Spain for more than 500 years, the Spanish have viewed their society as racially and ethnically homogeneous, until very recently. In fact the empirical research literature on intergroup attitudes has only emerged in the past few decades, and general societal concerns about ethnic attitudes have only taken hold in the past 10 years in Spain (Enesco et al., 2008). Moreover, the negative plight of the Gypsies has only recently been acknowledged as a broad-based societal issue.

Enesco and her colleagues (2008) have examined existing stereotypes that White Spanish children have about members of ingroups and outgroups, as well as judgments about exclusion and intergroup bias. In one of their studies, Spanish and Latin American children from second (7 years of age), fourth (9 years), and sixth (11 years) grades in Madrid ($N = 96$) reported their knowledge of positive and negative stereotypes as well as their personal beliefs regarding Spaniards, Gypsies, Latin American, and Chinese people (Enesco, Navarro, Paradela, & Guerrero, 2005). When asked what "other people think," children attributed positive stereotypes about Spaniards and Chinese and negative stereotypes about Latin Americans and Gypsies. In addition, Spanish children attributed more positive and fewer negative stereotypes to Chinese immigrants than to Latin American children. For example, stereotypes associated with Latin Americans and Gypsies were "drunk," "lazy," and "poor." Chinese were associated with "envious" but not much more.

Age-related changes indicated that older children reported more positive stereotypes about Gypsies than younger children and older Spanish children reported fewer positive stereotypes for their own group than their younger counterparts. In addition, regarding personal beliefs, older children's personal attitudes about Gypsies were less consistent with negative stereotypes than were younger children's attitudes. Older children also showed greater awareness about the distinction between their personal beliefs and stereotypes, being more able to recognize the existence of stereotypes as wrong than were younger children. These findings indicate that children have knowledge about negative stereotypes, and that incorporating these stereotypes into their personal beliefs decreases with age. Further, in a study on how Spanish children evaluate peer exclusion based on ethnic group, such as Gypsies and Africans, Spanish majority group children view it as wrong to exclude ostracized groups, applying moral reasoning to their judgments (Enesco et al., 2008).

What is unusual is that the Spanish majority children rarely applied conventional or personal reasoning for their justifications to exclude others, as has been shown in the United States by European-American majority children (Killen, Lee-Kim, McGlothlin, & Stangor, 2002). These authors suggested that this might be the case because there is little daily interaction between Spanish ethnic majority and Gypsies or Africans, suggesting that ethnic majority children idealize potential intergroup situations, despite their stereotypic expectations, because they rarely come into contact with members from subordinate groups. Furthermore, the authors point out that European studies on ingroup biases revealed that Spanish children have stronger ingroup bias than children from other European countries, even though they are also the recipients of negative attitudes from children in other European countries as well. Nonetheless, Spanish children develop racial awareness later than children in other Western countries, including the United States, and the authors have interpreted this finding as reflecting their lack of interaction with children from different ethnic minorities until very recently (after 1990).

To pursue the issue of stereotyping and exclusion, Monks and colleagues surveyed both Spanish and English children from diverse ethnic backgrounds about direct relational personal and cultural victimization (Monks, Ortega-Ruiz, & Rodriguez-Hidalgo, 2008). The direct personal victimization scenario involved a context in which one student excluded another from the same cultural background (interpersonal not intergroup exclusion). In the direct cultural victimization scenario social exclusion occurred between two students at school who were "from different cultures and have different color skin" (intergroup exclusion). The findings were that English (18% minority adolescents) as well as Spanish (11% minority adolescents) participants reported experiencing personal and cultural victimization, with a third of the participants reporting personal direct relational victimization, while only 4% reported cultural direct relational victimization. Participants were more negative about verbal and direct relational victimization when it was in a cultural context than when it was in a personal context. Among other forms of victimization, Spanish students disapproved of personal and cultural direct relational victimization significantly more than English students. Students also reported that cultural victimization occurred due to the victim being different rather than attributing negative behavior on behalf of the aggressor. While Spanish adolescents might disapprove of most forms of aggression more often than English adolescents, cultural minority adolescents in both cultures did report experiencing cultural victimization more often than majority students. Thus further investigation must be done to understand the link between majority children's attitudes and evaluations about exclusion and their exclusion behaviors towards peers belonging to minority groups.

An interesting phenomenon mentioned by Monks et al. (2008) that ought to be addressed in studies measuring intergroup exclusion is the personal/group discrimination discrepancy (Taylor, Wright, & Porter, 1994). Findings from this line of research have shown that when minority group participants are asked about their own experiences with discrimination they perceive themselves as experiencing less discrimination than other members of their group. This may explain why less cultural victimization was reported altogether. In addition, the finding that more personal victimization was reported by all participants could be an indication that children may not recognize forms of cultural victimization when it is directed at them and interpret it more in personal terms rather than stemming from their cultural affiliation. Research in social psychology has pointed to this type of pattern in adults, with the interpretation that individuals are reluctant to view themselves in the "victim" role, and this reluctance to adopt the "victim" role may extend to children. Future research should address this issue of children's and adolescents' own interpretations of experienced peer victimization. This can be done through the use of participant-generated definitions of personal and cultural peer exclusion in combination with hypothetical vignettes that incorporate responses to open-ended questions that will capture participants' interpretations. Perhaps participants in this study who did not judge the cultural victimization as being based on cultural identity may have found it difficult to take the perspective of a group when that perspective was so different to their own.

Immigrant children in Portugal

Research in Portugal has focused more squarely on White Portuguese children's racial bias, which reflects a cultural bias regarding attitudes about North Africans. In research on prejudice, Monteiro et al. (2009) analyzed children's biased behavior regarding resource allocation in a context in which they were asked to divide resources among two children (same-race and different-race). In one study, the researchers demonstrated that 6- to 7-year-old children were biased (giving more resources to same-race then different-race peers), whether an adult was present or absent. In contrast 9- to 10-year-olds were only biased in the adult-present condition, revealing a normative influence on their behavior. In a follow-up study, in which the researchers interviewed children and manipulated two norms, perceived intergroup similarity or dissimilarity ("he/she looks like me; does not look like me") and intergroup merit or equality ("give more to ingroup; give same to all"), younger children remained biased in both conditions whereas older children complied with the antiracist norm but not with the racist norm. Thus, different norms affected older children's (but not younger children's) allocation behavior, especially when the norms were made explicit (Monteiro et al., 2009). These results confirm findings on racial bias in the United States and United Kingdom, especially regarding the increase in awareness of equality norms and concerns with discrimination. In Portugal, older children were more sensitive to antiracist norms and showed less racism against North African immigrants than did younger children.

Muslim children in the Netherlands

Intergroup issues between northern African immigrants and indigenous Europeans have also contributed to prejudice in the Netherlands and

United Kingdom, particularly regarding asylum-seekers. Asylum-seekers refer to displaced families who have left their own country due to a lack of rights or safe environments to seek freedom in another country. In the Netherlands, asylum-seekers are often from northern Africa. In the Netherlands, Verkuyten and Steenhuis (2005) have studied ethnically Dutch preadolescents' understanding and reasoning about asylum-seeker peers and friendships. Verkuyten and colleagues have examined how Dutch children evaluate an asylum-seeker (from northern Africa) in comparison to a Moroccan and Dutch peer. Their findings revealed that asylum-seekers were viewed in more disparaging and negative terms than were children from the other groups. Further, the closer Dutch preadolescents lived to a center for asylum-seekers, the more likely they were to view the asylum-seeker peer negatively. Participants in the study gave reasons for the exclusion of an asylum-seeker based on personal and conventional reasons, not moral ones. Verkuyten (2008) has further designed intervention projects to reduce prejudice through his analysis of multicultural education in the Netherlands (and areas in Europe). The movement towards multiculturalism has been important given that negative attributions to asylum-seekers exist in other countries as well, such as in the United Kingdom, where recent research focusing on adolescents' views of the rights of asylum-seekers has revealed stereotypes and negative outlooks (Ruck, Tenenbaum, & Sines, 2007).

Learning about cultural history helps children to understand current-day patterns of housing, employment, and levels of schooling that challenge stereotypes based solely on group membership (Verkuyten, 2008). Such information has the potential to contribute to, or inhibit, stereotypes about groups that are often based on a lack of information about historical patterns of cultural group identities. This is because this information is highly related to group identity, and views about who counts as a member of the "ingroup" or the "outgroup" are often complex to decipher without a deep understanding about the cultural history.

Recent immigrants in Italy

The findings in Portugal and the Netherlands are also demonstrated in Italy (Castelli, De Amicis, & Sherman, 2007), and indicate that White Portuguese, Italian, and Dutch children have negative stereotypes regarding Black North African children. In the case of these countries, the influx of North Africans is recent, confounding immigrant status with race (Esses, Dovidio, Semenya, & Jackson, 2005), which becomes a complex problem to disentangle. This is because prejudice and stereotypes may be due to recent immigrant status, socioeconomic status, language, or race; pulling apart which variable is difficult. Not only that, but given that adults have trouble differentiating between these confounds (Gieling et al., 2010), it is not surprising that children do as well. Do children also have biases regarding immigrants of the same race, or of a higher socioeconomic status, or with the same language?

Cross-group friendships in Germany

In Germany, a pressing issue concerns treatment of Turkish children, who have been the target of exclusion and discrimination for several decades. This is due to the pattern of migration from Turkey to Germany when Turkish families moved to Germany as guest workers and often resettled in German cities without obtaining status as full citizens. Recent studies have examined the factors that contribute to facilitating or impeding biases about immigrants, and specifically Turkish children, in Germany (Feddes et al., 2009; Jugert, Noack, & Rutland, in press). Feddes et al. (2009) demonstrated how direct intergroup contact reduced prejudice amongst German children aged 7–11 years, as will be discussed in more detail in the next chapter on how to reduce prejudice. In the Feddes et al. (2009) study, prejudice was measured by attributions of positive adjectives (e.g., "friendly") to outgroup members. Again, as will be discussed in more detail in chapter 8, Jugert, Noack, and Rutland (in press) examined Turkish and German children's preferences for same-ethnic friendships in hetero-geneous schools over the course of a year and found that preferences decreased over the course of that time and were related to positive affective intergroup attitudes. However, it is important we also examine what factors predict intergroup contact or cross-group friendships. Empirical findings by Aboud and colleagues also found associations between cross-ethnic friendship and low levels of prejudice among ethnic majority but not ethnic minority children (Aboud, Mendelson, & Purdy, 2003).

Newly immigrated children in a homogeneous cultural context: Switzerland

A recent study, conducted by Malti et al. (in press) in Switzerland, was designed to explore Swiss majority adolescents' judgments about exclusion based on immigrant status, examining "status" differences, and controlling for race. In Switzerland, Serbians are recent immigrants who have been treated negatively and have experienced discrimination and, thus, the investigation of exclusion of Serbian children by Swiss national children as well as non-Swiss nationals provided an examination of the role of immigrant status, controlling for race. In this study, 247 children and adolescents (aged 11–13 and 14–16 years) in Switzerland (160 Swiss and 87 "non-Swiss") were interviewed regarding three types of exclusion contexts: (1) *gender* (an all-boys' gymnastics club that chose a boy instead of a girl to join a club); (2) *culture* (a group of Swiss (national) boys attending a football game choose a Swiss instead of a Serbian child to join); and (3) *personality trait* (a group of theater students chose an outgoing child instead of a shy child from joining).

As an example, the culture scenario was the following:

> Michael and some of his friends are going to a soccer game, Switzerland is playing against Serbia. Milan, a Serbian boy, and Markus, a Swiss boy, both want to go to the game too. Both know a lot about soccer. There is only one more ticket for the game. Michael and his friends invite the Swiss boy Markus to come along to the soccer game because they want to keep it a Swiss group who goes to see the match.

These three contexts were chosen as they represent familiar situations for children and adolescents and involve exclusion based on three types of characteristics, gender, culture, and personality. The study included both moral judgment assessments regarding whether it was all right or not all right to exclude, as well as participants' attributions of emotions regarding the excluded child as well as the excluder ("How will the excluder feel? How will the excluded person feel?").

Regarding exclusion based on nationality, most participants stated that it would be wrong. There were differences, however, for the two groups, with more Serbian adolescents than Swiss adolescents viewing it as wrong; Swiss adolescents justified exclusion based on group comfort and group identity: "It would be all right because the Serbian child would not fit in and would make the others uncomfortable." Yet, Serbian adolescents were more likely to invoke moral reasons, such as discrimination and negative feelings: "It's wrong because how will he feel? It just makes you want to go back home but you can't. It's not right to feel this way and it happens a lot." Even more striking were the emotions attributed to the excluder and the excluded, with Serbian adolescents more likely to attribute positive emotions to the Swiss excluder than were the Swiss participants. Swiss youth, with age, viewed the Swiss excluder as having positive feelings, such as pride, when excluding the non-Swiss, Serbian, peer from joining the group; whereas there were no age differences for emotion attributions for the non-Swiss sample. This is an example of how group identity, in the form of "national pride," can result in exclusionary acts that lead to prejudice and discrimination. Overall, children viewed exclusion based on gender and shyness as more legitimate then exclusion based on culture. With age, children viewed exclusion as all right, and boys viewed exclusion as more legitimate than did girls.

Social identity and status made a difference to children, viewing exclusion of a Serbian child as more legitimate than of a Swiss child in a peer activity involving group identity. Further, this study was novel in that two types of measures were made: moral judgments about whether it is wrong to exclude someone and emotion attributions, that is, the emotions attributed to excluders and the excluded. Combining judgments and emotion attributions in one study provided a picture of the factors that contribute to patterns of exclusion. For some children, using group membership to decide who to pick was legitimate, and the emotions that they attributed to the excluder were positive. In contrast, other children who viewed exclusion based on group membership as wrong, attributed negative feelings to the excluder. All children attributed negative emotions to the excluded peer, which indicates that children who viewed it as legitimate were also aware that the excluded child would feel bad. While the cultural category predicted responses to exclusion of a peer based on cultural membership (Swiss or non-Swiss), this was not the case for gender because girls viewed all forms of exclusion (gender, culture, personality trait) as more wrong than did boys.

These findings are interesting in light of the many educational programs that have been developed for educators in Macdonia, the successor state of former Yugolavia, from which it declared independence in 1991, and which has Albanian and Serbian children who come from countries previously at war. In the prior cultural context, Serbians were in the majority; thus, as new immigrants in other countries, such as Switzerland, their role is reversed and the consequences for children can be extreme, leading to victimization. Understanding the child's perspective from both viewpoints, as the majority and as the minority, is important for creating successful intervention programs (to be discussed in chapter 8).

Rejection, exclusion, and victimization in Korea and the United States

In a study designed to determine whether children differentiate peer rejection, exclusion, and victimization, Park and Killen (2010) interviewed

Korean ($N = 397$) and American ($N = 333$) children and adolescents (10 and 13 years of age) about peer exclusion based on personality (aggression, shyness) and group (gender, nationality) characteristics for three types of peer rejection. This study was different from the Swiss study because the salience of the exclusion varied from rejecting a friend to victimization. Children evaluated 12 scenarios in all: three peer rejection scenarios (friendship rejection, peer group exclusion, and peer victimization) in which exclusion based on personality and group membership occurred. The friendship rejection context was one in which one child did not want to be friends with another child (who was shy, aggressive, different nationality, or different gender). The exclusion context was one in which a group did not want a child to join them in their club (who was shy, aggressive, different nationality, or different gender); and the victimization context was one in which a group repeatedly teased and taunted a child (who was shy, aggressive, different nationality, or different gender).

Similar to the Swiss study, Park and Killen (2010) found that children evaluated peer rejection based on *group membership* (nationality, gender) as more unfair than peer rejection based on *personality traits* (shyness, aggression). In this study, nationality referred to two groups of equal status (Koreans and Americans). While Korean children were more willing to exclude based on nationality, American children were more willing to exclude based on gender. One of the primary findings of this study was that children viewed exclusion based on group membership as more wrong than exclusion based on personality traits, which supports our contention that group membership reflects a qualitatively different type of exclusion for individuals than does exclusion based on individual personality deficits (see also Park, Killen, Crystal, & Watanabe, 2003). When asked about why it was all right to exclude in a group context (excluding a child from joining a group), most children used social-conventional reasoning, and focused on group functioning. This study provided another example of the balance between group functioning, identity, and fairness judgments in the context of peer exclusion.

Intergroup Exclusion Based on Indigenous Groups

Research in Australia with Anglo-Australian, Aboriginal-Australian, and Pacific Islander children has revealed ingroup and outgroup attitudes towards recent immigrants as well as indigenous groups. As Griffiths and Nesdale (2006) explain, Australia has experienced several phases of migration: the first phase occurred when Anglo-Australian immigrants displaced Aboriginal people; the second phase occurred when other European groups migrated to Australia in the 1950s and 1960s; and the most recent group reflects Middle Eastern, Asian, and Pacific Islander ethnic groups.

In the Griffiths and Nesdale (2006) study, children aged 5–12 years of age from the ethnic majority group ($N = 59$, Anglo-Australian) and minority group ($N = 60$, Pacific Islanders) rated members of the Anglo-Australian, Pacific Islander, and Aboriginal (indigenous Australian) groups. There were two measures, an indirect and an explicit one. The explicit measure was a trait assignment task in which participants assigned positive and negative traits to members of ingroups and outgroups. The implicit measure was an assessment of how much the children would exclude individuals from each group. For this implicit measure, participants were given a talk in which nine houses were shown and children were told that the middle house was their own house. Children were asked to indicate which house they would allocate to an Anglo-Australian, a Pacific Islander, and an Aboriginal family. A distance score was calculated.

The findings for the explicit attitudes assessment revealed that the majority group rated the ingroup members more positively than the two outgroups, with the indigenous group rated the least positive. The ethnic minority group rated the ingroup and the ethnic majority outgroup equally, but rated the Aboriginal-Australian group the least positive. All children were more positive with age regarding their explicit ratings of the outgroups. For the implicit, "exclusion" task, Anglo-Australian children preferred ethnic ingroup neighbors rather than families from either ethnic outgroups. The youngest children (aged 6 years) did not differentiate between an ingroup family and the Anglo-Australian family, but the Anglo-Australian and Pacific Islander groups preferred these groups as neighbors over the Aboriginal families. Thus, with age, majority children preferred an ingroup family to live near them, and the minority immigrant group of children preferred their own group or the majority group to live near them rather than an indigenous Aboriginal group. As Griffiths and Nesdale (2006) indicate, little research has been done on exclusion based on indigenous groups. Measures of contact, and social reasoning assessments for what underlies these judgments, would be fruitful for future research.

Summary

The studies reviewed in this chapter reflect the very beginning of an important line of research revealing the origins of prejudice and bias in diverse cultural contexts. Social psychological research has been mostly laboratory-focused, typically using artificial groups to study prejudice. Actual groups are complicated by cultural history, levels of status, degree of contact, and experiences of exclusion. Yet, the research described in this chapter reveals systematic patterns that generalize across contexts, and at the same time, demonstrate unique considerations in various cultures regarding inclusion and exclusion. In all contexts, children made inclusion judgments, and viewed some forms of exclusion as unfair and wrong. Yet, stereotypic expectations were also revealed that were used to justify exclusion in contexts in which group functioning was threatened.

Unique contributions in these studies pertained to within-cultural-group variation, such as the different judgments by Arab children from Jordan, Israel, and the Palestinian Territories, which indicate that stress and other factors contribute to ingroup/outgroup distinctions. Further, a novel finding was the positive emotions attributed to the excluder in the Swiss-Serbian context, which reflects a newly immigrated group (within the past 5 years). Attributing positive emotions to the excluder may be a result of the recent immigration and the lack of recognition of what makes certain forms of exclusion wrong or unfair. Clearly the next step for research is to examine what types of interventions are effective for reducing prejudice and in the next chapter we review research on interventions designed to promote morality and positive intergroup attitudes.

Chapter 8

Increasing Inclusion, Reducing Prejudice, and Promoting Morality

This book so far has focused on the importance of morality, prejudice, and group identity in the development of social exclusion and inclusion in childhood. We have shown how moral reasoning can promote inclusion early in childhood, but we have also shown that different forms of prejudice emerge in childhood. Children exclude as well as include others in their everyday interactions and friendships. Now, in this chapter, we will examine how inclusion can be promoted and children can learn about what makes exclusion wrong or legitimate in group contexts. Our focus will be on how social experience and cultural diversity can act to facilitate social inclusion and help children to differentiate exclusion that is wrong from a moral viewpoint and exclusion that is part of making groups function well.

Research on social inclusion and exclusion in childhood has many applications to the areas of policy, programs, and applied interventions aimed at promoting fairness and reducing prejudice. In this chapter, we describe these various interventions to demonstrate the applications of research for addressing issues of exclusion, prejudice, and morality. Effective programs, designed to reduce prejudice and increase mutual respect, are those that rely closely on developmental research findings, and are developmentally appropriate. One of the principles of developmental theory is that children and adolescents understand the world qualitatively differently from adults, and thus, programs designed to be

Children and Social Exclusion: Morality, Prejudice, and Group Identity. Melanie Killen and Adam Rutland. © 2011 Melanie Killen and Adam Rutland. Published 2011 by Blackwell Publishing Ltd.

relevant for communicating messages to children must reflect the developmental abilities and the developmental context of childhood.

As an example, a program to facilitate fairness regarding the distribution of resources among children aged 6–8 years would not be effective if the content concerned the US Congress allocating funds to communities for improving their highways, as this reflects the content of the adult world, not the world of the young child. However, a program designed to facilitate fairness by asking children to decide how their peers should divide up toys among a group of children who have different claims to the toys would be a developmentally appropriate way to focus on fairness concepts that would be meaningful for children in their lives. When adults make allocation of resource decisions it is necessary to have as much information as possible, particularly when the content is unfamiliar. Children do not necessarily know how to ask for more information and thus it is essential to ensure that the information they are given is developmentally relevant for them and accessible.

Creating a developmentally appropriate program is more complex than simplifying the content, however, because it requires in-depth knowledge of recent developmental findings regarding children's reasoning about social exclusion, moral development, understanding of prejudice, and sense of group identity – topics that we have covered in this book. Unfortunately, interventions to tackle childhood exclusion and prejudice are often implemented by practitioners who are not informed by developmental research and the interventions are not systematically evaluated. For example, role-playing or empathy training is a technique widely used by educational practitioners. Role-playing typically involves the child adopting the role or taking the perspective of another child who is experiencing social exclusion. The child has to "walk in the shoes" of the other stigmatized child and feel firsthand what it is like to be discriminated against. This approach has received little empirical attention, however, and the limited research conducted suggests it does not significantly change children's empathy or the attitudes that may underlie social exclusion (see Aboud & Levy, 2000).

In contrast, within this chapter we will describe strategies to challenge social exclusion that are founded upon research, mentioned extensively throughout this book, on the development of children's moral reasoning, prejudice, and group identity. We will show how both explicit and implicit biases amongst children from a majority status group (e.g., European-American) can be reduced through the promotion of contact between groups, in particular cross-group friendships involving inclusive peer relationships (i.e., direct intergroup contact). We will also show, in line with our argument detailed in chapters 3 and 4, how the group and especially the group norm are important in the process by which direct contact reduces children's prejudice. Research will also be discussed showing intergroup factors that are crucial in bringing about cross-group friendships and encouraging positive contact between children from different groups. Concerns, however, will also be addressed about the effect of intergroup contact on the attitudes of minority status children (e.g., Turkish children living in Germany).

Next we will consider research that shows how positive contact between a child's group and other groups (i.e., extended intergroup contact), either through stories or via the mass media, can challenge a child's negative attitudes towards other groups and reduce exclusive group norms that prohibit the forming of cross-group friendships. We will also show that contact can facilitate moral reasoning (i.e., fairness) about exclusion, and enable adolescents to reject stereotypic expectations about others. Finally, we describe some research that shows how multicultural education can promote respect for cultural diversity, positive interactions between children from different groups, and tolerance to others from diverse cultures.

Intergroup Contact and Reducing Prejudice

There is a substantial history of research in both developmental and social psychology examining the most well known and effective approach to reducing prejudice and promoting social inclusion, namely the Contact Hypothesis (Allport, 1954). Here contact means individuals from one group (e.g., European-Americans) meeting and interacting with others from a different group (e.g., African-Americans). The underlying theory behind the Contact Hypothesis is that prejudice is a consequence of unfamiliarity with others from a different group which results in negative stereotyping and prejudice towards this group. Contact with others from another group should expose individuals to stereotype disconfirming information resulting in more positive attitudes, beliefs, and behaviors towards this group (Allport, 1954). Specifically, Allport proposed that contact between groups (i.e., intergroup contact) can help tackle intergroup bias if optimal conditions are established when individuals from different groups come into contact. Indeed, research suggests that intergroup contact is most effective when Allport's optimal conditions are met (Brown & Hewstone, 2005; Pettigrew & Tropp, 2006).

These optimal conditions (see Pettigrew & Tropp, 2006) include equal status between groups (i.e., no group is seen to be valued or respected more than another), support of institutional authorities like schools (i.e., authority figures are seen to support and promote positive contact between those from different groups), common goals (i.e., each group shares the same goals when individuals from each group meet), and cooperation rather than competition between groups (i.e., when the individuals from each group meet they work together to achieve their common goals). Although groups often vary in their degree of social status, research suggests that if the contact situation can be construed so each group thinks they have equal status with the other group (e.g., through creating a new activity in which both groups can excel or share a common sense of identity) then the likelihood of more positive intergroup attitudes will be higher (e.g., Schofield & Eurich-Fulcer, 2001). In fact, attitudes can be improved if institutional authorities (e.g., teachers, local government) help establish norms and standards for intergroup contact that make it more acceptable and, therefore, more likely to occur (see Pettigrew, 1998). Finally, contact between groups is most effective when groups cooperate together, working towards a common goal. When members of different groups work together and rely on each other such cooperative interdependence promotes positive intergroup attitudes (e.g., Maras & Brown, 1996; Slavin, 1995).

A famous study that demonstrated the value of cooperative interaction between groups was Sherif and colleagues' robber's cave study (Sherif, Harvey, White, Hood, & Sherif, 1961). Boys in an American summer camp were dived into arbitrary groups and competition between these groups was encouraged. This resulted in extremely negative behavior between groups, including verbal and physical abuse. These behaviors only receded when the two groups were given tasks requiring them to cooperate to reach a common goal. Many questions have been raised about these studies, though, which spawned a line of research on what happens to children in groups. Close analyses of the robber's cave study indicates that the adults played an instrumental role in the antagonism that resulted, and that the unique situation of an experimental summer camp may not be generalizable to children's everyday interactions in the playground.

Intergroup Contact and Children

Developmental researchers have investigated the Contact Hypothesis amongst children by seeing whether contact between different social groups under certain conditions reduces childhood prejudice (Aboud, 2005; Allport, 1954). A recent meta-analysis of studies examining the influence of contact on children's intergroup attitudes concluded that contact between children of different groups corresponds with less prejudice, especially when Allport's optimal conditions are established within the school environment (Tropp & Prenovost, 2008). The majority of studies included in this analysis examined children's ethnic or racial attitudes. This reflects the focus on racial or ethnic group as a possible basis for prejudice within the psychology literature and the growth of studies on the contact effect amongst children following the landmark 1954 Brown v. Board of Education decision in the United States. This decision declared that racially segregated schools were unconstitutional and began the process of dismantling state-imposed school segregation in the United States.

While there is evidence that contact changes children's ethnic or racial attitudes, there is less research into how contact may influence children's attitudes in relation to other categories (e.g., gender, nationality, disability, or religion). There seems to be no reason to think that intergroup contact could not change children's attitudes to groups, however, other than ethnic or racial ones. For example, Maras and Brown (1996) evaluated an intergroup contact intervention that involved children who had no disabilities taking part in regular everyday classroom collaborative activities (e.g., making a model) with children who had learning disabilities. Following the intervention, children expressed a greater liking for the outgroup members with disabilities compared to children who had had no contact with the outgroup. Cross-group contact has been incorporated into a number of prejudice-reduction interventions in the form of cooperative learning groups, bilingual education and racially integrated schooling, and vicarious contact through television and fictional stories (e.g., Graves, 1999; Maras & Brown, 2000; Wright & Tropp, 2005).

Cross-group Friendships and Prejudice

The Contact Hypothesis also suggests that intimate and personal cross-group friendships are particularly effective at reducing prejudice and challenging social exclusion (Brown, 1995; Pettigrew & Tropp, 2006). This involves more than casual contact (e.g., buying something from a minority group shopkeeper), instead cross-group friendships are close personal relationships in which individuals typically share intimate information about one another and feel free to express their thoughts or feelings. Indeed, cross-group friendships are related to less intergroup bias amongst children, and positive inter-ethnic attitudes predict a decrease in children's preference for same-ethnic friendships. Cross-ethnic friendship are considered to be especially powerful regarding attitude change as it is contact of high quality and meets several of the optimal conditions under which contact is supposed to lead to more positive intergroup attitudes (Allport, 1954; Pettigrew, 1998). In fact, Aboud, Mendelson, and Purdy (2003) reported that children's prejudice was related to their intergroup peer relationships. Specifically, children who had high-quality (e.g., involving companionship and intimacy) cross-group friendships and had interactive cross-group companions (i.e., friendships that were reciprocated by both children) showed less bias against different ethnic groups.

Typically, studies on the association between cross-group friendships and children's intergroup attitudes have relied on cross-sectional or correlational data, with researchers measuring children's reported level of contact at one moment in time and examining whether, for example, children with high contact show the least intergroup bias. This approach does not allow for a convincing test of directional hypotheses (Brown & Hewstone, 2005). Namely, it is difficult to determine whether having cross-group friendships leads to more positive attitudes toward other groups or, in fact, children's positive attitudes to these groups mean they seek more intergroup contact and cross-group friends. Longitudinal studies are needed to test whether cross-group friendships lead to positive attitudes or whether positive attitudes cause children to seek cross-group friends. Such studies are rare, though a recent study by Feddes and colleagues examined longitudinal cross-group friendship (or direct contact) effects on outgroup evaluations (Feddes, Noack, & Rutland, 2009).

This study examined whether, over time, direct cross-ethnic friendships caused children to have more positive evaluations of other groups. The study included German (i.e., majority status) and Turkish (i.e., minority status) children aged 7–11 years in ethnically non-mixed elementary schools at the beginning and end of the German school year. The Turkish population is the largest ethnic minority group in Germany, facing high levels of discrimination and rejection (Wagner, Van Dick, Pettigrew, & Christ, 2003). About 7% of the 6- to 10-year-old children in Germany have a Turkish migration background. Already, in elementary school, children with a Turkish migration background have been shown to perform worse than their German peers. It can, therefore, be assumed that Turkish children hold a lower social status position compared to

German children. This distinction is important as previous studies have found differences in associations between cross-group friendships and prejudice among minority and majority status groups (see Tropp & Pettigrew, 2005). We will return to this point later in the chapter.

In this study, the data were collected by Feddes and colleagues over a 7-month period in which children completed a questionnaire at two time points. Children were asked to write down the first names of their three best friends and to identify whether they were German, Turkish, or other nationalities. The children were also asked to attribute positive words to their ethnic outgroup to measure their explicit evaluations of this group.

Group norms and intergroup contact

Feddes and colleagues (2009) were also interested in *how* cross-group friendships might change children's evaluations of an ethnic outgroup. Some researchers have proposed that ingroup and outgroup norms about having cross-ethnic friendships are influenced by intergroup contact and in turn result in more positive attitudes towards other groups (e.g., Pettigrew, 1998). Evidence certainly suggests that children in middle childhood are sensitive to group norms about peer relations and actively reason about exclusion based on ethnicity. In addition, experimental studies have shown that social norms can directly affect children's intergroup attitudes and evaluations of deviant ingroup members. There-fore, it is likely that the experience of having a direct cross-group friendship going unsanctioned by peers over time is likely to reinforce the behavior which, in turn, is expected to generalize to more positive explicit attitudes toward the outgroup.

In their study, therefore, Feddes and colleagues (2009) measured children's social norms about having cross-ethnic friendships by asking children to imagine that a German/Turkish child was new in their class and to indicate what they thought *other German children* and *other Turkish children*, respectively, would think about them playing with the outgroup child.

It was found by Feddes et al. that amongst majority status German children, but not minority status Turkish children, more cross-group friendships predicted, over time, positive outgroup evaluations. This longitudinal study demonstrated for the first time the causal direction between greater direct contact (i.e., more cross-group friendships) and more positive outgroup attitudes amongst ethnic majority children. This association was partly mediated by perceived social norms about cross-ethnic friendship relations. This meant that the experience of direct contact, in part, made children's attitudes more positive by making them think that cross-ethnic friendships are more acceptable and to be encouraged by both groups. This finding demonstrates how the group and the norms about exclusion that define the group's identity are important for reducing prejudice through the promotion of direct intergroup contact. As we argued in chapters 3 and 4, any attempt to understand and eliminate social exclusion in children's lives by challenging their negative attitudes needs to consider group identity and norms.

Recent research has also shown that self-disclosure (sharing intimate and personal details with another person) in children's inter-ethnic friendships leads to more positive intergroup attitudes through increasing empathy and intergroup trust (Turner, Voci, & Hewstone, 2007, Study 4). This might be why cross-group *friendships* in particular are so important for changing intergroup attitudes: mere contact between groups, just attending ethnically mixed schools or youth clubs, may not provide the opportunity for those children involved to form close friendships and develop empathy and intergroup trust, or engage in self-disclosure (Pettigrew, 1998).

The multicultural and tolerant nature of the schools in the study by Feddes et al. (2009) was evident in the frequent opportunities for positive inter-ethnic contact over a prolonged time that were supported by the authorities, while equal status was emphasized (e.g., through a recognition of the minority group language by offering Turkish language courses). These conditions closely reflect Allport's (1954) optimal contact conditions, which should both allow the formation of cross-ethnic friendships and positive change in intergroup attitudes. Indeed, the longitudinal results found by Feddes and colleagues suggest that cross-ethnic friendships positively alter children's intergroup attitudes, rather than intergroup attitudes affecting children's cross-group friendships.

How do intergroup factors promote cross-group friendships?

The research described above suggests that cross-group friendships are important in the process of reducing prejudice and challenging negative attitudes that feed social exclusion in childhood. However, what intergroup factors are crucial in bringing about such friendships in the first place and encouraging positive contact between children from different groups? A recent study has examined why children seem to prefer same- over cross-ethnic friendships and what attitudes predict children's preference for same- over cross-ethnic friendships (Jugert, Noack, & Rutland, in press). This study measured children's friendships in ethnically heterogeneous secondary schools over the course of the first school year for German and Turkish children.

The children were asked to nominate their friends from within their school class using a peer-nomination technique common in the peer relations literature (see Aboud et al., 2003). This technique was used to calculate the number of same- and cross-ethnic companions in the class. Mutual friendships were determined by asking children to rate the friendship status of each same-sex class mate (i.e., on a scale where 1 = best friend, 2 = good friend, 3 = okay friend, 4 = okay kid who is not really a friend, and 5 = don't know very well). Jugert and colleagues decided to use a definition of friendship that was not limited to just best friends (see Aboud et al., 2003) but included good and 'okay' friends, too. This was because in the German school system children do not always go to the same secondary school as their classmates in elementary school. In fact, children are allocated to secondary schools based upon their grade point average at the end of elementary school so most secondary schools include children from many different elementary schools and neighborhoods. The assessment of friendship used was necessary as a limitation to only best friends would have been overly restrictive in a context of children entering their first year of secondary school in Germany.

Amongst other things, this study measured children's affective liking for their ethnic ingroup and outgroup, whether they thought their ethnic ingroup and outgroup thought cross-ethnic friendship were acceptable and normal (i.e., group norms), and children's perception of the extent to which Allport's (1954) optimal contact conditions were established within their school class.

This study found that children who held positive ethnic intergroup attitudes desired contact with the ethnic outgroup and thought their group would perceive cross-ethnic friendships as normal at the beginning of their first school year (i.e., held an inclusive group norm). These children then showed a lower preference for same-ethnic friendships at the end of the school year. Moreover, trends in both German and Turkish children's ethnic friendship preferences were linked to their intergroup attitudes and understanding of group norms about friendship; while intergroup contact conditions were only predictive of German children's ethnic friendship preferences. These findings show that interventions aimed at promoting positive ethnic attitudes and inclusive group norms, and that encourage openness to interacting with the ethnic outgroup, are likely to result in cross-ethnic friendships and so decrease examples of social exclusion.

These findings indicate that it is problematic to merely assume that perceived contact conditions are stable both over time and interindividually and have a uniform effect on all children's friendship choices (Molina & Wittig, 2006; Molina, Wittig, & Giang, 2004).

Intergroup Contact and Minority Status Children

This last point highlights how intergroup contact is not perceived in the same way by majority and minority ethnic groups, and cross-group friendships typically reduce the prejudice of majority group children (for an exception in which intergroup contact was related to minority adolescent exclusion attitudes, see Ruck, Park, Killen, & Crystal, in press). For example, Feddes and colleagues (2009) found that having more cross-group friendships did not predict over time positive outgroup evaluations amongst the minority status Turkish children. Such findings are in line with recent meta-analyses which included more than 500 studies investigating contact effects among children, adolescents, and adults (Pettigrew & Tropp, 2006; Tropp & Prenovost, 2008). These analyses have found the relationships between greater intergroup contact and reduced prejudice to be significantly weaker for members of minority status group than for members of majority status groups. Previous cross-sectional studies have also only shown positive associations between majority and not minority status children's cross-ethnic friendships and intergroup attitudes (Aboud et al., 2003; Turner et al., 2007, Study 1).

Aboud and colleagues (2003) reported a positive cross-sectional association between cross-ethnic friendship and intergroup attitudes among majority children but no such association among minority children. This study was conducted amongst ethnic majority status (e.g., White) and minority status (e.g., Black Caribbean) children from grades 1 to 6 in a multiracial English-language elementary school in Montreal. They also found that for these children, positive racial attitudes were significantly related to fewer cross-race exclusion friendships (i.e., when children rate each other as nonfriends) and that particularly high-quality cross-race friendships were associated with less bias. However, their analysis performed on the Black Caribbean children found no association between cross-race friendships and more positive racial attitudes.

Others have also noted that Allport's (1954) optimal contact conditions are being interpreted and defined differently across majority and minority status groups, and this might explain the failure to find a relationship between attitudes and intergroup contact amongst minority status children (Tropp & Pettigrew, 2005; Tropp & Prenovost, 2008). They suggest that minority status group members may be less convinced as to the extent to which optimal conditions are met compared to majority group members. This implies that, for example, Black Caribbean-Canadians or Turkish-Germans may have contact with White Canadians or White Germans but that the members of the minority groups do not perceive the groups to hold equal status, to share a common identity, or to be engaging in cooperation rather than competition during contact. Children from ethnic minority groups may also feel that any intergroup contact they experience is not fully supported and encouraged by figures and policies in powerful institutions (e.g., school, community organizations). In contrast, for example, children from ethnic majority groups are likely to hold a different view and believe that when intergroup contact occurs that optimal conditions are present. Optimal contact conditions might therefore be more effective in promoting positive intergroup attitudes among majority status group members compared to minority status group members.

In addition, the lack of contact effects on the intergroup attitudes of ethnic minority status children might reflect that this group is well aware of their group's lower status in many cultures and therefore are continuously aware of being a possible victim of prejudice (Crocker, Major, & Steele, 1998). Subsequently, they are less prone to develop positive attitudes towards the dominant majority status group after intergroup contact since they have a high and accessible level of perceived discrimination. It is worth noting that Nesdale and colleagues (e.g., Nesdale & Flesser, 2001) have shown that from a young age children are aware of social status differences and this affects their intergroup attitudes. This research has demonstrated that when children are randomly assigned to low- and high-status groups they use this information to inform their attitudes to others from different groups.

Other studies of "real" groups have found that ethnic minority children are highly aware of being stigmatized and report significant levels of perceived peer victimization based upon, for example, ethnic group membership. Studies by Verkuyten and colleagues have found high levels of perceived social exclusion amongst children from ethnic minority groups. In these studies Turkish children in the Netherlands are typically presented with a story in which a Turkish child is socially excluded because of ethnicity, and then asked "are you ever called names at school?" and "do you ever get teased at school?" or they ask the children "are you ever harassed at school or in the neighborhood because you are Turkish?" (Verkuyten, 2002a; Verkuyten & Thijs, 2002). Typically, Verkuyten and colleagues find that minority status Turkish children report significantly higher levels of perceived peer victimization or exclusion than majority status Dutch children.

Recently, some social psychologists have noted that amongst minority status adults (e.g., Israeli-Arabs), intergroup contact can result in false expectations about equality and fair treatment from the outgroup (Saguy, Tausch, Dovidio, & Pratto, 2009), together with a decreased desire for social change to challenge their disadvantaged position. These findings, combined with a significant body of evidence showing that intergroup contact reduces majority status children's prejudice and tendency to engage in social exclusion, might suggest that intergroup contact has the most positive and desirable effects in changing how majority groups think and behave. However, research on intergroup contact and children's social exclusion still needs to consider carefully the implications of contact for minority status children too since most contact situations involve majority and minority group children.

Reducing Implicit Biases through Intergroup Contact

We showed previously in chapter 3 that children have implicit and indirect biases from an early age. This begs the question, while intergroup contact seems to reduce majority status children's explicit prejudice, can it also decrease these children's implicit biases? Recent evidence suggests that implicit biases can be reduced by changing the social context, especially exposure to outgroups. For example, Turner and colleagues (2007) examined the attitudes of White majority status 8- to 11-year-old children living in ethnically homogenous areas towards the largest minority status group in the United Kingdom, namely South East Asian-British. This ethnic group consists of those of Indian, Pakistani, or Bangladeshi origin. A measure of cross-group friendship was obtained by asking children how often they spend time with South East Asian-British children outside school and how often they have these children around to their house. The children's implicit attitudes were measured using the Implicit Association Test (IAT). This was described in some detail in chapter 3. Turner and colleagues found that White British children who reported more cross-ethnic friendships with South East Asian-British children also showed more positive implicit outgroup attitudes measured using a version of the IAT. This finding suggests that while implicit biases might appear early in childhood (see chapter 3) they may not always be immune to contextual influences, since it is possible that repeated quality contact with an outgroup during the early part of life (i.e., before 8 years of age) might limit the formation of implicit biases. These intergroup contacts arguably may act to prevent the emergence of negative associations involving the outgroup (e.g., South East Asian–nasty or South East Asian–unfriendly), which will be picked up by the IAT.

Studies using indirect measures of attributional biases have also shown intergroup contact can reduce implicit biases. Drawing on previous methodologies (Lawrence, 1991; Sagar & Schofield, 1980), McGlothlin and colleagues used the ambiguous situations task (as described in chapter 3) to determine whether children used race to attribute intentions when evaluating familiar, everyday peer encounters (McGlothlin & Killen, 2005, 2006; McGlothlin, Killen, & Edmonds, 2005). This methodology is an indirect assessment of intergroup attitudes because the child is not told explicitly about race but only asked to describe what happened in interracial social situations. If biases are present, different interpretations of the same act performed by either a White character or a Black character will be given. These biases, even when subtle, affect social cognition and interracial relationships (see Aboud et al., 2003). For example, if an African-American child is perceived as more aggressive than a European-American child performing the same behavior then it is less likely that the African-American child will be considered a good candidate for a friend.

As described in chapter 3, McGlothlin and Killen (2006) presented an ambiguous situation task to 6- to 10-year-old European-American children living in an ethnically non-mixed area where over 90% of the school was European-American. Racial bias was only revealed by European-American children in non-mixed schools because McGlothlin and colleagues, using the same ambiguous situations methodology, found European-American children at the same age, and in the same school district, but enrolled in ethnically mixed schools, did not attribute more positive intentions to the ingroup than the outgroup; in fact, among this group, race was not used to attribute negative intentions (see also McGlothlin & Killen, 2010).

Reducing Prejudice through Extended Intergroup Contact

Direct intergroup contact, especially cross-group friendships, can reduce both explicit and implicit biases in favor of one group over another.

Compared to same-ethnic friendships, cross-ethnic friendships are relatively uncommon, are less stable than same-ethnic friendships, and decline with age (Kao & Joyner, 2004; Schneider, Dixon, & Udvari, 2007). Therefore, in the context of such segregation, it is reassuring to find evidence that merely being aware of cross-ethnic friendships between members of one's own group and another group can also reduce prejudice (Wright, Aron, McLaughlin-Volpe, & Ropp, 1997). This is known as the "extended contact" effect. Here a child's intergroup attitudes can become more positive by simply hearing that a member of their group has a friendship with a child from a different social group. This form of indirect contact means the child is experiencing intergroup contact via knowing their group is extending its boundaries to connect with outgroup children. For example, a British child may have some negative attitudes toward Iraqis but little experience of interacting with this group. Yet, according to the concept of extended contact, their attitude could be made more positive if they heard that another British child had formed a close cross-group friendship with an Iraqi refugee who had come to Britain.

There is evidence that extended contact can help tackle prejudice in both adolescents and young children. For example, in a series of studies, Cameron and colleagues developed extended contact interventions for children as young as 5 years (see Cameron & Rutland, 2008). These interventions exposed children to intergroup friendships through illustrated story reading that portrayed friendships between ingroup and outgroup members (e.g., White British children and non-White refugee children). Cameron and colleagues found that their extended contact intervention was effective in improving attitudes towards outgroups amongst 5- to 11-year-old children and across a number of different stigmatized outgroups, including the disabled, non-White refugees, and South East Asian-British.

Cameron and Rutland (2006) focused on improving British children's intergroup attitudes toward people with disabilities. This issue has become more significant in the UK, where the British government's policy of school inclusion in education (see Grubbs & Niemeyer, 1999) has fostered more direct contact among children both with and without disabilities. In this study, 5- to 10-year-old White British children who had no disabilities and went to schools where few children with disabilities were enrolled, participated in an extended contact intervention. The extended contact intervention involved children in groups of two or three reading (together with the researcher) three illustrated stories that portrayed friendships between children both with and without disabilities. The latter children had either a physical disability (e.g., were in a wheelchair) or a learning difficulty (e.g., Down syndrome).

Different forms of extended contact stories were tested by Cameron and Rutland. Some of these stories did not emphasize the social category the protagonists belonged to (i.e., the physically disabled) and instead stressed the characters' individual traits (i.e., their friendliness). This type of extended contact followed a decategorization approach in which the child's group membership was not empathized and the attention of the children reading the stories was drawn to the personal characteristics of those within the stories. According to the decategorization approach (Brewer & Miller, 1984), in order for positive attitude change to occur during cross-group contact, the outgroup member should not be perceived as being a member of the outgroup but instead should be treated as an individual. In this way, group boundaries will become irrelevant and people will be treated as individuals rather than as group members. There is, however, mixed evidence with regard to this approach (see Gonzalez & Brown, 2003).

In contrast, other stories highlighted both the child's social category and their personal characteristics. This form of extended contact took an intergroup approach, since the children were encouraged to focus on whether the children in the stories were disabled or not, in addition to their individual traits (Brown & Hewstone, 2005). The idea here was to make sure the children thought those in the stories were typical and reflective of others from their social category (i.e., disabled) making it hard for the children in the story to be subtyped (i.e., "she is friendly but is not like all other disabled children"). There was also a neutral or control intervention, which involved stories that drew no attention to the characters' individual qualities or to which social category they belonged to. After reading the story and while still in their small groups, the children with no disabilities took part in a group discussion of the stories, which was led by the researcher. The discussion emphasized the important and salient aspects of that intervention condition (i.e., individual characteristics or group membership, depending on the intervention condition). The intervention occurred once a week for six consecutive weeks.

It was found that, following the story reading, children had more favorable outgroup attitudes, and this was most pronounced when extended contact involved the intergroup approach. In addition, children, no matter what stories they read, expressed more positive intended behavior after the interventions (e.g., they said they were more likely to want to play with children with disabilities), but this was most evident with the stories that took an intergroup and decategorization approach. These findings support the use of extended contact as an intervention to improve young children's attitudes toward people with disabilities. They also contribute to the debate surrounding generalization and demonstrate the importance of maintaining group boundaries and heightening perceived typicality in order to obtain generalization from the contact situation to the whole outgroup. When children think the ingroup child in the story is typical of their group (i.e., not an unusual member of the group) they do not just show improved positive attitudes towards the outgroup member in the story, they also show more positive attitudes to the whole outgroup. This finding also concurs with the results of Wright et al. (1997) and Liebkind and McAlister (1999), who underscored the importance of emphasizing typicality during extended contact.

Another study by Cameron, Rutland, Brown, and Douch (2006) also varied what level of social categorization was salient using different models of story reading-based extended intergroup contact (Figure 8.1). This study examined majority status White English children's attitudes toward Black refugees. It was conducted in the southeast part of England, a region where tensions have periodically arisen between the majority status community and refugees due to the area's proximity to mainland Europe. Thus, children were likely to be aware of the negative attitudes and stereotypes towards refugees within their community. It was also set against a political context in which the British government was simultaneously seeking to

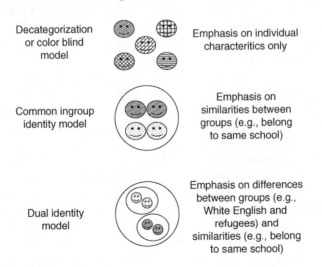

Figure 8.1 Different models for extended contact among children. (Source: Cameron et al., 2006.)

restrict the numbers of refugees to the country and stressing the importance of integrating them into British society.

First, in some stories the social categories of the characters were not mentioned and instead individual characteristics were emphasized (i.e., decategorization approach described above). In other stories, the super-ordinate (i.e., school) category membership of the story characters was stressed (i.e., common ingroup identity approach). This approach was developed by Gaertner and Dovidio (2000), who recommend that contact is most effective with the creation of a common ingroup that includes the ingroup (e.g., White English) and former outgroup (e.g., Black refugees) members in one superordinate category (e.g., the school they all attend). In this way, positive attitudes toward the ingroup members should then be extended to the new ingroup members, the erstwhile outgroup members. Research that supports this approach to contact comes from a variety of settings, including stepfamilies that are trying to become one family unit and minimal group studies (Banker & Gaertner, 1998; Gaertner, Jeffrey, Audrey, & Dovidio, 1989).

Finally, the protagonists' subgroup identities as White English and Black refugees were salient in other stories while also underlining their common school identity (i.e., dual identity approach). This approach is an amalgamation of the successful intergroup model used by Cameron and Rutland (2006) and the common ingroup approach. With this approach, Gaertner and Dovidio (2000) contend that it is possible for individuals to hold both the original ingroup identity and the common ingroup identity simultaneously. Thus, the goal of the dual identity approach is to invoke a superordinate identity while encouraging the retention of its constituent subgroup identities. The dual identity approach allows generalization through the maintenance of subgroup salience, and evidence is beginning to emerge that it is indeed associated with less intergroup bias, especially among adult minority groups (Gonzalez & Brown, 2003). There was also a control group of children who were exposed to no stories.

The results showed that all children who experienced the extended contact stories significantly increased their positive attitudes towards refugees compared to the children in the control group. Furthermore, dual identity extended contact was significantly better than the other forms of contact in achieving this attitude change. These findings show the value of promoting a common ingroup identity when trying to reduce children's prejudice, and are also compatible with the notion that contends children are more likely to generalize a positive outgroup attitude from the contact situation to the whole outgroup when subgroup categories remain salient. Thus, the process of extended contact operates by changing children's cognitive representations of social relations, and the self begins to treat ingroup members, to some extent, like the self (Cameron et al., 2006). Thus, when an ingroup member, who is seen as part of the self, has an outgroup close friendship, that person and perhaps the outgroup itself is seen positively as part of the self.

Recent research amongst children suggests that extended contact stories, and especially those involving friendships, improve intergroup attitudes by reducing anxiety about interacting with outgroup members (Cameron, Rutland, & Hossain, 2007). Cameron and colleagues also found that intergroup bias was reduced by extended contact stories through making children think that others like them think intergroup friendships are legitimate and normal (i.e., it changes the norm the children think their group has about having cross-group friendships). This is not surprising since we described research in chapter 4 which showed that in middle childhood children are sensitive to group norms for intergroup relations, what they should and should not do to "fit" in with the group. In fact children's perceived group norms about the appropriateness of intergroup friendships may be a major barrier to the formation of friendships between children from different groups. For example, Aboud and Sankar (2007) found that when children thought about who to be friends with they were concerned about what their ingroup peers would think about an outgroup friend, and whether they would get along with them. However, it appears that having positive extended contact changes the group norms for cross-group friendships, thereby making general attitudes more positive and reducing general anxiety or worries children have about intergroup contact itself.

Promoting Inclusion through the Mass Media

The studies on extended contact described above have shown how this approach promotes positive attitudes amongst children, though they have concentrated on relatively small-scale interventions based on story reading. Will this approach prove effective when challenging social exclusion on a larger scale and in a more hostile intergroup context in which groups are often in conflict and harbor very negative stereotypes? To answer this question one could look at broad-based media interventions which have been used throughout the world. Television serves as a source of information about the social world to children. As Bar-Tal and Teichman (2005) report, 87% of preschool-aged Israeli-Jewish children report learning about Arabs through television programs. While television may serve as a source of stereotypic information and result in social exclusion, high-quality programming can also work to combat such stereotypic information and promote social inclusion through the extended Contact Hypothesis. Educational television not only promotes cognitive skill acquisition and development but also promotes moral development and prosocial behaviors, including stereotype reduction (see Fisch & Truglio, 2001). For example, Graves (1999) reports that viewing a cartoon comprised of multi-ethnic characters led to positive changes in the attitudes of African-American children. These changes were represented by: (1) higher levels of identification with same-race messages; (2) recognition of positive emotions of a same-race character; and (3) recall of activities of the character along with cultural features of the character's environment (LaRose & Eisenstock, 1981). Moreover, European-American preschoolers, after 2 years of viewing *Sesame Street* when it first aired in the late 1960s, reported more positive attitudes towards African-Americans and Latino-Americans (Bogatz & Ball, 1971).

A major broadcast media intervention has been conducted by Sesame Workshop in the Middle East working with children in Israel (Israeli-Jewish), Gaza (Israeli-Palestinian), and the West Bank (Palestinian) to promote tolerance and reduce stereotypes (Cole et al., 2003). In the Middle East, research has demonstrated that young children have negative stereotypes about the outgroup, and that messages throughout the media reinforce negative attributes about the outgroup (Bar-Tal & Teichman, 2005; Brenick et al., 2010; Teichman & Zafrir, 2003). One of the program goals for Sesame Workshop is to collaborate with local broadcasters in troubled regions of the world to promote tolerance and mutual respect in young children (Cole, Labin, & del Rocio Galarza, 2008). The show produced in the Middle East called *Shara'a Simsim/ Rechov Sumsum* was a co-production of Israeli and Palestinian children's media providers with Sesame Workshop, and included bilingual episodes and cross-over segments in which characters from *Shara'a Simsim* (the Palestinian street) visited characters on *Rechov Sumsum* (the Israeli street) and vice versa. This broadcast involved characters from the Palestinian and Israeli communities engaging in positive interaction and forming friendships. Here there is, if not explicitly stated, a form of extended contact since children from each side of the conflict in the Middle East were learning of someone from their group having a positive friendship (e.g., holding hands, laughing and playing games together) with someone from the other group. These broadcasts also highlighted the religious and ethnic traditions of each respective society, illustrating such core themes as acceptance, friendship, and the appreciation of similarities and differences.

The results from these broadcasts revealed that following the viewing of *Shara'a Simsim/Rechov Sumsum*, the Israeli-Jewish and Israeli-Palestinian children significantly increased their positive views of members of the other culture, and the Israeli-Jewish children significantly decreased their negative views of members of the other culture. All three groups of children (Israeli-Jewish, Israeli-Palestinian, Palestinian) increasingly used prosocial reasoning, such as sharing toys or taking turns, when resolving peer conflict situations (Cole et al., 2003).

A program was created following this first intervention, called *Sesame Stories*, and was aired in 2003 with the same theme (Brenick, et al., 2007, 2010). A new evaluation project extended the prior study in several ways. First, the project evaluated children's exposure to *Sesame Stories*, a new production from Sesame Workshop. Second, this project targeted a large audience of children from four regions, including Tel Aviv, Gaza, the West Bank, and Aman, Jordan. The study added Jordanian preschoolers to the sample, creating four Arab groups, to allow for an even more detailed within-Arab group analysis.

Significantly, children's exposure to this new show was systematically examined by using a controlled viewing design, in which a group of children watched the show over 8 weeks, three times a week for 24 exposures to the program. A second group of children, who were matched to the intervention sample for age and culture, were not exposed to repeated viewings of the show in their classroom, and served as the control group. Finally, the project involved more comprehensive measurements of children's understanding of the characters as well as story comprehension, social goals, moral concepts, and conflict resolution judgments. The overall findings indicated that children from all four cultural contexts (Tel Aviv, Gaza, the West Bank, and Aman) had a very positive response to viewing of selected *Sesame Stories* programs regularly over a period of several weeks. Furthermore, the results revealed that children understood the moral themes embedded in the stories. When presented with moral reasoning problems (e.g., exclusion from a group based on gender or cultural membership) after exposure to *Sesame Stories*, a majority of children responded with positive or inclusive moral explanations (for more details about the results, see Brenick et al., 2007). Additionally, the interviews provided basic developmental information regarding how young children in the Middle East evaluate social conflict scenarios, particularly those that involve exclusion of children based on gender, cultural membership, and stereotypes. Thus, media intervention in the form of television shows geared for young children can have positive outcomes.

Sesame Street programming is an effective media intervention, in general, due to the fact that it allows children to identify with the characters by age, gender, and ethnicity, and offers familiar, child-relevant content, such as dealing with situations they would face in their everyday lives (Fisch & Truglio, 2001), as well as in this particular situation, because it is informed by research from developmental psychology and intergroup relations. In *Shara'a Simsim/Rechov Sumsum* exchanges and interactions between peers and "equals" (e.g., muppets and children) serve to provide key information about moral exchanges.

Similar effects from broadcast media interventions are seen with Macedonian, Albanian, Roma, and Turkish children who all showed increases in positive attitudes towards members of their own and the other group(s) after viewing *Nashe Maalo* (*Our Neighborhood*), a children's television program that represented children from each of the four ethnicities in an effort to promote mutual respect and understanding (Brenick et al., 2007). Other positive effects of viewing *Nashe Maalo* included higher ratings of self-perception, higher percentages of correctly identifying the other ethnic languages, and higher percentages of willingness to invite children from another ethnic group into their home (Common Ground Productions – Search for Common Ground in Macedonia and Sesame Workshop, 2000). These findings are all the more impressive given the high level of conflict between these groups. The *Shara'a Simsim/Rechov Sumsum* intervention in the Middle East also increased children's identification of cultural symbols, prosocial reasoning in regards to the peer social conflict scenarios, and decreased stereotyping (Brenick et al., 2010). Overall, the studies described above suggest that extended contact via mass media is effective when challenging social exclusion on a larger scale and hostile intergroup context, in which groups are often in conflict and harbor very negative stereotypes.

Intergroup Contact and Promoting Moral Reasoning in Children

Other research has also shown that as children encounter others from different ethnic and cultural backgrounds these cross-group friendships and interactions appear to promote moral reasoning about exclusion, and enable adolescents to reject stereotypic expectations about others (due to their understanding that their friendship peers do not hold the negative qualities promoted in societal stereotypic images). For example, Crystal and colleagues assessed the level of interracial interactions in the neighborhood and community together with the existence of cross-race friendships among 9- to 15-year-old racial majority and racial minority American children (Crystal, Killen, & Ruck, 2008). These children were shown scenarios depicting racial-based exclusion in cross-race relationships. There were three scenarios: lunch (exclusion during a lunch break where it was a personal choice between two friends with no external pressure); a sleepover (excluding a child from a sleepover due to parental discomfort); and a dance (excluding a child from cross-race dating in high school because of peer pressure). After hearing all the scenarios, children were asked to attribute a motive to the protagonist who did the excluding, judge the wrongfulness of the exclusion decision, and estimate the frequency of the type of exclusion observed among their peers.

Crystal and colleagues (2008) found that children with higher levels of intergroup contact gave higher ratings of the wrongfulness of exclusion and lower frequency estimations of race-based exclusion than did children reporting lower levels of contact. In addition, in two of the three scenarios, children with high contact were less likely than children with low contact to perceive the social exclusion as motivated by reasons that were not based on race, such as a lack of shared interests. These findings suggest that interracial contact not only influences children's ethnic attitudes but also impacts their social reasoning about race-based exclusion.

Another recent study also examined cross-race friendships and the use of stereotypes to explain interracial discomfort (Killen, Richardson, Kelly, Crystal, & Ruck, 2010). European-American participants at fourth (9 years of age), seventh (12 years) and 10th (15 years) grades ($N = 414$), attending high and low ethnically diverse public schools (with high and low self-reports of cross-race friendships, respectively), evaluated interracial peer encounters (e.g., at lunch). Participants enrolled in high-diversity schools were less likely to use stereotypes to explain racial discomfort and were more likely to view racial exclusion as being more wrong than were participants in low-diversity schools. Examples of stereotypic statements to explain interracial exclusion were: "He may not want to have lunch with him because they probably don't have the same interests because they're different looking" or "She isn't going to date him because when you're different skin color you just act differently." Children and adolescents who attended all-White schools were more likely to use such statements, reflecting their lack of contact and friendship with peers of different ethnic backgrounds. While there were no age differences for the explicit use of stereotypes, which was surprising, there were age differences for the recognition that peers used stereotypes to exclude others, which increased with age.

Intergroup contact within the school and community is important to the promotion of moral reasoning about social exclusion, which is known to result in positive attitudes towards different racial groups. Further, a high level of such contact aids children and adolescents to challenge negative societal attitudes about cross-race friendships and societal expectations about race-based exclusion.

Multicultural Education and Social Exclusion

A type of intervention commonly used in many societies is multicultural education. This approach, like the Contact Hypothesis, works under the assumption that prejudice and social exclusion is a result of ignorance about the outgroup (Hill & Augustinos, 2001). Multicultural approaches in the areas of education and societal change include the complex problem of both celebrating diversity by respecting cultural identities and, at the same time, recognizing that such identities are often viewed in negative terms by the majority group (Verkuyten, 2008). Multicultural interventions are not often founded upon research evidence drawn from psychology or any other social science. However, there are some examples of research that have examined in schools the use of a variety of socialization influences (e.g., story books, videos, games, activities) to promote multicultural awareness. For example, one intervention conducted with fourth grade (9 years of age) children in Hawaii, over a 10-week period, used a variety of methods (e.g. "multicultural bingo," "hands activity") to encourage children to address their ethnic and cultural differences and similarities (Salzman & D'Andrea, 2001). This study found the teachers, but not the children, reported more cooperative social interaction between the different ethnic groups. Other research suggests that multicultural interventions can often be ineffective and even have detrimental effects on children's intergroup attitudes. For example, these interventions, by highlighting certain stereotypic activities (e.g., songs or cultural practices), sometimes reinforces negative ethnic stereotypes (see for a review Bigler, 1999).

There has been, however, some research that suggests multicultural education helps create a school climate that promotes positive attention to cultural diversity, deals with negative interactions between children from different groups, and promotes tolerance to others from diverse cultures (see Verkuyten, 2008). For example, research in the United States shows that teaching 6- to 11-year-old European-American children explicitly about historical racial discrimination can improve their racial attitudes (Hughes, Bigler, & Levy, 2007). Hughes and colleagues (2007) showed that European-American children who learnt about historical racism held more positive and less negative attitudes towards African-Americans, and they also showed an increase in the degree to which they valued racial fairness.

The Dutch education system since 1985 has legally required schools to follow a multicultural curriculum to improve children's understanding of cultural differences, to limit prejudice and discrimination, and to promote moral reasoning about showing fairness to those from all groups. In reality, many Dutch schools implement little multicultural education and even when it is undertaken there is a lack of research examining effectiveness. Rare examples of such research are the studies by Verkuyten and colleagues into the effects of multicultural education on children's and adolescent's experiences of social exclusion and their intergroup attitudes (Kinket & Verkuyten, 1999; Verkuyten, 2003; Verkuyten & Kinket, 2000; Verkuyten & Thijs, 2001, 2002).

Ethnic victimization in the form of racist name-calling is a common form of bullying in schools (Smith & Shu, 2000). Verkuyten and Thijs (2002) examined how this type of social exclusion amongst Dutch, Turkish-Dutch, Moroccan-Dutch, and Surinamese-Dutch preadolescents is related to school (de)segregation and multicultural education. They surveyed 10- to 12-year-olds from 178 classrooms in 82 elementary schools across the Netherlands. A multilevel analysis showed that personal experience and perceptions of ethnic name-calling, teasing, and exclusion in the playground were determined independently by classroom settings and structure. In particular, Verkuyten and Thijs found that children experienced less exclusion if they believed they could tell the teachers about unfair behavior towards them and the teacher would take action (for a similar finding in the US, see Crystal, Killen, & Ruck, 2010). Dutch children also reported more awareness of ethnic exclusion if they said their classes spent more time discussing multicultural issues (e.g., the need to be fair to others from different countries and recognize different cultures within the class and society). Other studies (Kinket & Verkuyten, 1999; Verkuyten & Thijs, 2001) have also shown that

10- to 13-year-old Dutch and Turkish Dutch children reporting higher levels of multicultural education in the classroom, showed less ethnic intergroup bias.

These studies indicate that the local multicultural context within the classroom can help limit ethnic exclusion and the development of negative ethnic intergroup attitudes. Verkuyten (2008) contends that practices in the classroom (e.g., teachers who deal with examples of ethnic exclusion and discuss the need for fairness towards all cultures) help establish a positive inclusive group norm within the classroom that discourage social exclusion. In contrast, more formal aspects of multicultural education (e.g., teaching children about cultural traditions held by different ethnic groups) acted to limit negative attitudes by improving children's knowledge and understanding. Verkuyten and Thijs (2001, 2002) also found that ethnic minority Dutch children reported more ethnic victimization and exclusion if they attended ethnically non-mixed schools (i.e., where White Dutch children were clearly in the majority) and White Dutch children showed more ethnic intergroup bias if they attended these same ethnically non-mixed schools. Thus, the ethnic composition of a school influences the level of social exclusion and intergroup bias shown by children.

Factors that Reduce Childhood Bias

In order to show how research in developmental and social psychology can inform attempts to create such a social and normative environment, in Table 8.1 we have indicated the factors that play a role in the reduction of social exclusion in children's lives. Table 8.1 identifies intergroup contact and cross-group friendships, which we have discussed in depth within this chapter, however it also suggests that schools and communities need to promote moral and fairness-based reasoning, a sense of common identity with a shared purpose, and inclusive social norms that condemn the exclusion of others unless it is for legitimate reasons to make a group function effectively.

Firstly, there is a substantial body of research evidence (discussed in chapter 2) showing children's explicit moral judgments lead them to reject intergroup biases, as well as explicit social-conventional judgments and stereotypic expectations. These findings suggest that interventions that promote moral over social-conventional or stereotypical reasoning could help reduce children's prejudice and stereotyping which often leads them to condone social exclusion. Secondly, research has shown the

Table 8.1 Summary of key factors that reduce childhood bias. (© 2010 Adam Rutland and Melanie Killen)

Key factor	Examples of relevant empirical studies	Major conclusions
Moral judgment and fairness reasoning	Killen & Stangor (2001) Killen et al. (2002) Abrams et al. (2008) Killen et al. (2001)	Bias will decrease if children engage in moral reasoning and use moral principles (e.g. fairness) when evaluating all groups
Common ingroup identity	Dovidio et al. (2005) Banker & Gaertner (1998) Cameron et al. (2006)	Bias will diminish with the development of a common inclusive group identity
Social norms	Abrams et al. (2007) Rutland et al. (2005) Nesdale, Durkin. et al. (2005)	Bias will decrease amongst children who show self-presentation in line with inclusive social norms
Direct cross-group friendships	McGlothlin & Killen (2010) Crystal et al. (2008) Edmonds & Killen (2009) Turner et al. (2007)	Explicit and implicit bias will be reduced by direct intergroup contact involving cross-group friendships
Extended or indirect intergroup contact	Cameron & Rutland (2006) Cameron et al. (2006) Cameron et al. (2007)	Bias will reduce if children are aware of cross-group friendships between members of the ingroup and outgroup

development of a common inclusive social identity rather than singular exclusive social identity in both a family and school context can reduce children's intergroup biases and their tendency to engage in social exclusion. Thirdly, as we discussed in chapter 4, developmental psychologists have recently begun to demonstrate that group norms affect how children learn to control their explicit ethnic prejudice. Increasing children's *accountability* to their peer group, in the sense that their actions are visible and may have to be defended or could be criticized, typically makes anti-prejudice or inclusive social norms salient, thus it promotes positive intergroup judgments and decreases the likelihood of social exclusion. The factors shown in Table 8.1 all originate from robust research into the development of children's moral reasoning, prejudice, and group identity that we have reviewed and discussed comprehensively in the preceding chapters.

Summary

Intergroup contact interventions are a promising approach when attempting to reduce children's prejudice and challenge social exclusion. However, any educational strategy that will challenge social exclusion in childhood needs to foster an overall social climate and set of norms within the school and classroom that promote fairness and recognize the need for norms that make groups function harmoniously (Nucci, 2001).

In this chapter we have shown how interventions that focus on the need to encourage moral reasoning, reduce prejudice, and challenge exclusive group identities and norms will reduce social exclusion. In the next chapter, we describe our integrative theoretical model in depth, one that that has generated research on these different aspects of social exclusion, and one that will further generate new lines of research to understand social exclusion in childhood.

Chapter 9

Integration of Morality, Prejudice, and Group Identity: A New Perspective on Social Exclusion

Throughout this book we have described different approaches to understanding social inclusion and exclusion in children's lives. We have described this as a complex developmental phenomenon that reveals children's emerging morality and group identity, as well as prejudice and bias. The overarching question has been why do individuals exclude one another from social groups and what does it mean from the child's perspective? Why it is that children begin to exclude one another based on group membership, such as gender, race, ethnicity, and culture, and what are the forces that prompt children to be inclusive and to reject biases about groups that are often pervasive in children's worlds? What changes take place from early childhood and adolescence and what is the role of social influences?

Theories about Peer Relationships

The predominant developmental theories that have investigated children's experiences with exclusion have focused on peer relationships and social information processing, both of which focus on the individual and the individual in the context of group interactions. These theories do not focus on group dynamics and group identity, however, and do not address issues of prejudice, on the one hand, or morality, on the other

Children and Social Exclusion: Morality, Prejudice, and Group Identity. Melanie Killen and Adam Rutland. © 2011 Melanie Killen and Adam Rutland. Published 2011 by Blackwell Publishing Ltd.

hand. Yet, the predominant theories provide a wealth of information about how children understand peer relationships and their attribution of intentions, as well as a self concept, which are central for understanding all forms of exclusion.

As an example, research on peer relationships has pointed to the bases by which children make friendships, reject peers, and navigate the social landscape (see Rubin, Bukowski, & Parker, 2006). This body of research has pointed out what makes peer relationships complex, and how it is that children acquire social skills such as learning how to enter peer groups, establish friendships, and resolve conflicts. An important finding from this research has to do with the consequences of exclusion and peer rejection for children. Extensive experiences of peer rejection result in depression, anxiety, and loneliness (Bierman, 2004), and interventions that focus on social skills training have been beneficial for children who have trouble reading the social cues of others.

What we have focused on is peer exclusion where the source is not the individual social deficits of a child (e.g., lacking social skills) but general societal expectations about groups that lead to exclusion, and how this type of exclusion originates in childhood. It is common for adults to assume that exclusion based on race, religion, or gender is not part of childhood but reflective of the adult world. Yet, as has been described in detail in this book, exclusion based on group categories emerges early in childhood. The consequences for children who experience this type of exclusion has been shown to be similar to that experienced by children who are rejected by peers due to social deficits, making both types of exclusion important to understand and examine.

Social information processing research has also revealed extensive findings about children's social relationships, focusing on how children read cues from others and the attributions that they make about other children's behavior (Dodge et al., 2003). Much of this research has been devoted to understanding aggressive children, and what leads to bully–victim relationships. Moving away from the "bad seed" model, social information processing approaches have provided vast information regarding the complexity of the social profile of children who are identified as aggressive, or "bullies," as well as children who are identified as "victims" (Coplan, Girardi, Findlay, & Frohlick, 2007; Salmivalli & Peets, 2009). In fact, children who are bullies are often victims in other contexts. One particularly prominent finding has been to show that children who are susceptible to being aggressive overattribute negative intentions, referred to as the "hostile attribution bias" (Peets, Hodges, Kikas, & Salmivalli, 2007). These findings provide relevant information for understanding peer exclusion due to the consequences of negative attributions of intentions. In fact, as described in other chapters, minority children and adolescents are often the recipients of attributions of negative intentions based solely on their minority status, leading to prejudice and bias from the majority group not from children diagnosed as "aggressive." The measures used to demonstrate biases from the majority towards the minority have been derived from social information processing studies.

Theories about Social Exclusion

As described in chapters 2 and 5, domain-specific social-cognitive developmental models, which share a contextual foundation similar to many contemporary theories in developmental science (Keil, 2006; Kuhn & Siegler, 2006; Turiel, 2006), address issues of social exclusion. These approaches are ones that delve into how children understand the world and the meaning that they attribute to the wide range of events, interactions, and relationships that they experience in different social contexts. Children's social judgments determine their social behavior and reaction to events in the world, and their experiences then feed back to the formation of their judgments, much in the way that Piaget (1932), Vygotsky (1962), and other interactional theorists have explained development. These theories provide a basis to understand the complexity of children's experiences in social groups and how they view exclusion from groups in a range of normative as well as maladaptive contexts.

The main findings that have been highlighted are that, first, children often justify exclusion using conventional, not moral reasons, drawing on their interpretations of cultural traditions as well as hierarchies that are perpetuated and are often based on gender, race, and ethnicity. Conventional reasons are often heavily influenced by cultural messages and emphasized as important for maintaining group identity. Second, children understand that prejudicial behavior is unfair but often do not apply moral reasons to contexts that appear to be highly salient from a group identity perspective. This is due, in part, to children's recognition about the importance of groups as well as messages from the culture. Children enjoy being in groups, and spontaneously create many rules, customs, and traditions that guide their own peer group interactions. These rules are often constructed together, designed to create their own culture ("We like to do it this way!"). It is important for children to create groups and to figure out what it means to be a member of a group. What is difficult, though, is how to decide who can, will, or should be a member, and how inclusion and exclusion gets negotiated.

Third, group identity is both positive (affiliative) and negative (generating ingroup favoritism) and with age children understand these different aspects of social groups. Children want to be members of groups and quickly interpret exclusion or rejection negatively. Understanding that there are times when exclusion is legitimate is just as important as knowing when it is wrong. By late adolescence, individuals' differentiations of groups and the criteria for inclusion and exclusion become better understood. Yet, understanding the full scope of inclusion and exclusion is a life-long process. Adults find it difficult, and as parents sometimes overempathize with their children's rejection from groups. Examples of parents calling up coaches or teachers to complain about rejection are common, as well as contacting other parents to protest about their child's playgroup behavior regarding exclusion ("Why did your child not let my child play in his group at recess?").

Fourth, ingroup bias is often confused with outgroup dislike and disentangling this relationship is difficult for children as well as for adults. Preferring someone you know, who you identify with as being part of your own group, is not the same as disliking someone else who is associated with an outgroup, but this often gets interpreted as a non-benign decision, especially by a member of an outgroup who is excluded. Carefully differentiating these decisions is important for creating positive social relationships. Of course, there are many times when ingroup preference is related to outgroup dislike and the consequences are detrimental, but this connection is not automatic and requires close appraisal.

Fifth, children, with age, in fact will prefer a member of an outgroup who supports ingroup norms over an ingroup member who deviates from group norms. Children begin to switch their focus from group identity to group norms, and care more about the latter than the former, in some contexts. This change can be helpful as it creates more diversity in groups, especially when group identity is broadened to include other individuals. When a boy includes a girl in his group because she shares the group norm then the entire group's expectations about traits based on group identity can be altered and modified, which is a way of reducing stereotypes and prejudice.

Sixth, children like members of groups who support positive norms (such as voicing equality) more than those who support negative norms (such as voicing inequality). Children are more reluctant to exclude deviant members of groups who express positive rather than negative norms, and this is a fundamental aspect of understanding how groups work.

Finally, there are many ways in which both direct and extended intergroup contact provide a positive source of experience for children, which reduces prejudice in childhood. High-quality experiences with peers from different backgrounds and groups allow children to make their own inferences about people. This experience can show them that traits that they hear attributed to others based on group membership (that is, stereotypes) may be wrong. This process has been shown to reduce prejudice because it enables children to reject stereotypic expectations about others.

While there are many more distinctions and nuances to children's coordination of group identity and morality in the context of exclusion, we have highlighted a few findings that reveal how much children learn early on and have to understand to figure out when it is legitimate to exclude others, and when it is wrong or unfair. From this approach, children are active participants in their understanding of the social world. Parents play a role but are not the only source of information for children, nor do children passively adopt parental messages, even when it comes to exclusion, prejudice, and bias.

Children as Active Participants

While messages from adults and society are conveyed to children in both explicit and implicit ways, and children are significantly influenced by these messages, children display an amazingly strong resistance to being molded and shaped by adults. From the beginning children reject, resist, and challenge adult pressure and influence in the areas of prejudice and exclusion. This viewpoint about parent–child relationships runs counter to the predominant view that children do not "conform" enough to parental mandates and that parents need to socialize children to become good citizens (for reviews of parental socialization practices, see Grusec & Davidov, 2010; Grusec & Goodnow, 1994; Smetana & Turiel, 2003). This is because traditional views of parenting hold an assumption that parental values are always positive and that children are blank slates, or worse, aggressive and selfish. In contrast, studies over the past several decades in developmental science have demonstrated that parent–child relationships are bidirectional, and that children influence their parents as parents influence their children. In the area of morality this has been shown to be the case as described in chapter 2. Similarly, though, this is the case with prejudice as has been described by current developmental researchers (see Aboud & Amato, 2001; Killen, Richardson, & Kelly, 2010). There are times when parents hold traditional views that reflect prejudicial attitudes, when children can be a positive source of influence and promote change.

In fact, with age, children (particularly with certain types of experiences such as cross-race friends) reject parental messages that condone racial exclusion. Further, it has been shown that adolescents in heterogeneous schools reject parental messages about refraining from cross-race dating and friendships in adolescence (Edmonds & Killen, 2009). For some youth, it is wrong to refrain from bringing home a friend of a different race, for example, just because parents might feel uncomfortable about it ("Sometimes you have to teach your parents that it's wrong and it's racist"). Just because children state that it is wrong for parents to put this type of pressure on them does not mean, however, that this source of influence is not effective. Parents help children to understand the connections between acts and consequences, and this interactive process enables children to formulate principles of right and wrong, as well as to develop concepts about individuals, groups, and relationships. Children are influenced by parental attitudes, even when they do not want to be, and throughout the studies that we have reported children and adolescents also explain how you have to "listen to your parents" and "maybe they know something that you don't know." This was documented in studies in which children indicated that one should go along with parental desires to avoid cross-race dating or friendships (Killen, McGlothlin, & Lee-Kim, 2002).

Thus, while parental values and messages are influential, the direction of the message is not unidirectional and understanding children's values and beliefs are necessary for understanding the developmental process. Unlike often-stated theoretical expectations from social psychologists, in fact, very few studies have documented unidirectional correlations between parental and child forms of prejudice (see Aboud & Doyle, 1996; Castelli, Zogmaister, & Tomelleri, 2009). This lends further support to the view that children do not acquire prejudice by simply imitating their parents or from modeling parental attitudes, as was suggested by learning theory more than half a century ago. Allport (1954) in his foundational treatise on the nature of prejudice, recognized the bidirectionality, and made a distinction between *adopting* prejudice and *developing* prejudice, where the latter reflected notions similar to Piaget's theory of the acquisition of social knowledge, which Allport cited in his book.

Yet, parents and adults are influential, and contribute to children's development of prejudice, both in terms of hindering as well as facilitating it. Parent–child relationships are an important factor for whether children rely on moral values to reject prejudice or defer to conventional justifications to condone it. What makes these relationships crucial is the solid foundation by which children feel secure (through attachment) and confident to voice their own viewpoints, as we discussed in the chapter focused on the emergence of morality.

Judgments, Beliefs, Attitudes, Attributions of Emotions, and Behavior

Thus delving into what children think about inclusion, exclusion, prejudice, and discrimination is revealing about the extent to which they view exclusion based on race, for example, as contingent on rules and authority mandates (as conventional rules are understood) or as wrong due to unfairness and inequality (as moral transgressions are evaluated). The first step towards challenging prejudicial attitudes is to recognize the types of attitudes that are prejudicial and reflect different types of biases. Thus, determining when and how children recognize when attitudes about others reflect stereotypes and how judgments about ingroup favoritism can lead to negative outcomes is a central goal for social-cognitive developmental research. Without this analysis, discovering when children challenge and confront such beliefs will not occur.

Children's judgments, beliefs, and attitudes

Understanding children's evaluations of exclusion necessitates what type of exclusion should be examined, exclusion based on race, gender, ethnicity, culture, or religion (along with other categories). This endeavor reveals that children and adolescents evaluate exclusion differently depending on the target (who is being excluded?), the context (in what setting?), and the domain of exclusion (what is the nature of the consequences of exclusion and who is affected by it?). Answering these questions provides the basis for our contextual perspective because the phenomenon of exclusion takes many different forms.

Along with investigating how children interpret and reason about acts of inclusion and exclusion (when is it okay, when is it wrong, and why?), it is also necessary to understand what they know about groups, and how groups work. Which types of group norms are legitimate, which are wrong, and how does one's identification with a group factor into these types of attitudes and evaluations of group expectations? Thus, the other aspect of determining the origins of prejudice is to understand the origins of groups, and group identity. In this book, we have discussed how quickly group identity can set in, even in early childhood, and what this means for children's evaluations of group norms. Children's evaluations of group norms are strongly related to their group identity. Moreover, identifying with one group often means forming an ingroup bias, which may, but not necessarily, lead to outgroup negativity. Acting on this negative outgroup attitude can lead to prejudice, such as in acts of exclusion, victimization, and discrimination. These connections have to be examined extensively, as we have done in this book.

It is necessary to investigate and understand both judgment and behavior. This is because it is near impossible to fully dichotomize behavior and judgment. It is not feasible to know exactly what someone is thinking while they are in an actual situation; even neuroscience techniques, which have pushed the field forward in many important ways, record brain activation while the participant is lying inside a tube pressing buttons and responding to hypothetical vignettes rather than in an actual situation. What is behavior without some type of judgment or cognitive assessment? Humans are thinking, reasoning beings, making decisions, judgments, and evaluations every day through multiple interactions, exchanges, and encounters. What is judgment without behavior? Behavior and experience provide the "grist for the mill" and are essential for development and change (Turiel, 2002). Thus, understanding exclusion, prejudice, morality, and group identity in childhood requires conducting research on the interactive relationship between judgment and behavior.

In some cases the concerns about the relationship between judgment and action have to do with the validity of self-report data, and particularly with the predictive validity of self-report. When someone states that they would help someone in a dire situation of need there is a concern about social desirability, that the individual is stating this because they want to appear helpful and kind. This type of statement is a prediction about one's own behavior. Most studies on children's social cognition, however, do not collect self-report data, nor are the data collected predictions about one's own behavior. Instead, the data reflect, for the most part, how children and adolescents understand the social world, and particularly experiences and events involving exclusion, prejudice, group identity, and morality. These data have to do with what children reveal about their interpretations, evaluations, and beliefs about events, interactions, and encounters among individuals in familiar settings (in general).

Children can be asked to evaluate actual situations and to evaluate what others do ("Is it okay or not okay?"), their feelings about others, such as targets of exclusion or prejudice ("How much do you like him/her?"), group dynamics ("Do you think the group likes him/her?"), and social reasons for these judgments and decisions. In addition, children can attribute intentions of others, assign traits on the basis of group membership, respond to questions about their own identity and their viewpoint about the identity of others, as well as respond to more indirect measures about peer encounters. Thus, these measures are social cognitive because they reflect children's attitudes, judgments, and beliefs. These measures are not about children's prediction of their behavior but about their interpretation of events in their world.

Studies on social judgments provide an indication as to the types of contexts and behavioral situations that elicit stereotypic expectations, as well as exclusion and prejudice. For example, social psychologists, studying adults, have shown that stereotypes are often activated in situations that are ambiguous, complex, and multifaceted (Clark & Clark, 1947; Dovidio et al., 2001). This has also been demonstrated in studies with children. In situations with a clear-cut moral decision, for example, such as whether it is all right to hit a young child for no reason, the vast majority of children view it as wrong and give reasons such as the wrongfulness of inflicting pain on another person. In situations in which there is ambiguity or complexity, judgments are not as straightforward. Thus, when asked whether it is all right to hit someone back who hit you first, children, particularly those living in highly stressful contexts and exposed to violence, will judge it as legitimate, even when they view unprovoked hitting as wrong (see Ardila-Rey, Killen, & Brenick, 2009; Astor, 1994).

In the area of exclusion, most children view straightforward exclusion based on group membership as wrong, such as denying access to a group based solely on gender, race, or ethnicity. In complex or ambiguous situations, children often rely on stereotypic expectations or conventions to make decisions (as do adult as well). Further, in situations in which group identity is activated or made salient, children often exclude to maintain group identity and reinforce group boundaries or norms. Morality, prejudice, and group identity have many aspects to them that make them complex, and this contributes to why it is necessary to understand both judgments and actions regarding these areas of social development. So far, explicit judgments have been discussed, and yet implicit and indirect biases are part of what contributes to prejudice and exclusion as well.

Implicit and Indirect Measures of Prejudice and Exclusion

Research on implicit biases has demonstrated that young children hold such biases, and that these biases are similar to ones reflected in adulthood, and appear to vary depending on the context, target, and social experience, such as intergroup contact. What we have focused on is what happens at the social-evaluative level. Individuals hold biases but they do not always act on them. If implicit biases were the guiding force behind social interactions and relationships then there would be little positive behavior towards members of outgroups. Yet, adults as well as children are motivated to act in positive ways, and make judgments about the ethics of social interactions, relationships, and groups. The steps between implicit bias and behavior towards others are social cognitive and evaluative, from our viewpoint, and require close scrutiny.

Children's and adolescent's judgments, beliefs, and understanding of group dynamics are important checks on implicit biases that develop early in childhood. In fact, little evidence exists to confirm that the connection between implicit biases and behavior or action is automatic. Devine and her colleagues have demonstrated some of the factors that motivate adults to inhibit prejudicial biases (Devine, Plant, Amodio, Harmon-Jones, & Vance, 2002). We have pointed to different factors, such as the emergence of morality in childhood, as well as the forms and functions of group identity, to explain why it is that some children reject prejudicial attitudes and biases. Implicit biases have to be understood in relation to conscious judgment and decision-making, which is where the "stuff" of prejudice and bias occurs (excluding someone from a peer group or refusing to hire an individual in a work context). What do children do with implicit associations? How does it relate to their decisions about who to play with, who to be friends with, and who to include in a group? There are many instances in which children have stereotype knowledge but do not act on it. Why not? This question has been addressed in this book, and reflects the complex connections between implicit bias and explicit judgments, for which much more work is needed to fully understand this relationship.

An Integrative Social-Cognitive Developmental Perspective on Social Exclusion

The emergence of exclusion and inclusion involves a close interplay between the emergence of moral reasoning, concerns about group functioning, and the motivation to become fully integrated into a social group. Our perspective addresses the apparent contradiction between the early onset of *both* prejudice and morality in childhood, by showing that children simultaneously develop the ability to reason about the social world while considering notions of group identity, social-conventional norms, and morality.

Changes within domains have to do with the coordination of information, which can be viewed in terms similar to executive control, which has been a large and substantive focus within developmental science over the past decade (see Carlson, 2005; Zelazo, Carlson, & Kesek, in press). Children have to weigh various considerations when making judgments, such as decisions to include or exclude, and these decisions require coordinating information about the group, the target, morally salient issues, personal relationships, social influences, and the social context. The more variables that have to be weighed the more difficult the decision becomes, when one is aware of all of the variables. Children are often not aware of all of the variables, however, and this makes the decision easier, at times, but not necessarily more valid. In fact, young children often view group decisions solely in terms of fairness issues in contrast to older children, who also focus on group identity and group functioning. Without an analysis of children's attitudes and judgments, children's behavior might be misinterpreted and not well understood. Children come in to this world with moral predispositions and typically develop at an early age categories that distinguish "us" and "them." Many factors contribute to why it is that children exclude others, including their social-cognitive development, social environment, peer relationships, and parental messages.

This is a very different view from many other prominent theories and approaches to understanding prejudice and exclusion in childhood. What makes it different is that this viewpoint takes into account the active child. That is, what does the child think about when making decisions to exclude others, and what contextual factors bear on these decisions? Most research on prejudice has concentrated on parental influences, the salience of social categories, or cognitive developmental immaturity. Each of these viewpoints, while contributing to the emergence of prejudice and social exclusion in childhood, misses a central aspect of why children are not always prejudiced.

Childhood exclusion in the form of prejudice is not inevitable, either due to basic or instinctive bias or environmental influences that are blindly imitated by children. Nor is social exclusion due to an inherent, innate flaw in a person's moral character. Instead children *and* adults actively construct their attitudes about decisions involving exclusion and inclusion, using their social-cognitive understanding to navigate between moral principles and group identity concerns. Whether children's ingroup identity results in outgroup prejudice is determined by a number of factors, including a strong social foundation in the form of healthy attachments and parent–child relationships, positive peer relationships and friendships, opportunities for high-quality intergroup contact, and a strong emphasis on inclusive group norms, a secure social identity, and moral reasoning.

Social Experience Factors that Promote Inclusion

Intergroup contact, both direct and indirect, serves to reduce prejudice and promote inclusion. This has to do with the opportunities for cross-group friendship that reduce anxiety, challenge stereotypic expectations, increase empathy, induce perspective-taking, and foster moral reasoning about fairness and equal treatment. As discussed in chapter 7, this phenomenon has been studied in childhood (Tropp & Prenovost, 2008) and the findings have been positive regarding the role of intergroup contact on exclusion and inclusion. For example, cross-race friendships reduce prejudice and enable children to challenge stereotypic expectations of members of outgroups. Research with adults (Mendoza-Denton & Page-Gould, 2008) has demonstrated the ways that cross-race friendships reduce anxiety as well as stress (Mendes, Gray, Mendoza-Denton, Major, & Epel, 2007).

Further, in a series of studies by Cameron and colleagues, children who have extended contact (hearing stories about children who have friendships with members of outgroups) show improved intergroup relations. One of the important outcomes of these findings has to do with the relationship between social experience (behavior) and judgment. Further, these studies indicate that developmental intergroup research has provided ways in which children's understanding of exclusion can be addressed through methods such as the promotion of intergroup contact, inclusive common identities and social norms, social-cognitive skills training, moral reasoning, and tolerance.

Exclusion and Prejudice

It is important to distinguish exclusion and prejudice; we do not use these terms interchangeably. We have delineated these examples in previous chapters such as in situations involving practical considerations (only 10 classmates can play a game together due to space), talent (only the fastest runners will join the track team), and merit (only students with the highest grades will be admitted to the Honor Society), to name a few. These decisions involve agreed-upon criteria and are recognized as dimensions that serve to increase group coherence and group goals.

The potential for exclusion decisions reflecting prejudice and bias occurs when the decision to exclude appears to be justifiable but, in fact, reflects the use of irrelevant criteria (e.g., group membership) that cannot be defended on any moral grounds. Thus, in the example of the game at recess, a group may exclude others due to the physical constraints of the space but if the group deliberately or unconsciously refrains from inviting children who are not the same race or ethnicity then this would be viewed as unjustified exclusion. Or if high grades are not assigned to girls in science due to stereotypic expectations then exclusion from the Honor Society may, in fact, reflect a history of prejudice or bias. Whether these decisions are a result of group identity or prejudice has to be determined, and cannot be assumed. Further, there are many contextual considerations, such that targets of exclusion in one context may be the excluders in another context. Disentangling practical considerations, merit, and talent, along with categories such as gender, race, and ethnicity are complicated for adults, and even more so for children. Our hope is that new lines of research in psychological science will provide more information for understanding the developmental origins, emergence, and manifestations of exclusion and inclusion in childhood.

Summary

Human history has shown that morality and prejudice often exist side by side. Social groups that have committed horrendous acts of violence towards others often provide nurture and assistance for members of the "ingroup." This nurture is provided to strengthen the ingroup while perpetuating extreme derogation of the outgroup. This juxtaposition of good and evil appears incomprehensible to most individuals. Yet, in a more normative context, one can ask how does the strengthening of the ingroup provide a justification for exclusion of the outgroup, especially when exclusion results in harm to others? This question has been the focus of many social psychology investigations, and, more recently, for developmental psychology.

Even more complicated are examples of moral leaders, who while striving for equality, justice, and fairness, treat an "outgroup" as less than human, which may also serve to strengthen the ingroup. Fiske and her colleagues have written about the dehumanization that often accompanies prejudice and discrimination (Fiske, 2002). The general point is that this prejudice, which exists alongside moral goals, is not justified by the morality but appears to be differentially applied to individuals along group identity lines, hence a domain distinction. Rather than interpreting these orientations as a confusion, individuals often evaluate these types of decisions from a domain-specific viewpoint, that is, the moral acts are distinct from actions that strengthen group identity (often resulting in derogation of the outgroup). For example, children and adolescents in schools often celebrate how notions of equality, justice, and fairness are central to being human, and yet, at the same time, may exclude their peers from social clubs when the peers look and act differently – such as students who are gay, from another religious group (Muslim in France or the Netherlands), from a different country (northern Africans in Spain), or recent immigrants (Latinos in the United States). We do not imply that all forms of exclusion and prejudice emerge from group identity, outgroup derogation, or ingroup bias. Clearly, there are forms of prejudice and exclusion that are the result of psychopathology and extreme deviance, with no logic or coherence or connection to group identity.

Navigating the social world poses many challenges for children and research over the past 25 years has revealed the complexity of children's social knowledge and their social understanding. No longer do we characterize the infant's world, for example, as a "bloomin', buzzin', confusion" (James, 1890) as was done in the dawn of psychology. Nor do we characterize the young child as "egocentric, selfish, and asocial," as was often suggested in child-rearing books from the latter part of the last century (Shelov, Remar, & Altmann, 1978). Children come into the world with a social predisposition and are highly tuned to social stimuli and social messages from parents, caregivers, and family members.

One of the most difficult and complex social decisions that children, adolescents, and adults make throughout their lives involves inclusion and exclusion of others. These decisions involve an understanding of others' perspectives, how groups function and become cohesive, what it means to show prosociality, when to apply principles of morality and fairness, when to understand interactions in the context of groups, conventions, and cultural histories. These are all key aspects of social development that connect the child to the world of others. Throughout this book we have provided a window into this process and hopefully we have shown how we can all help children figure out the complexities of social exclusion and inclusion. Social exclusion and inclusion allow children to learn about the social world, and indeed about whom they are and how they want to be defined. They are an essential part of becoming a social being. Understanding the complexity of social exclusion in childhood will help to alleviate not only the injustices that occur on the playgroup, but will provide the foundations of the trajectories of morality, prejudice, and group identity from childhood to adulthood. Social justice and injustice is part of the daily human existence, and shedding light on the developmental process is fundamental for moving towards a just and fair society, culture, and shared community.

References

Aboud, F. E. (1988). *Children and prejudice*. Oxford, England: Blackwell.

Aboud, F. E. (2005). The development of prejudice in childhood and adolescence. In J. F. Dovidio, P. Glick, & L. Rudman (Eds.), *On the nature of prejudice: Fifty years after Allport* (pp. 310–326). Malden, MA: Blackwell.

Aboud, F. E., & Amato, M. (2001). Developmental and socialization influences on intergroup bias. In R. Brown & S. Gaertner (Eds.), *Blackwell handbook of social psychology: Intergroup relations* (pp. 65–85). Oxford, England: Blackwell Publishers.

Aboud, F. E., & Doyle, A. B. (1996). Parental and peer influences on children on children's racial attitudes. *International Journal of Intercultural Relations, 20*, 371–383.

Aboud, F. E., & Levy, S. R. (2000). Interventions to reduce prejudice and discrimination in children and adolescents. In S. Oskamp (Ed.), *Reducing prejudice and discrimination* (pp. 269–293). Mahwah, NJ: Lawrence Erlbaum Associates.

Aboud, F. E., Mendelson, M. J., & Purdy, K. T. (2003). Cross-race peer relations and friendship quality. *International Journal of Behavioral Development, 27*, 165–173.

Aboud, F. E., & Sankar, J. (2007). Friendship and identity in a language-intergrated school. *International Journal of Behavioral Development, 31*, 445–453.

Abrams, D., & Hogg, M. A. (2001). Collective self. In M. A. Hogg & S. Tindale (Eds.), *Blackwell handbook of social psychology: Vol. 3, Group processes* (pp. 425–461). Oxford, England: Blackwell.

Abrams, D., Hogg, M. A., & Marques, J. M. (2005). A social psychological framework for understanding social inclusion and exclusion. In D. Abrams,

M. A. Hogg, & J. M. Marques (Eds.), *The social psychology of inclusion and exclusion* (pp. 1–24). New York, NY: Psychology Press.

Abrams, D., & Rutland, A. (2008). The development of subjective group dynamics. In S. Levy & M. Killen (Eds.), *Intergroup attitudes and relations in childhood through adulthood* (pp. 47–65). Oxford, England: Oxford University Press.

Abrams, D., Rutland, A., & Cameron, L. (2003). The development of subjective group dynamics: Children's judgments of normative and deviant in-group and out-group individuals. *Child Development, 74*, 1840–1856.

Abrams, D., Rutland, A., Cameron, L., & Ferrell, J. (2007). Older but wilier: In-group accountability and the development of subjective group dynamics. *Developmental Psychology, 43*, 134–148.

Abrams, D., Rutland, A., Cameron, L., & Marques, J. (2003). The development of subjective group dynamics: When in-group bias gets specific. *British Journal of Developmental Psychology, 21*, 155–176.

Abrams, D., Rutland, A., Ferrell, J. M., & Pelletier, J. (2008). Children's judgments of disloyal and immoral peer behavior: Subjective group dynamics in minimal intergroup contexts. *Child Development, 79*, 444–461.

Abrams, D., Rutland, A., Pelletier, J., & Ferrell, J. (2009). Children's group nous: understanding and applying peer exclusion within and between groups. *Child Development, 80*, 224–243.

Allport, G. W. (1954). *The nature of prejudice.* New York, NY: Doubleday Anchor Books.

Almas, I., Cappelen, A. W., Sörensen, E. O., & Tungodden, B. (2010). Fairness and the development of inequality acceptance. *Science, 328*, 1176–1178.

Ardila-Rey, A., Killen, M., & Brenick, A. (2009). Displaced and non-displaced Colombian children's reasoning about moral transgressions, retaliation, and reconciliation. *Social Development, 18*, 181–209.

Arsenio, W. F., & Gold, J. (2006). The effects of social injustice and inequality on children's moral judgments and behavior: Towards a theoretical model. *Cognitive Development, 21*, 388–400.

Arsenio, W. F., & Kramer, R. (1992). Victimizers and their victims: Children's conceptions of the mixed emotional consequenes of victimization. *Child Development, 63*, 915–927.

Arthur, A. E., Bigler, R. S., Liben, L. S., Gelman, S. A., & Ruble, D. N. (2008). Gender stereotyping and prejudice in young children: A developmental intergroup perspective. In S. Levy & M. Killen (Eds.), *Intergroup attitudes and relations in childhood through adulthood* (pp. 66–86). Oxford, England: Oxford University Press.

Astington, J., & Olson, D. R. (1995). The cognitive revolution in children's understanding of mind. *Human Development, 38*, 179–189.

Astor, R. A. (1994). Children's moral reasoning about family and peer violence: The role of provocation and retribution. *Child Development, 65,* 1054–1067.

Augoustinos, M., & Rosewarne, D. L. (2001). Stereotype knowledge and prejudice in children. *British Journal of Developmental Psychology, 19,* 143–156.

Baird, J. A., & Astington, J. W. (2004). The role of mental state understanding in the development of moral cognition and moral action. *New Directions for Child and Adolescent Development, 103,* 37–49.

Banaji, M., Baron, A. S., Dunham, Y., & Olson, K. (2008). Some experiments on the development of intergroup social cognition. In S. R. Levy & M. Killen (Eds.), *Intergroup relations: An integrative developmental and social psychological perspective* (pp. 87–104). Oxford, England: Oxford University Press.

Bandura, A. (1977). *Social learning theory.* Englewood Cliffs, NJ: Prentice-Hall.

Bandura, A. (1986). *Social foundations of thought and action: A social cognitive theory.* Englewood Cliffs, NJ: Prentice-Hall.

Banerjee, R. (2002). Audience effects on self-presentation in childhood. *Social Development, 11,* 487–507.

Banerjee, R., & Yuill, N. (1999a). Children's explanations of self-presentational behaviour. *European Journal of Social Psychology, 29,* 105–111.

Banerjee, R., & Yuill, N. (1999b). Children's understanding of self-presentational display rules: Associations with mental-state understanding. *British Journal of Developmental Psychology, 17,* 111–124.

Banker, B. S., & Gaertner, S. L. (1998). Achieving stepfamily harmony: An intergroup relations approach. *Journal of Family Psychology, 12,* 310–325.

Bar-Haim, Y., Ziv, T., Lamy, D., & Hodes, R. M. (2006). Nature and nurture in own-race face processing. *Psychological Science, 17,* 159–163.

Baron-Cohen, S., O'Riordan, M., Stone, V., Jones, R., & Plaisted, K. (1999). Recognition of faux pas by normally developing children and children with asperger syndrome or high-functioning autism. *Journal of Autism and Developmental Disorders, 29,* 407–418.

Baron, A. S., & Banaji, M. R. (2006). The development of implicit attitudes. *Psychological Science, 17,* 53–58.

Bar-Tal, D., & Teichman, Y. (2005). *Stereotypes and prejudice in conflict: Representations of Arabs in Israeli Jewish society.* New York, NY: Cambridge University Press.

Bennett, M., Barrett, M., Karakosov, R., Kipiani, G., Lyons, L., & Pavlenko, V. (2004). Young children's evaluations of the ingroup and of outgroups: A multi-national study. *Social Development, 13,* 124–141.

Bennett, M., Lyons, E., Sani, F., & Barrett, M. (1998). Children's subjective identification with the group and in-group favoritism. *Developmental Psychology, 34,* 902–909.

Bennett, M., & Sani, F. (Eds.). (2004). *The development of the social self*. New York, NY: Psychology Press.

Bennett, M., & Sani, F. (2008). Children's subjective identification with social groups. In S. Levy & M. Killen (Eds.), *Intergroup attitudes and relationships from childhood through adulthood* (pp. 19–31). Oxford, England: Oxford University Press.

Bennett, M., & Yeeles, C. (1990). Children's understanding of the self-presentational strategies of ingratiation and self-promotion. *European Journal of Social Psychology, 20,* 455–461.

Bierman, K. L. (2004). *Peer rejection: Developmental processes and intervention strategies*. New York, NY: Guilford Press.

Biernat, M. (2003). Toward a broader view of social stereotyping. *American Psychologist, 58,* 1019–1027.

Bigler, R. S. (1999). The use of multicultural curricula and materials to counter racism in children. *Journal of Social Issues, 55,* 687–705.

Bigler, R. S., Brown, C. S., & Markell, M. (2001). When groups are not created equal: Effects of group status on the formation of intergroup attitudes in children. *Child Development, 72,* 1151–1162.

Bigler, R. S., & Liben, L. (2006). A developmental intergroup theory of social stereotypes and prejudice. In R. Kail (Ed.), *Advances in child psychology* (pp. 39–90). New York, NY: Elsevier.

Blair, R. J. R. (1995). A cognitive development approach to morality: Investigating the psychopath. *Cognition, 57,* 1–29.

Blakemore, S. J., Winston, J., & Frith, U. (2004). Social cognitive neuroscience: Where are we heading? *Trends in Cognitive Sciences, 8,* 216–222.

Bogatz, G., & Ball, S. (1971). *The second year of Sesame Street: A continuing evaluation*. Princeton, NJ: Educational Testing Service.

Boivin, M., Hymel, S., & Bukowski, W. M. (1995). The roles of social withdrawal, peer rejection, and victimization by peers in predicting loneliness and depressed mood in children. *Development and Psychopathology, 7,* 765–786.

Brenick, A., Killen, M., Lee-Kim, J., Fox, N., Leavitt, L., Raviv, A., Masalha, S., Murra, F., & Smadi, Y. (2010). Social understanding in Young Israeli-Jewish, Israeli-Palestinian, Palestinian, and Jordanian children: Moral judgments and stereotypes. *Early Education and Development, 21,* 1–26.

Brenick, A., Lee-Kim, J., Killen, M., Fox, N. A., Leavitt, L. A., & Raviv, A. (2007). Social judgments in Israeli and Arabic children: Findings from media-based intervention projects. In D. Lemish & M. Gotz (Eds.), *Children, media and war* (pp. 287–308). Cresskill, NJ: Hampton Press.

Brewer, M. B. (1979). Ingroup bias in the minimal intergroup situation: A cognitive-motivational analysis. *Psychological Bulletin, 86,* 307–324.

Brewer, M. B. (1999). The psychology of prejudice: Ingroup love or outgroup hate? *Journal of Social Issues, 55*, 429–444.

Brewer, M. B., & Brown, R. (1998). Intergroup relations. In D. T. Gilbert, S. T. Fiske, & G. Lindzey (Eds.), *The handbook of social psychology* (Vol. 2, pp. 554–594). New York, NY: McGraw-Hill.

Brewer, M. B., & Miller, N. (1984). Beyond the contact hypothesis. In N. Miller & M. B. Brewer (Eds.), *Groups in contact* (pp. 281–302). New York, NY: Academic Press.

Brown, R. (1995). *Prejudice: Its social psychology.* Oxford, England: Blackwell.

Brown, R., & Hewstone, M. (2005). An integrative theory of intergroup contact. *Advances in Experimental Social Psychology, 37*, 255–343.

Buhs, E. S., & Ladd, G. W. (2001). Peer rejection as antecedent of young children's school adjustment: An examination of mediating processes. *Developmental Psychology, 37*, 550–560.

Bukowski, W. M., & Sippola, L. K. (2001). Groups, individuals, and victimization: A view of the peer system. In J. Juvonen & S. Graham (Eds.), *Peer harassment in school: The plight of the vulnerable and victimized* (pp. 355–377). New York, NY: Guilford Press.

Cairns, E. (1989). Social identity and inter-group conflicts in Northern Ireland: A developmental perspective. In J. Harbison (Ed.), *Growing up in Northern Ireland* (pp. 115–130). Belfast, Northern Ireland: Stranmillis College.

Cairns, E., & Hewstone, M. (2002). The impact of peacemaking in Northern Ireland on intergroup behavior. In G. Salomon & B. Nevo (Eds.), *The nature and study of peace education* (pp. 217–228). Hillsdale, NJ: Lawrence Erlbaum Associates.

Cameron, L., & Rutland, A. (2006). Extended contact through story reading in school: Reducing children's prejudice towards the disabled. *Journal of Social Issues, 62*, 469–488.

Cameron, L., & Rutland, A. (2008). An integrative approach to changing children's intergroup attitudes. In S. Levy & M. Killen (Eds.), *Intergroup attitudes and relations in childhood through adulthood* (pp. 191–203). Oxford, England: Oxford University Press.

Cameron, L., Rutland, A., Brown, R. J., & Douch, R. (2006). Changing children's intergroup attitudes toward refugees: Testing different models of extended contact. *Child Development, 77*, 1208–1219.

Cameron, L., Rutland, A., & Hossain, L. (2007). *Prejudice-reduction through story-reading: Indirect contact in the classroom.* Paper presented at the 37th Annual Meeting of the Jean Piaget Society, Amsterdam, the Netherlands.

Carlson, S. M. (2005). Developmentally sensitive measures of executive function in preschool children. *Developmental Neuropsychology, 28*, 595–616.

Carpendale, J., & Lewis, C. (2006). *How children develop social understanding.* Oxford, England: Blackwell.

Cassidy, J. (2008). The nature of the child's ties. In J. Cassidy & P. R. Shaver (Eds.), *Handbook of attachment: Theory, research and clinical applications* (2nd ed., pp. 3–22). New York, NY: Guilford Press.

Castelli, L., De Amicis, L., & Sherman, S. J. (2007). The loyal member effect: On the preference for ingroup members who engage in exclusive relations with the ingroup. *Developmental Psychology, 43,* 1347–1359.

Castelli, L., Zogmaister, C., & Tomelleri, S. (2009). The transmission of racial attitudes within the family. *Developmental Psychology, 45,* 586–591.

Chandler, M. J., Sokol, B. W., & Wainryb, C. (2000). Beliefs about truth and beliefs about rightness. *Child Development, 71,* 91–97.

Chang, L. (2004). The role of classroom norms in contextualizing the relations of children's social behaviors to peer acceptance. *Developmental Psychology, 40,* 691–702.

Clark, K. B., & Clark, M. P. (1947). Racial identification and preference in Negro children. In E. M. Maccoby, T. M. Newcomb & E. L. Hartley (Eds.), *Readings in social psychology* (3rd ed., pp. 602–622). New York: Holt Rinehart & Winston.

Colby, A., & Kohlberg, L. (1987). *The measurement of moral judgment:* Vol. 1, *Theoretical foundations and research validation.* New York, NY: Cambridge University Press.

Cole, C., Arafat, C., Tidhar, C., Zidan, W. T., Fox, N. A., Killen, M., Leavitt, L., Lesser, G., Richman, B.A., Ardila-Rey, A., & Yung, F. (2003). The educational impact of Rechov Sumsum/Shara'a Simsim, a television series for Israeli and Palestinian children. *International Journal of Behavioral Development, 27,* 409–422.

Cole, C. F., Labin, D. B., & del Rocio Galarza, M. (2008). Begin with the children: What research on Sesame Street's international coproductions reveals about using media to promote a new more peaceful world. *International Journal of Behavioral Development, 32,* 359–365.

Common Ground Productions – Search for Common Ground in Macedonia and Sesame Workshop (2000). *Lessons from Nashe Maalo: A research report on what ethnic Albanian, Madedonian, Roma and Turkish youth learned from watching Nashe Maalo.* Common Ground Production – Search for Common Ground in Macedonia and Sesame Workshop. Washington, DC: Author.

Coplan, R., Girardi, A., Findlay, L. C., & Frohlick, S. L. (2007). Understanding solitude: Young children's attitudes and responses toward hypothetically withdrawn peers. *Social Development, 16,* 390–409.

Crick, N., & Dodge, K. A. (1994). A review and reformulation of social information-processing mechanisms in children's social adjustment. *Psychological Bulletin, 115,* 74–101.

Crocker, J., Major, B., & Steele, C. (1998). Social stigma. In D. Gilbert, S. T. Fiske, & G. Lindzey (Eds.), *The handbook of social psychology* (4th ed., Vol. 2, pp. 504–553). New York: McGraw-Hill.

Crouter, A. C., Bumpus, M. F., Head, M. R., & McHale, S. M. (2001). Implications of overwork and overload for the quality of men's family relationships. *Journal of Marriage and Family*, 63, 404–416.

Crouter, A. C., Head, M. R., Bumpus, M. F., & McHale, S. M. (2001). Household chores: Under what conditions do mothers lean on daughters? In A. Fuligni (Ed.), *Family assistance and obligation during adolescence. New directions in child development*. San Francisco, CA: Jossey-Bass.

Crouter, A. C., Manke, B., & McHale, S. M. (1995). The family context of gender intensification in early adolescence. *Child Development*, 66, 317–329.

Crystal, D., Killen, M., & Ruck, M. (2008). It's who you know that counts: Intergroup contact and judgments about race-based exclusion. *British Journal of Developmental Psychology*, 26, 51–70.

Crystal, D. S., Killen, M., & Ruck, M. R. (2010). Fair treatment by authorities is related to children's and adolescents' evaluations of interracial exclusion. *Applied Developmental Science*, 14, 125–136.

Damon, W. (1977). *The social world of the child*. San Francisco, CA: Jossey-Bass.

Damon, W., & Killen, M. (1982). Peer interaction and the process of change in children's moral reasoning. *Merrill-Palmer Quarterly*, 28, 347–367.

Dasgupta, N., & Asgari, S. (2004). Seeing is believing: Exposure to counterstereotypic women leaders and its effect on the malleability of automatic gender stereotyping. *Journal of Experimental Social Psychology*, 40, 642–658.

Degner, J., & Wentura, D. (2010). Automatic prejudice in childhood and early adolescence. *Journal of Personality and Social Psychology*, 98, 356–374.

Devine, P. G. (1989). Stereotypes and prejudice: Their automatic and controlled components. *Journal of Personality and Social Psychology*, 56, 5–18.

Devine, P. G., Plant, E. A., Amodio, D. M., Harmon-Jones, E., & Vance, S. L. (2002). The regulation of explicit and implicit race bias: the role of motivations to respond without prejudice. *Journal of Personality and Social Psychology*, 82, 835–848.

Dixon, J., Durrheim, K., & Tredoux, C. (2005). Beyond the optimal contact strategy. *American Psychologist*, 60, 697–711.

Dodge, K. A., Lansford, J. E., Burks, V. S., Bates, J. E., Pettit, G. S., Fontaine, R., & Price, J. M. (2003). Peer rejection and social information-processing factors in the development of aggressive behavior problems in children. *Child Development*, 74, 374–393.

Dovidio, J. F., & Gaertner, S. L. (1991). Changes in the expression and assessment of racial prejudice. In K. H. Knopke, R. H. Norrrell, & R. W.

Rogers (Eds.), *Opening doors: Perspectives on race relations in contemporary America* (pp. 119–148). Tuscaloosa, AL: University of Alabama Press.

Dovidio, J. F., Gaertner, S. L., Hodson, G., Houlette, M. A., & Johnson, K. M. (2005). Social inclusion and exclusion: Recategorization and the perception of intergroup boundaries. In D. Abrams, M. A. Hogg & J. M. Marques (Eds.), *The social psychology of inclusion and exclusion* (pp. 245–264). New York: Psychology Press.

Dovidio, J. F., Gaertner, S. L., & Validizic, A. (1998). Intergroup bias: Status, differentiation, and a common in-group identity. *Journal of Personality and Social Psychology, 75,* 109–120.

Dovidio, J. F., Kawakami, K., & Beach, K. (2001). Implicit and explicit attitudes: Examination of the relationship between measures of intergroup bias. In R. Brown & S. L. Gaertner (Eds.), *Blackwell handbook of social psychology: Vol. 4, Intergroup processes* (pp. 175–197). Oxford, England: Blackwell.

Doyle, A. B., & Aboud, F. E. (1995). A longitudinal study of white children's racial prejudice as a social-cognitive development. *Merrill-Palmer Quarterly, 41,* 209–228.

Doyle, A. B., Beaudet, J., & Aboud, F. E. (1988). Developmental patterns in the flexibility of children's ethnic attitudes. *Journal of Cross Cultural Studies, 19,* 3–18.

Dunham, Y., Baron, A. S., & Banaji, M. (2007). Children and social groups: A developmental analysis of implicit consistency in Hispanic Americans. *Self and Identity, 6,* 238–255.

Dunn, J. (1988). *The beginnings of social understanding.* Cambridge, MA: Harvard University Press.

Dunn, J. (2006). Moral development in early childhood and social interaction in the family. In M. Killen & J. G. Smetana (Eds.), *Handbook of moral development* (pp. 331–350). Mahwah, NJ: Lawrence Erlbaum Associates.

Durkin, K. D. (1995). *Developmental social psychology: From infancy to old age.* Oxford, England: Blackwell.

Edmonds, C., & Killen, M. (2009). Do adolescents' perceptions of parental racial attitudes relate to their intergroup contact and cross-race relationships? *Group Processes and Intergroup Relations, 12,* 5–21.

Eisenberger, N. I., & Lieberman, M. D. (2004). Why rejection hurts: A common neural alarm system for physical and social pain. *Trends in Cognitive Sciences, 8,* 294–300.

Ellemers, N. (1993). The influence of socio-structural variables on identity management strategies. *European Review of Social Psychology, 4,* 22–57.

Enesco, I., Guerrero, S., Callejas, C., & Solbes, I. (2008). Intergroup attitudes and reasoning about social exclusion in majority and minority children in Spain. In S. Levy & M. Killen (Eds.), *Intergroup attitudes and relations in childhood through adulthood* (pp. 105–125). Oxford, England: Oxford University Press.

Enesco, I., Navarro, A., Paradela, I., & Guerrero, S. (2005). Stereotypes and beliefs about different ethnic groups in Spain: A study with Spanish and Latin American children living in Madrid. *Journal of Applied Developmental Psychology, 26,* 638–659.

Esses, V. M., Dovidio, J. F., Semenya, A. H., & Jackson, L. M. (2005). Attitudes towards immigrants and immigration: The role of national and international identity. In D. Abrams, M. A. Hogg & J. M. Marques (Eds.), *The social psychology of inclusion and exclusion* (pp. 317–337). New York, NY: Psychology Press.

Feddes, A. R., Noack, P., & Rutland, A. (2009). Direct and extended friendship effects on minority and majority children's interethnic attitudes: A longitudinal study. *Child Development, 80,* 377–390.

Fiedler, K., Freytag, P., & Unkelbach, C. (2007). Pseudocontingencies in a simulated classroom. *Journal of Personality and Social Psychology, 92,* 665–677.

Fisch, S. M., & Truglio, R. T. (2001). Why children learn from Sesame Street. In S. M. Fisch & R. T. Truglio (Eds.), *"G" is for growing: Thirty years of research on children and Sesame Street* (pp. 233–244). Mahwah, NJ: Lawrence Erlbaum Associates.

Fiske, S. T. (2002). What we know now about bias and intergroup conflict, the problem of the century. *Current Directions in Psychological Science, 11,* 123–128.

FitzRoy, S., & Rutland, A. (2010). Learning to control ethnic intergroup bias in childhood. *European Journal of Social Psychology, 40,* 679–693.

Frankenberg, E., & Orfield, G. (Eds.). (2007). *Lessons in integration: Realizing the promise of racial diversity in American schools.* Charlottesville, VA: University of Virginia Press.

Fuegan, K., Biernat, M., Haines, E., & Deaux, K. (2004). Mothers and fathers in the workplace: How gender and parental status influence judgments of job-related competence. *Journal of Social Issues, 60,* 737–754.

Fuligni, A. J., Witkow, M., & Garcia, C. (2005). Ethnic identity and the academic adjustment of adolescents from Mexican, Chinese, and European backgrounds. *Developmental Psychology, 41,* 799–811.

Gaertner, S. L., & Dovidio, J. F. (2000). *Reducing intergroup bias: The Common Ingroup Identity Model.* Philadelphia, PA: Psychology Press.

Gaertner, S. L., Jeffrey, M., Audrey, M., & Dovidio, J. F. (1989). Reducing intergroup bias: The benefits of recategorization. *Journal of Personality and Social Psychology, 57,* 239–249.

Garandeau, C. F., & Cillessen, A. H. N. (2006). From indirect aggression to invisible aggression: A conceptual view on bullying and peer manipulation. *Aggression and Violent Behavior, 11,* 612–625.

Gazelle, H., & Ladd, G. W. (2003). Anxious solitude and peer exclusion: A diathesis-stress model of internalizing trajectories in childhood. *Child Development, 74,* 257–278.

Gelman, S. A. (2009). Learning from others: Children's construction of concepts. *Annual Review of Psychology, 60,* 115–140.

Gelman, S. A., Collman, P., & Maccoby, E. (1986). Inferring properties from cognitive versus inferring categories from properties: The case of gender. *Child Development, 57,* 396–404.

Gelman, S. A., Heyman, G. D., & Legare, C. H. (2007). Developmental changes in the coherence of essentialist beliefs about psychological characteristics. *Child Development, 78,* 757–774.

Gelman, S. A., & Wellman, H. (1991). Insides and essences: Early understandings of the nonobvious. *Cognition, 38,* 213–244.

Gieling, M., Thijs, J., & Verkuyten, M. (2010). Tolerance of practices by Muslim actors: An integrative social-developmental perspective. *Child Development, 81,* 1384–1399.

Gjerde, P. F. (2004). Culture, power, and experience: Toward a person-centered cultural psychology. *Human Development, 47,* 138–157.

Gonzalez, R., & Brown, R. (2003). Generalization of positive attitude as a function of subgroup and superordinate group identifications in intergroup contact. *European Journal of Social Psychology, 33,* 195–214.

Goodman, M. E. (1952). *Race awareness in young children.* New York, NY: Collier.

Graves, J. L. (2001). *The emperor's new clothes: Biological theories of race at the millennium.* New Brunswick, NJ: Rutgers University Press.

Graves, S. B. (1999). Television and prejudice reduction: When does television as a vicarious experience make a difference? *Journal of Social Issues, 55,* 707–725.

Greenfield, P. M., & Cocking, R. R. (Eds.). (1994). *Cross-cultural roots of minority child development.* Mahwah, NJ: Lawrence Erlbaum Associates.

Greenwald, A. G., McGhee, D. E., & Schwartz, J. L. K. (1998). Measuring individual differences in implicit cognition: The Implicit Association Test. *Journal of Personality and Social Psychology, 74,* 1464–1480.

Greenwald, A. G., Poehlman, T. A., Uhlmann, E., & Banaji, M. (2009). Understanding and using the Implicit Association Test: III. Meta-analysis of predictive validity. *Journal of Personality and Social Psychology, 97,* 17–41.

Griffiths, J., & Nesdale, D. (2006). In-group and out-group attitudes of ethnic majority and minority children. *International Journal of Intercultural Relations, 30,* 735–749.

Grubbs, P. R., & Niemeyer, J. A. (1999). Promoting reciprocal social interactions in inclusive classrooms for young children. *Infants and Young Children, 11,* 9–18.

Grusec, J. E., & Davidov, M. (2010). Integrating different perspectives on socialization theory and research: A domain-specific approach. *Child Development, 81,* 687–709.

Grusec, J. E., & Goodnow, J. J. (1994). Impact of parental discipline methods on the child's internalization of values: A reconceptualization of current point of view. *Developmental Psychology, 30,* 4–19.

Hamlin, J. K., Wynn, K., & Bloom, P. (2007). Social evaluation by preverbal infants. *Nature, 450,* 557–560.

Harris, P., Johnson, C. N., Hutton, D., Andrews, G., & Cooke, T. (1989). Young children's theory of mind and emotion. *Cognition and Emotion, 3,* 379–400.

Hartshorne, H., & May, M. (1928–1930). *Studies in the nature of character: Vol. I, Studies in deceit, Vol. II, Studies in self-control, Vol. III, Studies in the organization of character.* New York, NY: Macmillan.

Hawker, D. S. J., & Boulton, M. J. (2000). Twenty years' research on peer victimization and psychosocial maladjustment: A meta-analytic review of cross-sectional studies. *Journal of Child Psychology and Psychiatry, 41,* 441–455.

Hay, D. F. (2006). Yours and mine: Toddlers' talk about possessions with familiar peers. *British Journal of Developmental Psychology, 24,* 39–52.

Helwig, C. (1995a). Social context in social cognition: Psychological harm and civil liberties. In M. Killen & D. Hart (Eds.), *Morality in everyday life: Developmental perspectives* (pp. 166–200). Cambridge, England: Cambridge University Press.

Helwig, C. (1995b). Adolescents' and young adults' conceptions of civil liberties: Freedom of speech and religion. *Child Development, 66,* 152–166.

Helwig, C. (2008). The moral judgment of the child reevaluated: Heteronomy, early morality, and reasoning about social justice and inequalities. In C. Wainryb, J. G. Smetana & E. Turiel (Eds.), *Social development, social inequalities, and social justice* (pp. 27–52). New York, NY: LEA Taylor and Francis Group.

Hewstone, M., Cairns, E., Voci, A., Paolini, S., McLernon, F., Crisp, R., & Craig, J. (2005). Intergroup contact in a divided society: Challenging segregation in Northern Ireland. In D. Abrams, M. A. Hogg & J. M. Marques (Eds.), *The social psychology of inclusion and exclusion* (pp. 265–292). New York, NY: Psychology Press.

Hill, M. E., & Augustinos, M. (2001). Stereotype change and prejudice reduction: Short- and long-term evaluationof a cross-cultural awareness programme. *Journal of Community and Applied Social Psychology, 11,* 243–262.

Hinde, R. A., Titmus, G., Easton, D., & Tamplin, A. (1985). Incidence of "friendship" and behavior toward strong associates versus nonassociates in preschoolers. *Child Development, 56,* 234–245.

Hitti, A., Mulvey, K. L., & Killen, M. (in press). Evaluation of social exclusion: The role of group norms, group identity, and fairness. *Anales de Psicologia* (Special Issue).

Hogg, M. A. (2001). Social identity and the sovereignty of the group: A psychology of belonging. In C. Sedikides & M. Brewer (Eds.), *Individual self, relational self, collective self* (pp. 123–143). New York, NY: Psychology Press.

Horn, S. S. (2003). Adolescents' reasoning about exclusion from social groups. *Developmental Psychology, 39,* 71–84.

Horn, S. S. (2006). Group status, group bias, and adolescents' reasoning about the treatment of others in school contexts. *International Journal of Behavioral Development, 30,* 208–218.

Horn, S.S. (2007). Leaving LGBT (Lesbian, Gay, Bisexual, and Transgender) students behind. In C. Wainryb, J. Smetana & E. Turiel (Eds.), *Social development, social inequality, and social justice* (pp. 131–153). New York, NY: Lawrence Erlbaum Associates.

Horn, S. S. (2008). The multifaceted nature of sexual prejudice: How adolescents reason about sexual orientation and sexual prejudice. In S. Levy & M. Killen (Eds.), *Intergroup attitudes and relations in childhood through adulthood* (pp. 173–190). Oxford, England: Oxford University Press.

Horn, S.S., & Nucci, L. P. (2003). The multidimensionality of adolescents' beliefs about and attitudes toward gay and lesbian peers in school. *Equity and Excellence in Education, 36,* 136–147.

Hughes, D., Rodriguez, J., Smith, E. P., Johnson, D. J., Stevenson, H. C., & Spicer, P. (2006). Parents' ethnic-racial socialization practices: A review of research and directions for future study. *Developmental Psychology, 42,* 747–770.

Hughes, J. M., Bigler, R. S. & Levy, S. R. (2007). Consequences of learning about historical racism among European American and African American children. *Child Development, 78,* 1689–1705.

Hymel, S., Bowker, A., & Woody, E. (1993). Aggressive versus withdrawn unpopular children: Variations in peer and self-perceptions in multiple domains. *Child Development, 64,* 879–896.

James, W. (1890). *The principles of psychology.* Cambridge, MA: Harvard University Press.

Jugert, P., Noack, P., & Rutland, A.(in press). Trajectories of friendship choices among German and Turkish preadolescents entering ethnically heterogeneous schools: A one-year longitudinal study. *Child Development.*

Juvonen, J., & Gross, E. F. (2005). The rejected and the bullied: Lessons about social misfits from developmental psychology. In K. D. Williams, J. P. Forgas, & W. von Hippel, W. (Eds.), *The social outcast: Ostracism, social exclusion, rejection, and bullying.* (pp. 155–170). New York, NY: Psychology Press.

Kant, I. (1785/1981) *Foundations of the metaphysics of morals (1785)*. Translated by James Elllington. Indianapolis, IN: Hackett Publishing Company.

Kao, G., & Joyner, K. (2004). Do race and ethnicity matter among friends? Activities among interracial, interethnic, and intraethnic adolescent friends. *Sociological Quarterly, 45*, 557–573.

Katz, P. A. (1976). The acquisition of racial attitudes in children. In P. A. Katz (Ed.), *Towards the elimination of racism* (pp. 125–154). New York, NY: Pergamon.

Keil, F. (2006). Cognitive science and cognitive development. In W. Damon, R. Lerner, D. Kuhn, & R. Siegler (Eds.), *Handbook of child psychology: Cognition, perception, and language* (6th ed., Vol. 2, pp. 609–635). Hoboken, NJ: Wiley.

Kelly, D. J., Quinn, P. C., Slater, A. M., Kang, L., Gibson, A., Smith, M., & Pascalis, O. (2005). Three-month-olds, but not newborns, prefer own-race faces. *Developmental Science, 8*, 31–36.

Kelly, D. J., Quinn, P. C., Slater, A. M., Kang, L., Liezhong, G., & Pascalis, O. (2007). The other-race effect develops during infancy: Evidence of perceptual narrowing. *Psychological Science, 18*, 1084–1089.

Kelly, M., & Duckitt, J. (1995). Racial preference and self-esteem in black South African children. *South African Journal of Psychology, 25*, 217–223.

Killen, M. (2007). Children's social and moral reasoning about exclusion. *Current Directions in Psychological Science, 16*, 32–36.

Killen, M., Breton, S., Ferguson, H., & Handler, K. (1994). Preschoolers' evaluations of teacher methods of intervention in social transgressions. *Merrill-Palmer Quarterly, 40*, 399–416.

Killen, M., Henning, A., Kelly, M. C., Crystal, D., & Ruck, M. (2007). Evaluations of interracial peer encounters by majority and minority US children and adolescents. *International Journal of Behavioral Development, 31*, 491–500.

Killen, M., Kelly, M., Richardson, C., Crystal, D., & Ruck, M. (2010). European-American children's and adolescents' evaluations of interracial exclusion. *Group Processes and Intergroup Relations, 13*, 283–300.

Killen, M., Kelly, M., Richardson, C. B., & Jampol, N. (2010). Attributions of intentions and fairness judgments regarding interracial peer encounters. *Developmental Psychology, 46*, 1206–1213.

Killen, M., Lee-Kim, J., McGlothlin, H., & Stangor, C. (2002). How children and adolescents evaluate gender and racial exclusion. *Monographs of the Society for Research in Child Development* (Serial No. 271, Vol. 67, No. 4). Oxford, England: Blackwell.

Killen, M., Margie, N. G., & Sinno, S. (2006). Morality in the context of intergroup relationships. In M. Killen & J. G. Smetana (Eds.), *Handbook of moral development* (pp. 155–183). Mahwah, NJ: Lawrence Erlbaum Associates.

Killen, M., McGlothlin, H., & Henning, A. (2008). Explicit judgments and implicit bias: A developmental perspective In S. R. Levy & M. Killen (Eds.), *Intergroup attitudes and relations in childhood through adulthood* (pp. 126–145). New York, NY: Oxford University Press.

Killen, M., McGlothlin, H., & Lee-Kim, J. (2002). Between individuals and culture: Individuals' evaluations of exclusion from social groups. In H. Keller, Y. Poortinga, & A. Schoelmerich (Eds.), *Between biology and culture: Perspectives on ontogenetic development* (pp. 159–190). Cambridge, England: Cambridge University Press.

Killen, M., Mulvey, K. L., Richardson, C. B., Jampol, N., & Woodward, A. (in press). The "accidental transgressor": Morally-relevant theory of mind. *Cognition*.

Killen, M., & Naigles, L. (1995). Preschool children pay attention to their addressees: The effects of gender composition on peer disputes. *Discourse Processes, 19*, 329–346.

Killen, M., Pisacane, K., Lee-Kim, J., & Ardila-Rey, A. (2001). Fairness or stereotypes? Young children's priorities when evaluating group exclusion and inclusion. *Developmental Psychology, 37*, 587–596.

Killen, M., Richardson, C., & Kelly, M. C. (2010). Developmental perspectives. In J. F. Dovidio, M. Hewstone, P. Glick & V. M. Esses (Eds.), *Handbook of prejudice and discrimination* (pp. 97–114). Thousand Oaks, CA: Sage Publishers.

Killen, M., Rutland, A., & Jampol, N. (2008). Social exclusion in middle childhood and early adolescence. In K. H. Rubin, W. Bukowski & B. Laurenson (Eds.), *Handbook of peer interactions, relationships and groups* (pp. 249–266). New York, NY: Guilford Press.

Killen, M., Rutland, A., Abrams, D., Mulvey, K. L., & Hitti, A. (2010). *Social reasoning and group dynamics regarding intergroup exclusion*. College Park: University of Maryland.

Killen, M., Sinno, S., & Margie, N. G. (2007). Children's experiences and judgments about group exclusion and inclusion. In R. V. Kail (Ed.), *Advances in child development and behavior* (pp. 173–218). New York, NY: Elsevier.

Killen, M., & Smetana, J. G. (1999). Social interactions in preschool classrooms and the development of young children's conceptions of the personal. *Child Development, 70*, 486–501.

Killen, M., & Smetana, J. G. (Eds.). (2006). *Handbook of moral development*. Mahwah, NJ: Lawrence Erlbaum Associates.

Killen, M., & Stangor, C. (2001). Children's reasoning about social inclusion and exclusion in gender and race peer group contexts. *Child Development, 72*, 174–186.

Killen, M., & Turiel, E. (1991). Conflict resolution in preschool social interactions. *Early Education and Development, 2*, 240–255.

King, M. L. (1957/1986) *I have a dream: Writings and speeches that changed the world*. Edited by James Melvin Washington. San Francisco, CA: Harper Collins.

Kinket, B., & Verkuyten, M. (1999). Intergroup evaluations and social context: A multilevel approach. *European Journal of Social Psychology, 29*, 219–237.

Kohlberg, L. (1971). From is to ought: How to commit the naturalistic fallacy and get away with it in the study of moral development. In T. Mischel (Ed.), *Psychology and genetic epistemology* (pp. 151–235). New York, NY: Academic Press.

Kohlberg, L. (1984). *Essays on moral development*: Vol. 2, *The psychology of moral development – The nature and validity of moral stages*. San Francisco, CA: Harper and Row.

Kuhn, D., & Franklin, S. (2006). The second decade: What develops (and how). In W. Damon, R. M. Lerner, D. Kuhn, & R. S. Siegler (Eds.), *Handbook of child psychology: Cognition, perception, and language* (6th ed., Vol. 2, pp. 953–993). Hoboken, NJ: Wiley.

Lagattuta, K. H. (2005). When you shouldn't do what you want to do: Young children's understanding of desires, rules, and emotions. *Child Development, 76*, 713–733.

Lagattuta, K.H., Nucci, L., & Boascaki, S. (2010). Bridging theory of mind and the personal domain: Children's reasoning about resistance to parental control. *Child Development, 81*, 616–635.

Lambert, W. E., & Klineberg, O. (1967). *Children's views of foreign peoples: A cross-national study*. New York, NY: Meredith Publishing.

Langlois, J. H., Ritter, J. M., Roggman, L. A., & Vaughn, L. S. (1991). Facial diversity and infant preferences for attractive faces. *Developmental Psychology, 27*, 79–84.

LaRose, R., & Eisenstock, B. (1981, August). *Techniques for testing the effectiveness of minority portrayals in multicultural children's programming*. Paper presented at the annual meeting of the International Communication Association, Minneapolis, MN.

Lawrence, V. W. (1991). Effect of socially ambiguous information on White and Black children's behavioral and trait perceptions. *Merrill-Palmer Quarterly, 37*, 619–630.

Leary, M. R. (1996). *Self-presentation: Impression management and interpersonal behaviour*. Boulder, CO: Westview Press.

Leavitt, L. A., & Fox, N. A. (1993). *The psychological effects of war and violence on children*. Mahwah, NJ: Lawrence Erlbaum Associates.

Lemerise, E., & Arsenio, W. F. (2000). An integrated model of emotion processes and cognition in social information processing. *Child Development, 71*, 107–118.

Leslie, A., Knobe, J., & Cohen, A. (2006). Acting intentionally and the side-effect effect: Theory of mind and moral judgment. *Psychological Science, 17*, 421–427.

Levine, J. M. (1989). Reaction to opinion deviance in small groups. In P. B. Paulus (Ed.), *Psychology of group influence* (Vol. 2, pp. 187–231). Hillsdale, NJ: Lawrence Erlbaum Associates.

Levy, S. R., Chiu, C. Y., & Hong, Y. Y. (2006). Lay theories and intergroup relations. *Group Processes and Intergroup Relations, 9,* 5–24.

Levy, S. R., & Killen, M. (2008). *Intergroup attitudes and relations in childhood through adulthood.* Oxford, England: Oxford University Press.

Liben, L. S., & Bigler, R. S. (2002). The developmental course of gender differentiation: Conceptualizing, measuring and evaluating constructs and pathways. *Monographs of the Society for Research in Child Development* (Serial No. 269, Vol. 67, No. 2). Oxford, England: Blackwell.

Lieberman, M. D. (2007). Social cognitive neuroscience: A review of core processes. *Annual Review of Psychology, 58,* 259–289.

Liebkind, K., & McAlister, A. (1999). Extended contact through peer modeling to promote tolerance in Finland. *European Journal of Social Psychology, 29,* 765–780.

Malti, T., Gasser, L., & Buchmann, M. (2009). Aggressive and prosocial children's emotion attributions and moral reasoning. *Aggressive Behavior, 35,* 90–102.

Malti, T., Gummerum, M., Keller, M., & Buchmann, M. (2009). Children's moral motivation, sympathy, and prosocial behavior. *Child Development, 80,* 442–460.

Malti, T., Killen, M., & Gasser, L. (in press). Social reasoning and emotion attributions regarding peer exclusion in Switzerland. *Child Development.*

Maras, P., & Brown, R. (1996). Effects of contact on children's attitudes toward disability: A longitudinal study. *Journal of Applied Social Psychology, 26,* 2113–2134.

Maras, P., & Brown, R. (2000). Effects of different forms of school contact on children's attitudes toward disabled and non-disabled peers. *British Journal of Educational Psychology, 70,* 337–351.

Marques, J. M., Yzerbyt, V. Y., & Leyens, J.-P. (1988). The black sheep effect: Judgmental extremity towards ingroup members as a function of ingroup identification. *European Journal of Social Psychology, 18,* 1–16.

Martin, C. L. (1995). Stereotypes about children with traditional and nontraditional gender roles. *Sex Roles, 33,* 727–751.

McGarty, C. (1999). *Categorization in social psychology.* London, England: Sage.

McGlothlin, H., & Killen, M. (2005). Children's perceptions of intergroup and intragroup similarity and the role of social experience. *Journal of Applied Developmental Psychology, 26,* 680–698.

McGlothlin, H., & Killen, M. (2006). Intergroup attitudes of European American children attending ethnically homogeneous schools. *Child Development, 77,* 1375–1386.

McGlothlin, H., & Killen, M. (2010). How social experience is related to children's intergroup attitudes. *European Journal of Social Psychology: Special Issue: Children's Intergroup Attitudes* (Guest editors: J. Degner & Y. Dunham), *40*, 625–634.

McGlothlin, H., Killen, M., & Edmonds, C. (2005). European-American children's intergroup attitudes about peer relationships. *British Journal of Developmental Psychology, 23*, 227–249.

McHale, S. M., Bartko, W. T., Crouter, A. C., & Perry-Jenkins, M. (1990). Children's housework and psychosocial functioning: The mediating effects of parents' sex role behaviors and attitudes. *Child Development, 61*, 1413–1426.

Mendes, W. B., Gray, H. M., Mendoza-Denton, R., Major, B., & Epel, E. S. (2007). Why egalitarianism might be good for your health: Physiological thriving during stressful intergroup encounters. *Psychological Science, 18*, 991–998.

Mendoza-Denton, R., & Page-Gould, E. (2008). Can cross-group friendships influence minority students' well-being at historically White universities? *Association for Psychological Science, 19*, 933–939.

Miller, J. G. (2001). Culture and moral development. In D. Matsumoto (Ed.), *The handbook of culture and psychology* (pp. 151–169). New York, NY: Oxford University Press.

Molina, L. E., & Wittig, M. A. (2006). Relative importance of contact conditions in explaining prejudice reduction in a classroom context: Separate and equal? *Journal of Social Issues, 62*, 489–509.

Molina, L. E., Wittig, M. A., & Giang, M. T. (2004). Mutual acculturation and social categorization: A comparison of two perspectives on intergroup bias. *Group Processes and Intergroup Relations, 7*, 239–265.

Monks, C. P., Ortega-Ruiz, R., & Rodriguez-Hidalgo, A. J. (2008). Peer victimization in multicultural schools in Spain and England. *European Journal of Developmental Psychology, 5*, 507–535.

Monteiro, M. B., de Franca, X. D., & Rodriques, R. (2009). The development of intergroup bias in childhood: How social norms can shape children's racial behaviours. *International Journal of Psychology, 44*, 29–39.

Muldoon, O. T., McLaughlin, K., & Trew, K. (2007). Adolescents' perceptions of national identification and socialization: A grounded analysis. *British Journal of Developmental Psychology, 25*, 579–594.

Mulvey, K. L., Hitti, A., & Killen, M. (2010). The development of stereotyping and exclusion. *Wiley Interdisciplinary Reviews: Cognitive Science, 1*, 597–606.

Nesdale, D. (2001a). Development of prejudice in children. In M. Augoustinos & K. J. Reynolds (Eds.), *Understanding prejudice, racism and social conflict*. London, England: Sage.

Nesdale, D. (2001b). Language and development of children's ethnic prejudice. *Journal of Language and Social Psychology, 20,* 90–110.

Nesdale, D. (2004). Social identity processes and children's ethnic prejudice. In M. Bennett & F. Sani (Eds.), *The development of the social self* (pp. 219–245). New York, NY: Psychology Press.

Nesdale, D. (2007). The development of ethnic prejudice in early childhood: Theories and research. In O. Saracho & B. Spodek (Eds.), *Contemporary perspectives on socialization and social development in early childhood education.* Charlotte, NC: Information Age Publishing.

Nesdale, D. (2008). Social identity development and children's ethnic attitudes in Australia. In S. Quintana & C. McKown (Eds.), *Handbook of race, racism and the developing child* (pp. 313–338). New York, NY: Wiley.

Nesdale, D., Durkin, K., Maass, A., & Griffiths, J. (2005). Threat, group identification, and children's ethnic prejudice. *Social Development, 14,* 189–205.

Nesdale, D., & Flesser, D. (2001). Social identity and the development of children's group attitudes. *Child Development, 72,* 506–517.

Nesdale, D., Maass, A., Durkin, K., & Griffiths, J. (2005). Group norms, threat, and children's racial prejudice. *Child Development, 76,* 652–663.

Nesdale, D., Maass, A., Kiesner, J., Durkin, K., Griffiths, J., & Ekberg, A. (2007). Effects of peer group rejection, group membership, and group norms, on children's outgroup prejudice. *International Journal of Behavioral Development, 31,* 526–535.

Nucci, L. P. (2001). *Education in the moral domain.* Cambridge, England: Cambridge University Press.

Nucci, L. P., & Turiel, E. (1978). Social interactions in the context of moral and conventional transgressions. *Child Development, 49,* 400–407.

Nucci, L. P., & Turiel, E. (1993). God's word, religious rules and their relation to Chrisitian and Jewish children's concepts of morality. *Child Development, 64,* 1485–1491.

Nucci, L. P., & Turiel, E. (2000). The moral and personal: Sources of conflicts. In L. Nucci, G. Saxe & E. Turiel (Eds.), *Culture, thought, and development* (pp. 115–140). Mahwah, NJ: Lawrence Erlbaum Associates.

Nucci, L. P., & Weber, E. K. (1995). Social interactions in the home and the development of young children's conceptions of the personal. *Child Development, 66,* 1438–1452.

Nussbaum, M. C. (1999). *Sex and social justice.* Oxford, England: University of Oxford Press.

Ojala, K., & Nesdale, D. (2004). Bullying and social identity: The effects of group norms and distinctiveness threat on attitudes towards bullying. *British Journal of Developmental Psychology, 22,* 19–35.

Okin, S. M. (1989). *Justice, gender, and the family.* New York, NY: Basic Books.

Olson, M. A., & Fazio, R. H. (2004). Reducing the influence of extrapersonal associations on the Implicit Association Test: Personalizing the IAT. *Journal of Personality and Social Psychology, 86*, 653–677.

Opotow, S. (1990). Moral exclusion and injustice: An introduction. *Journal of Social Issues, 46*, 1–20.

Palkovitz, R. (2002). Involving fathering and child development: Advancing our understanding of good fathering. In C. Tamis-LaMonda & N. Cabrera (Eds.), *Handbook of father involvement* (pp. 119–140). Mahwah, NJ: Lawrence Erlbaum Associates.

Park, Y., & Killen, M. (2010). When is peer rejection justifiable? Children's understanding across two cultures. *Cognitive Development, 25*, 290–301.

Park, Y., Killen, M., Crystal, D., & Watanabe, H. (2003). Korean, Japanese, and American children's evaluations of peer exclusion: Evidence for diversity. *International Journal of Behavioral Development, 27*, 555–565.

Park, Y., Lee-Kim, J., Killen, M., Park, Y., & Kim, J. (2009). *Korean children's reasoning about parental expectations regarding gender-stereotypic activities.* National Institutes of Child Health and Human Development (submitted).

Peets, K., Hodges, R., Kikas, E., & Salmivalli, C. (2007). Hostile attributions and behavioral strategies in children: Does relationship type matter? *Developmental Psychology, 43*, 889–900.

Pettigrew, T. F. (1998). Intergroup contact theory. *Annual Review of Psychology, 49*, 65–85.

Pettigrew, T. F. (2010). Commentary: South African contributions to the study of intergroup relations. *Journal of Social Issues, 66*, 417–430.

Pettigrew, T. F., & Tropp, L. R. (2005). Allport's intergroup contact hypothesis: Its history and influence. In J. F. Dovidio, P. Glick & L. Rudman (Eds.), *Reflecting on the nature of prejudice: Fifty years after Allport* (pp. 262–277). Malden, MA: Blackwell.

Pettigrew, T. F., & Tropp, L. R. (2006). A meta-analytic test of intergroup contact theory. *Journal of Personality and Social Psychology, 90*, 751–783.

Pfeifer, J. H., Ruble, D. N., Bachman, M. A., Alvarez, J. M., Cameron, J. A., & Fuligni, A. J. (2007). Social identities and intergroup bias in immigrant and nonimmigrant children. *Developmental Psychology, 43*, 496–507.

Piaget, J. (1932). *The moral judgment of the child.* New York, NY: Free Press.

Piaget, J. (1952). *The origins of intelligence in children.* New York, NY: International Universities Press.

Quinn, P. C., Yahr, J., Kuhn, A., Slater, A. M., & Pascalis, O. (2002). Representation of the gender of human faces by infants: A preference for female. *Perception, 31*, 1109–1121.

Ross, H., Ross, M., Stein, N., & Trabasso, T. (2006). How siblings resolve their conflicts: The importance of first offers, planning, and limited opposition. *Child Development, 77*, 1730–1745.

Rothbart, M., Ellis, L., & Posner, M. I. (2004). Temperament and self-regulation. In R. F. Baumeister & K. D. Vohs (Eds.), *Handbook of self-regulation: Research, theory and application* (pp. 357–370). New York, NY: Guilford Press.

Rubin, K., Bukowski, W., & Parker, J. (2006). Peers, relationships, and interactions. In W. Damon, R. Lerner, & N. Eisenberg (Eds.), *Handbook of child psychology: Social, emotional and personality development* (6th ed., Vol. 3, pp. 571–645). Hoboken, NJ: Wiley.

Ruble, D. N., Alvarez, J., Bachman, M., Cameron, J., Fuligni, A., & Coll, C. G. (2004). The development of a sense of "we": The emergence and implications of children's collective identity. In M. Bennett & F. Sani (Eds.), *The development of the social self* (pp. 29–76). Hove, England: Psychology Press.

Ruble, D. N., & Martin, C. L. (1998). Gender development. In W. Damon & N. Eisenberg (Eds.), *Handbook of child psychology: Social, emotional and personality development* (5th ed., Vol. 3, pp. 933–1016). New York, NY: Wiley.

Ruble, D. N., Martin, C. L., & Berenbaum, S. (2006). Gender development. In W. Damon, R. Lerner, & N. Eisenberg (Eds.), *Handbook of child psychology: Social, emotional, and personality development* (6th ed., Vol. 3, pp. 858–932). New York, NY: Wiley.

Ruck, M. D., Abramovitch, R., & Keating, D. P. (1998). Children's and adolescents' understanding of rights: Balancing nurturance and self-determination. *Child Development, 69,* 404–417.

Ruck, M. D., Park, H., Killen, M., & Crystal, D. S. (in press). Intergroup contact and evaluations of race-based exclusion in urban minority children and adolescents. *Journal of Youth and Adolescence.*

Ruck, M. D., Tenenbaum, H. R., & Sines, J. (2007). British adolescents' views about the rights of asylum-seeking children. *Journal of Adolescence, 30,* 687–693.

Rutland, A. (1999). The development of national prejudice, ingroup favouritism and self stereotypes in British children. *British Journal of Social Psychology, 38,* 55–70.

Rutland, A. (2004). The development and self-regulation of intergroup attitudes in children. In M. Bennett & F. Sani (Eds.), *The development of the social self* (pp. 247–265). New York, NY: Psychology Press.

Rutland, A., Cameron, L., Milne, A., & McGeorge, P. (2005). Social norms and self-presentation: Children's implicit and explicit intergroup attitudes. *Child Development, 76,* 451–466.

Rutland, A., & Cinnirella, M. (2000). Context effects on Scottish national and European self-categorization: The importance of category accessibility, fragility, and relations. *British Journal of Social Psychology, 39,* 495–519.

Rutland, A., Killen, M., & Abrams, D. (2010). A new social-cognitive developmental perspective on prejudice: The interplay between morality and group identity. *Perspectives on Psychological Science*, 5, 279–291.

Sagar, H. A., & Schofield, J. W. (1980). Racial and behavioral cues in Black and White children's perceptions of ambiguously aggressive acts. *Journal of Personality and Social Psychology*, 39, 590–598.

Saguy, T., Tausch, N., Dovidio, J., & Pratto, F. (2009). The irony of harmony: Intergroup contact can produce false expections of equality. *Psychological Science*, 20, 114–121.

Salmivalli, C., & Peets, K. (2009). Bullies, victims, and bully–victim relationships in middle childhood and early adolescence. In K. H. Rubin, W. M. Bukowski & B. Laursen (Eds.), *Handbook of peer interactions, relationships, and groups* (pp. 322–340). New York, NY: Guilford Press.

Salzman, M., & D'Andrea, M. (2001). Assessing the impact of a prejudice prevention project. *Journal of Counseling and Development*, 79, 341–347.

Schachter, S. (1951). Deviation, rejection and communication. *Journal of Abnormal and Social Psychology*, 46, 190–207.

Schlenker, B. R. (1980). *Impression management: The self-concept, social identity, and interpersonal relations*. Monterey, CA: Brooks-Cole.

Schneider, B. H., Dixon, K., & Udvari, S. (2007). Closeness and competition in the inter-ethnic and co-ethnic friendships of early adolescents in Toronto and Montreal. *Journal of Early Adolescence*, 27, 115–138.

Schofield, J. W., & Eurich-Fulcer, R. (2001). When and how school desegregation improves intergroup relations. In R. J. Brown & S. L. Gaertner (Eds.), *Blackwell handbook of social psychology*: Vol. 4, *Intergroup processes* (pp. 475–494). Oxford, England: Blackwell.

Schuette, C., & Killen, M. (2009). Children's evaluations of gender stereotypic household chores. *Early Education and Development*, 20, 693–712.

Selman, R. (1980). *The growth of interpersonal understanding: Developmental and clinical analyses*. New York, NY: Academic Press.

Shelov, S. P., Remer, T., & Altmann, M. D. (Eds.) (1998). *American Academy of Pediatrics: Caring for your baby and young child: Birth to age 5*. New York: Bantam Books.

Sherif, M., Harvey, O. J., White, B. J., Hood, W. R., & Sherif, C. W. (1961). *Intergroup conflict and cooperation: The robber's cave experiment*. Norman: University of Oklahoma Press.

Simon, B., Loewy, M., Stuermer, S., Weber, U., Freytag, P., Habig, C., & Spahlinger, P. (1998). Collective identification and social movement participation. *Journal of Personality and Social Psychology*, 74, 646–658.

Sinno, S., & Killen, M. (2009). Moms at work and dads at home: Children's evaluations of parental roles. *Applied Developmental Science*, 13, 16–29.

Sinno, S., & Killen, M.(in press). Social reasoning about second-shift parenting. [Special Section: *Gender Relationships,* Ed. by H. Tenenbaum & P. Leman.] *British Journal of Developmental Psychology.*

Slavin, R. E. (1995). Cooperative learning and intergroup relations. In J. A. Banks & C. A. M. Banks (Eds.), *Handbook of reserach on multicultural education* (pp. 628–634). New York, NY: Macmillan.

Smetana, J. G. (1981). Preschool children's conceptions of moral and social rules. *Child Development, 52,* 1333–1336.

Smetana, J. G. (1993). Understanding of social rules. In M. Bennett (Ed.), *The development of social cognition: The child as psychologist* (pp. 111–114). New York, NY: Guilford Press.

Smetana, J. G. (1995). Morality in context: Abstractions, ambiguities, and applications. In R. Vasta (Ed.), *Annals of child development* (Vol. 10, pp. 83–130). London, England: Jessica Kingsley Publishers.

Smetana, J. G. (2006). Social-cognitive domain theory: Consistencies and variations in children's moral and social judgments. In M. Killen & J. G. Smetana (Eds.), *Handbook of moral development* (pp. 119–154). Mahwah, NJ: Lawrence Erlbaum Associates.

Smetana, J. G., & Asquith, P. (1994). Adolescents' and parents' conceptions of parental authority and personal autonomy. *Child Development, 65,* 1147–1162.

Smetana, J. G., Schlagman, N., & Adams, P. (1993). Preschoolers' judgments about hypothetical and actual transgressions. *Child Development, 64,* 202–214.

Smith, P. K., & Shu, S. (2000). What good schools can do about bullying: Findings from a survey of English schools after a decade of research and action. *Childhood, 7,* 193–212.

Staub, E. (1990). Moral exclusion, personal goal theory, and extreme destructiveness. *Journal of Social Issues, 46,* 47–64.

Tajfel, H. (1970). Experiments in intergroup discrimination. *Scientific American, 223,* 96–102.

Tajfel, H. (1978). Social categorization, social identity and social comparison. In H. Tajfel (Ed.), *Differentiation between social groups: Studies in the social psychology of intergroup relations* (pp. 61–76). London, England: Academic Press.

Tajfel, H., Jahoda, G., Nemeth, C., Rim, Y., & Johnson, N. (1972). The devaluation by children of their own national and ethnic group: Two case studies. *British Journal of Social and Clinical Psychology, 11,* 235–243.

Tajfel, H., & Turner, J. C. (1979). An integrative theory of intergroup conflict. In W. G. Austin & S. Worchel (Eds.), *The social psychology of intergroup relations* (pp. 33–47). Monterey, CA: Brooks-Cole.

Tamis-LaMonda, C. S., & Cabrera, N. (Eds.). (2003). *Handbook of father involvement: Multidisciplinary perspectives.* Mahwah, NJ: Lawrence Erlbaum Associates.

Taylor, D. M., Wright, S. C., & Porter, L. E. (1994). Dimensions of perceived discrimination: The personal/group discrimination discrepancy. In M. P. Zanna & J. M. Olson (Eds.), *The psychology of prejudice: The Ontario symposium* (Vol. 7, pp. 233–255). Hillsdale, NJ: Lawrence Erlbaum Associates.

Taylor, M. G. (1996). The development of chidlren's beliefs about social and biological aspects of gender differences. *Child Development, 67,* 1555–1571.

Taylor, M. G., Rhodes, M., & Gelman, S. A. (2009). Boys will be boys; cows will be cows: Children's essentialist reasoning about gender categories and animal species. *Child Development, 80,* 461–481.

Teichman, Y. (2001). The development of Israeli children's images of Jews and Arabs and their expression in human figure drawings. *Developmental Psychology, 37,* 749–761.

Teichman, Y., & Zafrir, H. (2003). Images held by Jewish and Arab children in Israel of people representing their own and the other group. *Journal of Cross-Cultural Psychology, 34,* 658–676.

Theimer, C. E., Killen, M., & Stangor, C. (2001). Young children's evaluations of exclusion in gender-stereotypic peer contexts. *Developmental Psychology, 37,* 18–27.

Thompson, R. A. (2006). The development of the person: Social understanding, relationships, conscience, self. In W. Damon, R. Lerner, & N. Eisenberg (Eds.), *Handbook of child psychology: Social, emotional, and personality development* (6th ed., Vol. 3, pp. 24–98). Hoboken, NJ: Wiley.

Thompson, R. A., Laible, D. J., & Ontai, L. L. (2003). Early understainding of emotion, morality, and self: Developing a working model. *Advances in Child Development and Behavior, 31,* 137–171.

Tisak, M. S. (1986). Children's conceptions of parental authority. *Child Development, 57,* 166–176.

Tomasello, M., Carpenter, M., Call, J., Behne, T., & Moll, H. (2005). Understanding and sharing intentions: The ontogeny and phylogeny of cultural cognition. *Behavioural and Brain Sciences, 28,* 675–691.

Trew, K. (2004). Children and socio-cultural divisions in Northern Ireland. *Journal of Social Issues, 60,* 507–522.

Tropp, L. R., & Pettigrew, T. F. (2005). Relationships between intergroup contact and prejudice among minority and majority status groups. *Psychological Science, 16,* 951–957.

Tropp, L. R., & Prenovost, M. A. (2008). The role of intergroup contact in predicting children's inter-ethnic attitudes: Evidence from meta-analytic and field studies. In S. Levy & M. Killen (Eds.), *Intergroup attitudes and relations in childhood through adulthood* (pp. 236–248). Oxford, England: Oxford University Press.

Turiel, E. (1983). *The development of social knowledge: Morality and convention*. Cambridge, England: Cambridge University Press.

Turiel, E. (1998). The development of morality. In W. Damon & N. Eisenberg (Eds.), *Handbook of child psychology: Social, emotional and personality development* (5th ed., Vol. 3, pp. 863–932). New York, NY: Wiley.

Turiel, E. (2002). *The culture of morality: Social development, context, and conflict*. Cambridge, England: Cambridge University Press.

Turiel, E. (2006). The development of morality. In W. Damon, R. Lerner, & N. Eisenberg (Eds.), *Handbook of child psychology: Social, emotional, and personality development* (6th ed., Vol. 3, pp. 789–857). Hoboken, NJ: Wiley.

Turiel, E., Killen, M., & Helwig, C. C. (1987). Morality: Its structure, functions, and vagaries. In J. Kagan & S. Lamb (Eds.), *The emergence of morality in young children* (pp. 155–243). Chicago, IL: University of Chicago Press.

Turner, J. C., Hogg, M. A., Oakes, P. J., Reicher, S. D., & Wetherell, M. S. (Eds.). (1987). *Rediscovering the social group: A self-categorisation theory*. Oxford, England: Basil Blackwell.

Turner, R. N., Voci, A., & Hewstone, M. (2007). Reducing explicit and implicit outgroup prejudice via direct and extended contact: The mediating role of self-disclosure and intergroup anxiety. *Journal of Personality and Social Psychology, 93*, 369–388.

Vaish, A., Carpenter, M., & Tomasello, M. (2009). Sympathy through affective perspective taking and its relation to prosocial behavior in toddlers. *Developmental Psychology, 45*, 534–543.

Verkuyten, M. (2001). National identification and intergroup evaluations in Dutch children. *British Journal of Developmental Psychology, 19*, 559–571.

Verkuyten, M. (2002a). Ethnic attitudes among minority and majority children: The role of ethnic identification, peer group victimization and parents. *Social Development, 11*, 558–570.

Verkuyten, M. (2002b). Perceptions of ethnic discrimination by minority and majority early adolescents in the Netherlands. *International Journal of Psychology, 37*, 321–332.

Verkuyten, M. (2003). Ethnic in-group bias among minority and majority early adolescents: The perception of negative peer behaviour. *British Journal of Developmental Psychology, 21*, 543–564.

Verkuyten, M. (2005). Ethnic group indentification and group evaluation among minority and majority groups: Testing the multiculturalism hypothesis. *Journal of Personality and Social Psychology, 88*, 121–138.

Verkuyten, M. (2008). Multiculturalism and group evaluations among minority and majority groups. In S. Levy & M. Killen (Eds.), *Intergroup attitudes and relations in childhood through adulthood* (pp. 157–172). Oxford, England: Oxford University Press.

Verkuyten, M., & Kinket, B. (2000). Social distances in a multi ethnic society: The ethnic hierarchy among Dutch preadolescents. *Social Psychology Quarterly*, *63*, 75–85.

Verkuyten, M., & Slooter, L. (2008). Muslim and non-Muslim adolescents' reasoning about freedom of speech and minority rights. *Child Development*, *79*, 514–528.

Verkuyten, M., & Steenhuis, A. (2005). Preadolescents' understanding and reasoning about asylum seeker peers and friendships. *Journal of Applied Developmental Psychology*, *26*, 660–679.

Verkuyten, M., & Thijs, J. (2001). Ethnic and gender bias among Dutch and Turkish children in late childhood: The role of social context. *Infant and Child Development*, *10*, 203–217.

Verkuyten, M., & Thijs, J. (2002). Racist victimization among children in the Netherlands: the effect of ethnic group and school. *Ethnic and Racial Studies*, *25*, 310–331.

Vygotsky, L. (1962). *Thought and language*. Cambridge, MA: MIT Press.

Wagner, U., Van Dick, R., Pettigrew, T. F., & Christ, O. (2003). Ethnic prejudice in East and West Germany: The explanatory power of intergroup contact. *Group Processes and Intergroup Relations*, *6*, 22–36.

Wainryb, C. (1993). The application of moral judgments to other cultures: Relativism and universality. *Child Development*, *64*, 924–933.

Wainryb, C. (2006). Moral development in culture: Diversity, tolerance, and justice. In M. Killen & J. G. Smetana (Eds.), *Handbook of moral development* (pp. 211–240). Mahwah, NJ: Lawrence Erlbaum Associates.

Warneken, F., & Tomasello, M. (2007). Helping and cooperation at 14 months of age. *Infancy*, *11*, 271–294.

Wellman, H. M. (1990). *The child's theory of mind*. Cambridge, MA: MIT Press.

Williams, J. E., Best, D. L., Boswell, D. A., Mattson, L. A., & Graves, D. J. (1975). Preschool racial attitude measure II. *Educational and Psychological Measurement*, *35*, 3–18.

Woodward, A. L. (2008). Infants grasp of others intentions. *Current Directions in Psychological Science*, 1–11.

Woodward, A. L. (2009). *Infants' learning about intentional action*. New York, NY: Oxford University Press.

Wright, S. C., Aron, A., McLaughlin-Volpe, T., & Ropp, S. A. (1997). The extended contact effect: Knowledge of cross-group friendships and prejudice. *Journal of Personality and Social Psychology*, *73*, 73–90.

Wright, S. C., & Tropp, L. R. (2005). Language and intergroup contact: Investigating the impact of bilingual instruction on children's intergroup attitudes. *Group Processes and Intergroup Relations*, *8*, 309–328.

Yee, M. D., & Brown, R. (1994). The development of gender differentiation in young children. *British Journal of Social Psychology, 33*, 183–196.

Zelazo, P. D., Carlson, S. M., & Kesek, A.(in press). The development of executive function in childhood. In C. Nelson & M. Luciana (Eds.), *Handbook of Developmental Cognitive Neuroscience*. Cambridge, MA: MIT Press.

Zelazo, P. D., Helwig, C. C., & Lau, A. (1996). Intention, act, and outcome in behavioral prediction and moral judgment. *Child Development, 67*, 2478–2492.

Index

Page numbers in *italics* refer to figures; page numbers in **bold** refer to tables